IRISHBATT

The Story of Ireland's Blue Berets in the Lebanon

HENRY McDONALD

Gill & Macmillan

Published in Ireland by
Gill & Macmillan Ltd
Goldenbridge
Dublin 8
with associated companies throughout the world
© Henry McDonald 1993
0 7171 2134 8
Index compiled by Helen Litton
Print origination by Seton Music Graphics, Bantry, Co. Cork
Printed by ColourBooks Ltd, Dublin

A catalogue record for this book is available from
the British Library.

1   3   5   4   2

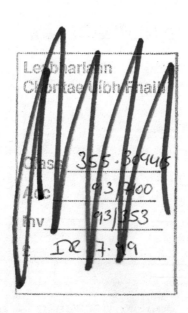

CONTENTS

Peace with honour? There can never be dishonour in peace.
(Jim Larkin)

ACKNOWLEDGMENTS

George Orwell compared writing a book to suffering from a long bout of painful illness. Now that this writer's suffering is over I wish to thank all of those who helped through the dark days. They include those who provided interviews, documents, photographs, books, names, addresses and helpful suggestions. They also include those who provided material and emotional support during the exhausting months of research and writing.

Firstly, a big thank you to Gill & Macmillan—in particular Fergal Tobin—for backing the idea. In uniform I am indebted to Lt-Col Des Travers, Captain Tom Aherne, Comdts Dave Ashe and Wally Young, Lt-Col Coleman Goggin, Lt-Col Colm Mangan, Comdt Peter Young and his staff at Military Archives, Comdt Connie Ryan, Comdt Noel Loughnane, Captain Johnny McMahon, Captain Brendan McAndrew and to all those hundreds of other soldiers who gave interviews and anecdotes about their tours of duty in Lebanon. However, I would have to single out two men in particular, still serving in the Defence Forces, who were extremely helpful in this book—CQMS Jim Clarke and Private Phillip Thorpe—whose kindness, courtesy and good humour I will never forget.

Retired soldiers also played their part in this work. Specifically I would like to thank John O'Mahony, Lt-Gen. William Callaghan (retired), Donal O'Laoire, Eddie Johnston, Tony Norris and all those other members of the United Nations Veterans Association who helped me out. Other ex-forces members I should mention in dispatches are Brendan and Martin Hamill.

Among many others there were: Jim Cusack, Ed O'Loughlin, the staff at the *Irish Times* library, Mick Sharkey, Kathleen Higgins (*Irish News* library), Stephen O'Reilly, Ruth O'Reilly, Tom O'Dwyer

Acknowledgments

(*Jerusalem Post*), Steve Hindy, the *Irish Press* photo library, Rosie Cowan, Ehud Ya'an', Danny Ben Moshe, Ori Orr, Abu Gawas (Amal), Abbas Fawas, Colonel Fawas (Lebanese army), Brian Hamilton, Marie Toft and cousin Grainne, Michael McAleavey and Michael Martin.

To those others whom I haven't mentioned, many apologies and many thanks for all your help. Finally I am indebted to my mother, father and sister Cathy and last but by no means least Emma, for all their moral support over the last few years of research and writing this book. Without their shoulders to lean on I would never have come through.

GLOSSARY

AEs: Armed Elements. Umbrella title for all groups whether Palestinian or Lebanese opposed to Israel and the DFF

Amal: Meaning hope. The largest and more moderate Shia Moslem militia and political group in Lebanon led by American educated Nabbi Berri

APC: Armoured Personnel Carrier

BMR: Battalion Mobile Reserve. Armoured response unit used as back up by Irishbatt

DFF: De Facto Forces or South Lebanon Army (SLA), a mainly Christian pro-Israel militia currently led by General Antoine Lahad

EOD: Engineer Ordnance Disposal. The Irishbatt teams which destroy suspect devices and unexploded ordnance throughout their area

Hizbollah: Radical pro-Iranian Shia Moslem organisation. Opposes peace with Israel and the UN presence

IDF: Israeli Defence Force

Irishbatt: Acronym for the Irish Battalion

Mossad: Israel's renowned external intelligence body. The head of Mossad opposed Ariel Sharon's plans during the 1982 invasion of Lebanon

OGL: Observer Group Lebanon. Unarmed UN mission policed by officers. It has been in Lebanon since 1958

ONUSAL: United Nations Mission El Salvador

Glossary

PFLP: Popular Front for the Liberation of Palestine. Breakaway faction from PLO led by former gynaecologist Dr George Habash

PLO: Palestinian Liberation Organisation. The mainstream Palestinian nationalist guerilla movement

Shin Bet: Israel's internal intelligence agency. Mainly operating in Israel proper and Occupied Territories of West Bank and Gaza, but did play an active role in Lebanon post 1982 invasion

SST: Specialist Search Teams. Used by Irishbatt to search and clear routes of ordnance and road side bombs in south Lebanon

UNAVEM: United Nations Angola Verifications of Elections Mission

UNDOF: United Nations Disengagement Observer Force. Based on the Golan Heights to separate and observe the truce between the Israeli and Syrian armies

UNEF: United Nations Emergency Force. Deployed to police the ceasefire lines between Israeli and Arab forces after wars of 1967 and 1973

UNIFCYP: United Nations peacekeeping force in Cyprus

UNIFIL: United Nations Interim Force in Lebanon

UNTAC: United Nations Transitional Authority in Cambodia

UNTSO: United Nations Treaty Supervision Organisation. The oldest UN mission in the Middle East based in several regional capitals including Jerusalem, Damascus, Beirut, Cairo and Amman. Unarmed and primarily an observer mission

South Lebanon—from the Mediterranean coast to the Golan Heights, a strategic cockpit in the wider Arab-Israeli conflict.

Tibnin—the 'capital' of Irishbatt zone.

Marajayoun—the headquarters town of the Israeli-backed 'South Lebanon Army'.

Naquorra—UN headquarters.

Tyre—former Palestinian stronghold now under the nominal control of the Lebanon army.

Reproduced with permission from *The Irish Times*

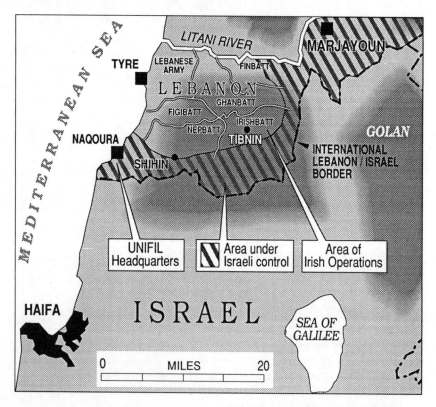

The United Nations headquarters in Naquorra—trapped inside
Israel's self-declared security zone. To the east is the Irish battalion
area and its regional capital Tibnin. Part of Irishbatt area is still in
Israeli-occupied territory. Since 1978 Irish and other UN forces
have failed to fulfil their mandate and take control of the entire south
Lebanon region. Reproduced with permission from *The Irish Times*

MISSING PRESUMED DEAD

Inisheer, 9 March 1993

Every year the elderly residents on Inisheer sleep beside their ancestors. They bed down for the night of 14 June in the island's graveyard overlooking the Atlantic. After dawn the local parish priests celebrate mass among the tombstones. The vigil is held to celebrate a saint's feast day but it probably pre-dates Christianity as it comes exactly one week before the traditional pagan festival of the summer solstice.

The locals lie on the sandy soil beside the grave of Inisheer's patron saint, St Chaomhain, who is allegedly buried in the cemetery. He is famed for bringing Christianity to the island and built a church there at the same time as the Crusaders were reconquering the Holy Land from the armies of Islam.

Red, white and yellow roses adorn the flat stone under which the saint is meant to have been laid to rest. Flat circular candles are placed on St Chaomhain's resting place. The flowers and the candles are laid in reverence to Chaomhain and the islanders' own descendants rooted deep at rest in the quiet Inisheer earth.

Around the ageing pilgrims who sleep out in honour of their saint are the decaying gravestones of deceased islanders. Some of the graves date back several centuries. One flat stone bears the name of a John Joyce who died in 1815—the year of Napoleon's defeat at Waterloo. The annual ritual demonstrates the fragile but cherished link between the living and the dead on Inisheer.

There is one memorial stone missing from the graveyard built around the ruins of St Chaomhain's tenth-century church. The memory of only the second ever islander to serve in the Irish army overseas lies suspended in the penumbral category of 'Missing Presumed Dead'.

If, as senior army intelligence officers believe, Private Kevin Joyce is indeed dead, it seems unlikely he will ever be laid to rest alongside his ancestors in the dry limestone earthmound beside the ocean. His remains have never been found. His fate continues to be a mystery casting its shadow over his family, home and the army he joined in June 1979.

Long before Brian Keenan was kidnapped in Beirut, Kevin Joyce was Ireland's first hostage in Lebanon. He disappeared in a country where thousands of civilians and combatants have gone missing and never returned since the outbreak of civil war in 1975. The cemetery where he should have been laid to rest is only a few hundred yards from his home.

The peace and silence of Inisheer is a far cry from the vicious religious and ethnic violence of Lebanon. But for a brief period in the past the ruins of O'Brien's Castle perched on the highest point on Inisheer was the scene of many fratricidal clashes between warring clans when the 'ferocious O'Flahertys' disturbed the peace. The fifteenth-century castle was built by the O'Briens who ruled the island for about 450 years until they were defeated by the O'Flahertys in 1585.

There are other surprising similarities between south Lebanon and the smallest of the Aran islands, the most obvious being the geological parallels. South Lebanon, known in Arabic as Jebel Amil, has the same harsh soil as the Burren. The dry limestone earth soaks up the rain in both regions. It is good land only for staples such as potatoes and tobacco. Isolated either by being stuck in the hills or cut off from the mainland by the sea, people in both regions have eked out a living despite the odds nature has stacked against them. When the sun beats down on a summer's day in the Burren you could almost imagine yourself in south Lebanon.

The economic backbone of both communities is peasant farming. Life revolves around strong simple faith and ritual. Even with the most modern links to the outside world a sense of isolation still permeates both places.

Kevin Joyce left his family home in Castlevillage for the last time in October 1980 to serve with the 47th Irish battalion in Lebanon. He enlisted at home with the 1st infantry battalion in Galway. A fluent Irish speaker, he was detailed to work with the signals section in Lebanon. He manned one of the radio outposts in the zone controlled by the United Nations peacekeeping force. By the time the

20-year-old soldier arrived in Lebanon four Irishmen had already lost their lives in the cause of peace, including Private Stephen Griffin who was buried in a church graveyard on 16 April 1980 beside the Connemara coast facing out to the Aran islands.

Almost exactly one year after Stephen Griffin's funeral, Kevin Joyce was manning an Irish observation post in the Lebanese village of Dyar Ntar. Alongside him was Private Hugh Doherty, also 20, from Letterkenny, Co. Donegal. Their task was to monitor movements in the wadis (dried up river beds) that cut into the area under Irish control. The soldiers had to report to Irish headquarters if any armed guerilla groups were trying to infiltrate into the United Nations zone. At that time in the eastern sector of the Irish battalion area Palestinian resistance organisations were attacking the Israelis who had invaded Lebanon three years before. Dyar Ntar was the Irish battalion's 'eyes and ears' into that strategic area. The Palestinian fighters operating under orders from Tyre city on the Mediterranean coast were determined to knock out the listening post. It was an irritating barrier between them and their Israeli enemies.

The previous November the intentions of one Palestinian faction towards the United Nations Interim Force in Lebanon were clear to see in an incident in which a number of soldiers from Senegal were murdered. The Senegalese, all Moslems, were shot dead at point blank range by an assassin for the Popular Front for the Liberation of Palestine (PFLP) under direct orders from one Colonel Billal in Tyre. Billal had indicated on several ocasions that UNIFIL should move its posts out of the area east of Tyre which became known as 'The Iron Triangle'. According to Irish officers who met him, Billal saw the UN posts not only as a major obstacle to Palestinian operations against the Israelis and their Christian allies in south Lebanon but also an affront to his own personal standing. Posturing and not being seen to lose face in front of a perceived enemy are articles of faith in Arab military culture.

Irish officers were shocked by the cold-blooded way the murders were carried out. The African peacekeepers had been killed while sleeping in their camp beds inside a canvas tent. It was clearly the work of a cold psychopath. Irishmen would have the misfortune to encounter this man and his gang six months later.

The Senegalese killings took place at the height of Palestinian power in south Lebanon. The guerillas extended over the region launching rocket and ground attacks on Israel proper. They also dominated their Lebanese hosts, running their war effort from the proceeds of extortion and protection rackets, robberies and drugs. In fact the myriad of Palestinian factions had set up a state within a state in Lebanon, even managing to establish a fledgling regular army organised around conventional military brigades with anti-quated Soviet tanks and artillery.

Part of the United Nations soldiers' brief was to curb Palestinian guerilla activity in the south. The UN's belief was that attacks on the Israeli army or Israel's northern settlements would result in massive retaliatory military strikes with ordinary Lebanese and Palestinian civilians ending up as the main losers. Preventing escalating conflict on both sides was part of the original orders given to UN commanders in south Lebanon. Despite this, there was relatively good contact between the mainstream Palestinian Liberation Organisation led by Yasser Arafat and UNIFIL. Meetings took place on a regular basis. Soldiers recalled playing football matches against Palestinians in Tyre. Gunner Eddie Johnston from Co. Kildare remembered a bizarre inci-dent when he was praised by a well-known PFLP fighter in Brashit village for the IRA's assassination of Lord Mountbatten and the killing of 18 British soldiers in Warrenpoint on 27 August 1979. Gunner Johnston said the guerilla, who was on first-name terms with Irish soldiers, shook their hands that day and said their comrades had done 'an excellent job' back in Ireland. Eddie never got a chance to explain that the Irish army was not the Provisional IRA and that it was ranged against all subversive paramilitary organisations back in Ireland. Relations were further cemented with the Palestinians when Irish Foreign Minister Brian Lenihan recognised the PLO as the 'sole legitimate representative of the Palestinian people' during a speech in Bahrain in 1980.

In the first three years of the United Nations mission in Lebanon the Irish contingent lost three men in action, all killed by the pro-Israeli militia. Many Irishmen who met the PLO and its splinter factions on the ground found it difficult to believe that Palestinians would kill their comrades. But as successive battalions in Lebanon have learned, the Irish soldier frequently finds himself shot at by both sides. By late 1993 the Defence Forces had lost sixteen soldiers killed in action in Lebanon, seven at the hands of Palestinian or Lebanese Moslem factions.

On the evening of Monday, 27 April Kevin Joyce and Hugh Doherty were holed up in the Dyar Ntar post. Doherty had only arrived in Lebanon just six days before with the 49th battalion. He had said goodbye to his widowed mother Elizabeth at their home in Ballymacool Terrace, Letterkenny and joined the advance party of the battalion forming up in Dublin later that day.

He had spent three years in the army and was normally based in his home barracks of Rockhill. Private Doherty had just turned 20 the previous August. Like Kevin Joyce it was his first tour of Lebanon. The Letterkenny man actually began his tour on the same day as his brother-in-law, Sergeant John Touhy, who was married to his sister Phyllis. Joyce, however, had only about a week left to serve before going home.

That fateful evening a fellow signals man noticed something strange happening in the battalion area. UN veteran Paul Smith had been manning the communications centre in the Irish battalion's headquarters near the largest town in south Lebanon, Tibnin. Paul, a Dubliner with 25 years service in the army, started to get suspicious after the lights in villages close to the Dyar Ntar listening post went off.

'I could see what was happening from headquarters,' he recalled. 'When the lights go out in the south you know something is going to happen or has happened.'

His suspicions were heightened when he carried out a check over the radio of all the isolated Irish observation posts around the area of operations. Joyce and Doherty failed to respond to his constant calls. He told his commander who immediately ordered a patrol to investigate what was going on at Dyar Ntar. When the patrol arrived they found Hugh Doherty dead with three bullet wounds on his back. Kevin Joyce was nowhere to be seen. The attackers had taken two Irish standard issue FN rifles and a radio pack with them.

It had been only just over a year since two other Irish soldiers, Privates Derek Smallhorne and Thomas Barrett, had been abducted and murdered by a pro-Israeli militia in south Lebanon. Troops serving in the same battalions as Kevin Joyce and Hugh Doherty believed it was happening all over again.

Paul Smith, who had seen action abroad in United Nations peacekeeping missions in the Congo and Cyprus, remembered hearing the reaction of his comrades when they heard about Dyar Ntar. It was shortly after 7.00 p.m. local time.

'We had just finished our dinner and all the lads decided to go down to a local corner shop for a beer. As we got up to leave the camp I remember I was called out by my sergeant-major. He told me to bring the lads back into camp as something terrible had happened at Dyar Ntar. He said there was one dead and one missing.' As well as lights going out across parts of the Irish area Paul said phone lines to 'C' company (Joyce and Doherty's unit while in Lebanon) had been cut. It was clear the attack on Dyar Ntar had been carefully planned.

Feelings at Irish headquarters were running very high when word came through about the two men. Paul Smith said a lot of his colleagues wanted to strike back. 'A lot of the lads had been out in Lebanon when Barrett and Smallhorne were killed. Their attitude was "It's starting up again. So let's get out there this time and blow the fuck out of them." In the end good sense and discipline prevailed.'

Even if they had been allowed to hit back, Irish troops had first to discover who exactly was behind the attack. Ballistic tests later showed that a Kalashnikov AK-47 rifle was used to murder Hugh Doherty. At the time it was an automatic weapon generally used by Palestinian groups and their left wing Lebanese allies. This at least suggested that the pro-Israeli (mainly Christian) militia group behind the Barrett and Smallhorne killings were not responsible for this incident. Of course investigating officers had to keep an open mind: one militia group often captured a rival organisation's weapons and used them for their own murderous purposes.

Villages in the area were searched throughout the week. Rumours were rife. There were reports that Joyce had been spotted in a number of different places. A special team of unarmed United Nations officers known as Observer Group Lebanon (OGL) was dispatched to Tyre to negotiate with senior Palestinian figures over the abduction. It was all to no avail. The Palestinians were either unaware of the young soldier's whereabouts or were keeping quiet.

What exactly happened on that fateful night remains clouded. Army officers investigating the Dyar Ntar incident were, however, able to piece together a sketchy account of the killing and kidnap. The men on the post were probably not surprised at the sight of armed men walking towards their position. There were known to be many bands of bird fowlers hunting in the area. According to intelligence gleaned after the incident the gang which captured Kevin Joyce posed as hunters as they approached the OP to win the Irishmen's trust. It was not until they got to the post itself that they tried to overpower the two soldiers. In the ensuing panic the less experienced Irishman bolted.

The fact that Hugh Doherty had been shot in the back and lay in the place where he normally left his rifle suggested he had been running for his weapon when the guerillas stormed the post. The investigating officers believe to this day that Private Doherty's reaction was typical of a soldier with hardly any experience of life on the ground in Lebanon. The fact that the guerillas had not killed Kevin Joyce on the spot seemed strange.

The investigating team concluded the Palestinian group's aim had been to kidnap both soldiers. The captured troops would then have been a powerful bargaining chip in their hands. The price of their freedom would be the closure of the Dyar Ntar post. Things did not quite work out like that. Doherty's death complicated the guerillas' plans. But they still kept Joyce alive which suggested at least in the early days that they were willing to negotiate his release.

Joyce was believed to have been taken to Tyre by his captors. Within a matter of days of the abduction, senior UN officers were informed that he was being held in one of the Palestinian refugee camps that ring the ancient coastal city. There was one specific report to Irish headquarters that a white man had been spotted in Rashidya camp, a Palestinian stronghold which was devastated by the Israelis in the second invasion of Lebanon just over a year later. No one could be sure that the white man was Kevin Joyce. There were numerous reports of white western men in the Palestinian camps. Some troops claimed to have met Irishmen connected with various republican paramilitary groups at home in Lebanon training with Palestinian guerillas. There was also the possibility that the mysterious 'white man' in Rashidya was an Israeli soldier captured by one of the Palestinian factions. Every report therefore had to be treated with a high degree of scepticism. In Lebanon giving information is a cottage industry. The Americans were known to have spent millions of dollars in the mid to late 1980s in order to secure the whereabouts of their nationals seized by kidnappers in Beirut, usually without any positive results. Thousands of ordinary Lebanese had been the victims of kidnap gangs who bartered their lives with money and privileges they could exact from their captives' families, sects or communities.

In the first week of May the search for Private Joyce was concentrated in the villages of Jwyya, Mahrounah and Mazraat al Mushrif. Representatives of the PLO, Amal and the Lebanese leftist/Moslem National Movement co-operated with UNIFIL. But there was no sign of the young soldier anywhere.

While the search for Kevin Joyce continued Private Doherty's remains were flown home for burial. His funeral, with full military honours, took place on 3 May in his home town. Thousands turned out to pay their last respects to the young soldier shot dead the week before. His coffin was taken from his home to St Eunan's Cathedral led by the band of the army's Western Command with a guard of honour from his home battalion, the 28th Infantry.

The chaplain of his home unit, the Rev. Alan Ward, was the principal celebrant during Requiem Mass for Private Doherty. He told mourners that the murdered soldier's family, friends and comrades in the Defence Forces should be proud of the young private. In his homily, Fr Ward contrasted the sacrifice made by the soldier in Lebanon to the work of fellow Irishmen involved in paramilitary violence during one of the most violent periods of the current Northern troubles—the summer of the 1981 hunger strikes. 'Hugh Doherty's family should look back with pride in his memory because he was aware of the dangers involved in his mission in Lebanon but he did not hesitate because of this. He showed the courage of a good soldier. His sacrifice stands in sharp contrast to those in this country who think little of taking life. Hugh did not take life. He gave his life in the cause of peace.'

Unlike the Dohertys, the Joyce family had to live on in the cruel uncertainty about whether Kevin was alive or dead. He was never given a full Christian burial. The islanders understood this kind of loss. Kevin Joyce's fate was comparable to that of a fisherman lost at sea. Tragically, his family would never know for sure what exactly happened to him.

Officers were still certain that he was alive one month after his disappearance. One of the officers heading the investigation, who at that time was working for the unarmed United Nations Truce Supervision Organisation (UNTSO), was told that the young soldier had been taken away from Tyre and spirited north to Beirut. He was also told that Joyce had been given a change of clothing. There was even an unconfirmed report from the Lebanese capital that Joyce was seen wearing jeans, a beige sweatshirt and sneakers while being taken out of a car into a Palestinian stronghold in the city. If there was any truth in these reports it is also certain that Kevin Joyce spent a birthday in captivity—he was 21 years of age on 27 May 1981.

The team investigating the young soldier's disappearance was in touch with a number of different sources in Lebanon. These included contacts with the mainstream PLO, the indigenous Lebanese Shia Moslem organisation, Amal, the Lebanese army's intelligence branch in Beirut, the Deuxieme Bureau, and, at a later stage, the Israelis. The UN was frustrated at the conspiracy of denial among the various Palestinian splinter organisations under suspicion. Each denied any involvement in the murder and abduction at Dyar Ntar. What was only clear in hindsight was that Kevin Joyce's usefulness to the gang that snatched him was running out.

About eight weeks after his abduction an incident which did not even directly involve Irish troops probably sealed Kevin Joyce's fate. Another former British colony, the Pacific island state of Fiji, also sent a battalion to south Lebanon to serve with the UN. The area under the Fijians' control bordered the 'Iron Triangle' and was the focus of several armed clashes between the UN and Palestinian guerillas. Less than a week before the killing and kidnap at Dyar Ntar Fijian troops came under fire from armed elements believed to be connected with a Palestinian guerilla group operating in nearby Quana village. In April alone Fijian checkpoints denied entry to 76 armed men belonging to the Palestinians and their allies. The UN also confiscated 44 pistols, 7 AK-47 rifles, 1 FN rifle and assorted military equipment such as walkie-talkies, magazines, ammunition and trip wire. There was no love lost between Palestinian fighters on the ground and UN soldiers.

During one exchange on 19 June near the village of Deir Amiss, which is close to Dyar Ntar, a major gun battle broke out between the Fijians and the Palestinians. Three Palestinians were killed in the shoot-out. Three Fijians, including one officer, were also captured by gunmen. The Fijian officer was eventually handed over and according to a UN report was described as 'out of his mind with fear' after his ordeal. He was manhandled after attempting to escape. His two comrades were murdered by their captors. A follow-up investigation found that during the incident the Fijian post was ransacked and uniforms, personal documents, watches and money were stolen. Prior to Deir Amiss there had been high level contacts between the UN and the PLO and some of its offshoot factions. These broke down temporarily after the Fijians killed the Palestinian fighters. Relations between the Palestinian factions and UNIFIL were at an all-time low. Things were so serious that an emergency meeting was held between the UN force commander, the Irish General William Callaghan and PLO chairman Yasser Arafat in Beirut on 21 June.

Irish officers are convinced the Deir Amiss shoot-out had a direct bearing on Kevin Joyce's fate. The Defence Forces of course have never issued a decisive statement about the soldier's final end. As no physical evidence has yet to be produced to show that he is in fact dead, the military authorities cannot make any absolute pronoucement about him. Two senior officers working as intelligence officers

for the Irish battalion and the UN in Lebanon, however, have told the
author they believe that Kevin Joyce was killed sometime between the
Deir Amiss incident and the period before the second Israeli invasion
of June 1982.

Before the breakdown in communications between the Palestinians
and UNIFIL, Irish officers were informed that Kevin Joyce was being
treated well by his captors and would soon be released. All that
changed after Deir Amiss. By the time the Israelis invaded on 6 June
1982 the Irish UNIFIL contingent was offered fresh information on
the soldier. During a conversation with an officer working with
UNTSO, a Lebanese army intelligence operative claimed Kevin Joyce
had been killed during an Israeli air raid on the southern capital. His
story was that during an air strike on Sidon an Israeli bomb destroyed
a PLO office. According to this version Private Joyce was being held
in an underground basement at Ein Hilweh refugee camp and was
killed along with the rest of the occupants in the office. The answer
was too simple. 'The Israeli barbarians', as the Lebanese officer described them, had been responsible for the Irish soldier's death. Blame
was shifted from Beirut to Jerusalem.

The Irish UNTSO officer, who to this day cannot be named,
told his Lebanese counterpart, 'Surely you don't expect me to
believe that?' The Lebanese officer informed him that this was the
only story he was going to get and simply smiled when the Irishman continued to doubt the story.

Blame and counter-blame was part of the political landscape in
Lebanon. No one, least of all the PLO or any of its factions, was
going to admit that they were suspected of coldly executing Kevin
Joyce after Deir Amiss. The unfortunate soldier was no longer an
asset in his captors' hands. In their eyes he had lost all usefulness.
So they simply disposed of him in a lonely, cruel fashion.

But who exactly was behind the kidnap of Kevin Joyce and the
murder of Hugh Doherty? It is difficult for any army, peacekeepers
or war-makers, to pinpoint the men who physically pulled the
trigger or planted the bomb. But in the Dyar Ntar incident senior
officers in the Irish Defence Forces have been aware for almost a
decade of a prime suspect! Their attention from very early on
focused not on a Palestinian but rather on a Lebanese man who
served the PFLP and Colonel Billal. His name is Abu Amin Dayk.

Dayk came from the village of Jwyya which is inside the area controlled by the Fijian battalion. The village's name comes from the
French word for joy, *joie*. It derived from French Crusaders who were

no doubt eternally grateful for services rendered by the women of the area during their occupation in the tenth century. Dayk's home was only three kilometres south-east of Dyar Ntar.

Dayk first came to the attention of UNIFIL following the murder of the Senegalese soldiers in November 1980. He was known by UN intelligence to be one of Colonel Billal's main assassins and took part in the point-blank murders of the African soldiers. Like many other Lebanese he had joined one of the Palestinian factions when the PLO was at the height of its power. He was known to be a ruthless man who instilled fear and hatred amongst his fellow Lebanese.

His name kept cropping up in conversations Irish officers had with various factions when the subject of Kevin Joyce's disappearance was raised. Incredibly, just over two years after the Dyar Ntar incident Dayk himself sought the help of the Irish battalion in Lebanon. This might appear to have been the ultimate in arrogance. But Lebanon is a country where your enemy today could be your friend tomorrow. The Lebanese have a saying: 'He killed him and then marched in his funeral procession.'

The battalion's chief intelligence officer was summoned to a meeting with him in the village of Tair Zibna along with a Dutch colleague who could speak Arabic. For the first time since Hugh Doherty's murder and Kevin Joyce's disappearance an Irish soldier—now retired from the Defence Forces—came face to face with the prime suspect behind the crime.

'Dayk was in his mid-thirties. He was of slight build. He had black hair and spoke in a very deep monosyllabic tone. I remember during that meeting he appeared to be very nervous. You could tell he was aware that his enemies were closing in. It was weird being in the same room as the man we suspected had been behind the Dyar Ntar attack. He was very uneasy during the meeting. He kept looking out the window. When people like Dayk sought a meeting with UNIFIL you could be sure their power was waning,' the former Irish officer recalls.

The Palestinian hitman packed a pistol in a hip-holster during the meeting held inside a house he had taken over. The only other person in the house was a woman who remained in the kitchen, only appearing once to offer Dayk's guests tea. Incredibly he wanted help from the UN to protect him against his enemies. After the Israelis pushed out the PLO and their off-shoots, new indigenous Lebanese movements became the power in south Lebanon. Locals who were at the sharp end of Palestinian dominance and arrogance prior to the 1982 invasion were seeking revenge. One of their prime targets was Abu

Amin Dayk. He was to become a casualty of the changing power structures in south Lebanon a year later.

Amal was now the rising force both in Beirut and the south. In the capital it had fought running battles with the PLO, besieging two Palestinian refugee camps for several weeks and killing hundreds of ordinary civilians in the fighting. In the south its fighters attacked the retreating Israeli army which was pulling back from most of the country into its self-declared security zone. It was also exacting revenge. Amal arrested Abu Amin Dayk in May 1984 holding him in a make-shift jail in the village of Marrakeh inside the Fijian battalion area. He was tried on a number of charges relating to the killing of native Lebanese on behalf of the PLO. Within hours of his trial Dayk was publicly hanged. Amal actually invited an Irish commandant to attend the hanging. What passes for justice in Lebanon is normally carried out in a crude brutal fashion without recourse to a legal defence or a right to appeal. The Shia Moslem militia group's leader known as Daoud Daoud even went as far as to point the finger at Dayk for the murder of the two Irish soldiers during the attack on the Dyar Ntar post. Despite this, the Irish officer declined. A French UN commander did, however, attend the summary execution in the village.

All this of course is of little comfort to the Joyce family back on Inisheer. His father Michael, mother Mary and brothers and sisters were told several stories relating to Kevin's disappearance. There were other theories about his abduction. One rather fanciful but groundless story was that he had joined up with his captors and was reported to be fighting alongside the Palestinians when the Israeli army besieged Beirut. The only sound explanation about what happened to the young soldier, however, is the one relating to the role of Abu Amin Dayk. It is not the only theory but it is the most plausible and widely held.

Nothing has ever been found to confirm that Kevin Joyce is dead or alive. His family broke their silence about him only once during the summer of 1990. On 10 July, Ireland waited as Lebanese kidnappers announced they were poised to release a western hostage they had seized in Beirut. Irish diplomats in the Middle East believed that Brian Keenan was about to be set free after years in captivity. Less than a month later their optimism was proved correct.

Hope and happiness for Keenan's family, particularly his two sisters who worked tirelessly for his freedom, sparked heartbreaking memories for the Joyces. His brother, 32-year-old Michael, wished the Keenans well but said the focus on the Belfast man's fate only reminded his family about Kevin's disappearance.

Michael said that what his elderly parents wanted most was finally to give their son a Christian burial if indeed he was dead. During the euphoria over Brian Keenan's release most of Ireland seemed to forget that Kevin had been the country's first hostage in Lebanon.

'I hope people will remember my brother especially at this time. My parents were devastated when Kevin went missing. They'll never get over it. It's very difficult for all of us, but what can you do?' said Michael. Asked about the daily deluge of news about Brian Keenan during that time, Michael Joyce added: 'Every time I hear that it just keeps bringing my thoughts back to Kevin.'

Lebanon remains Ireland's longest and most costliest overseas mission to date. Thirty-three men have died in the region since it began in 1978. At least all their deaths have been accounted for. In some cases the Defence Forces have even been aware of the names of the men who killed Irish troops in south Lebanon but unable to do anything to bring the killers to justice.

Only Kevin Joyce's fate however remains an unclosed chapter in the annals of Irish military history. While there is no body there might be a miracle. After all, hundreds of American families are still clinging to the desperate hope that loved ones who went missing in action in Vietnam almost two decades ago may one day turn up alive and well. Perhaps, officially at least, Kevin Joyce is doomed to remain like those American MIAs in that limbo world of 'Missing Presumed Dead'.

TOTAL RECALL

Sergeant Patrick Mulcahy lay bleeding in the back of a makeshift ambulance truck. He had been in the Congo less than a fortnight. Like the rest of the 36th Irish battalion, he had been pitched into the horrors of a vicious civil war in a far-off land.

In 1960 the Congo gained independence from its imperial masters, the Belgians. As with many other newly emerging African states the Congo was fractured along tribal lines. Coupled with this were the rich mineral deposits including diamond mines in the south of the country. These were still under the control of foreign multinationals. With the support of outside governments and financial interests a tribal leader called Moise Tshombe declared the southern region of the Congo the independent state of Katanga.

Under his leadership Katanga broke away from the central government in the old colonial capital, Leopoldville. The United Nations voted only to recognise the central government which had official jurisdiction over the entire former colony, including Katanga. After Tshombe continued to defy the UN and the Congolese government, the security council decided to dispatch a multinational force under the organisation's blue flag to stop the country breaking up. It was called a peacekeeping operation but in reality it was more of a peace-enforcing mission.

As in the Lebanon more than eighteen years later, Irish troops went to the Congo under the UN flag to protect a nation which was fragmenting due to the ambition of a regional warlord and the connivance of foreign powers.

For three years Irish, along with other troops mainly from neutral nations, battled with Katangan irregulars known as the gendarmerie and foreign mercenaries.

On 12 December 1961, Irish troops received orders to storm a railway tunnel in an area of Elisabethville, Katanga's capital and the Congo's second city, which was held by the Katangan forces. The military engagement turned out to be one of the key turning points in the conflict. The Battle of the Tunnel was a bloody, brutal affair and Paddy Mulcahy was wounded early on. But despite his injuries, he stayed with his platoon and while looking for missing men, was wounded again, taking a lump of shrapnel round in the leg after a mortar landed on the Irish position.

He was hit badly this time, worse than he himself thought. 'Is that you Mick?' he cried into the darkness as the battle raged. He was still looking for other wounded comrades. It wasn't Mick, however, but 19-year-old Dubliner Jim Clarke who came upon him. It was the first time Jim Clarke had ever seen a military casualty in the heat of battle. He was one of the many young lads who in the 36th battalion thought the world of Paddy Mulcahy, an old soldier who took the lads under his wing, gave them tips and cared for them beyond the call of duty.

Sergeant Mulcahy was laid on a stretcher in a trench near the front line while the ambulance was called up. Clarke was ordered to drive him to the nearest Irish field hospital several kilometres away. He set off with his casualty in the back, driving slowly through the darkness of the African bush, with the headlights turned off in order to avoid enemy fire.

Paddy Mulcahy took four days to die. Gangrene set in. A few days before the Battle of the Tunnel, he had written home to his wife Marie to say that he was fine, that the battalion had arrived safely and that they had settled in. She got that letter on the morning of the same day that later brought news of his death. Bad news travels fast.

Jim Clarke, now himself a company quartermaster sergeant at the Supply and Transport corps in Dublin's McKee barracks, remembers how he felt when learning about Paddy Mulcahy's death.

'At first I thought he would be saved but then I learned on 16 December that he had died. That was a terrible day. He had been an old soldier who looked after the younger lads in 'A' Company. It was an awful blow to all of us.'

That first battlefield experience failed, however, to put Jim Clarke off army life. During his thirty-three years in the Irish Defence Forces he continued to volunteer for dangerous overseas missions with the United Nations, including Lebanon.

Seventeen of Patrick Mulcahy's comrades from 'A' Company who fought in the Battle of the Tunnel in December 1961 are still serving in the army, some with years of overseas duty under their belts, including the Lebanon.

The heaviest loss of life in the Congo was the Niemba massacre when Baluba tribesmen killed nine Irish soldiers in November 1960. Those who fell that day are still remembered. The United Nations Veterans Association named their headquarters in Dublin's Stoney-batter area Niemba House in honour of the men slaughtered during that ambush.

Despite such heavy Irish losses so early on in the mission the morale of troops remained high, according to a top-secret letter Lt-Col Eoghan O'Neill sent to the army chief of staff in Dublin. The letter, only released into the public domain in January 1992, had nothing but praise for Irish soldiers but warned that their equipment was hopelessly out of date compared to other UN contingents such as the Scandinavian battalions. Lt-Col O'Neill revealed that the troops were issued with old-fashioned weapons and only had papier mâché helmets to protect them in battle!

The 36th Irish battalion was stationed in Elisabethville where they had seized control back from Katangan rebels with relatively little bloodshed. 'I have never seen soldiers in better form,' he wrote. 'They are in wonderful spirits and most willing. But FN rifles will be necessary. They must have bayonets. Bazookas will be necessary in each company. The Swedes have steel helmets. We only have papier mâché ones.'

Lt-Col O'Neill also had a warning about the age of soldiers sent to the Congo. 'Seventeen or eighteen is much too young for conditions here. Sentries of seventeen are much too nervous . . . and the next battalion cannot bank upon the chance of training here before action commences.'

His concern for the relative youth of soldiers in the Congo contrasts with today where senior army officers are worried that Ireland now has the oldest troops on average in Europe. Latest army statistics show that the average age of a soldier serving with the United Nations in Lebanon is around thirty.

One of the men who had to escort the bodies from the Niemba massacre was Michael Colton who served as a quartermaster in the 33rd battalion. Speaking in Niemba House in September 1992, his voice went hoarse when he told how the only way home on leave for him was to sit with the coffins containing his comrades on the 24-hour flight via Libya to Ireland. 'It lived with me for years after. I remember the bodies were brought to Leopoldville and onto the

American chartered plane back home in wooden crates which weighed around 1,200 lbs.

'They needed a crane to haul them up into the aircraft. I stood on the tarmac that day feeling numb. One of the dead was a good friend of mine. Corporal Pete Kelly and I knew the rest of them from training with them back home. I was 28 at the time and had some experience in the army but meeting their relatives was unbearable. It took me a long time to get over it. I had been given a dreadful task.'

It was an adventure for which the men were not always ready. Nothing could prepare them for the incredible tropical heat. Michael said he couldn't bear to speak about what happened out in the Congo while home on leave. "I was glad to get home, to see everyone again. But when family and friends asked me what was going on all I could say was "I don't know". They couldn't believe it when I informed them I was going back. To me it was all an adventure despite the danger.'

One of his comrades, fellow Dubliner Colum Deveney, recalled a similar macabre experience on the tarmac of Leopoldville airport the day he arrived in the Congo in January 1961. He remembers the belting heat as he stepped out of the American Globemaster after a gruelling 24-hour flight from Ireland via Wheeler airbase in Libya. He and his colleagues were still wearing their Irish winter kit, comprising of, among other things, a woollen hairshirt buttoned up to the neck!

The first sight that he saw as he walked away from the plane was rows and rows of empty coffins. 'I thought, "Jesus, this is some reception." I'll never forget beside the empty coffins were hundreds of crates of Pepsi cola in the store.

'On the Sunday after I arrived we were in Kamina and were marched to Mass in our winter uniforms. It was 120 degrees but I don't remember anyone collapsing despite the fact we were even wearing woollen underpants. We got suntanned that day but got plenty of blisters as well. Things improved throughout the mission. I suppose we learned as it went along.'

During their 'occupation' of Elisabethville, Colum recalls the locals exploding into laughter at the site of men marching in mohair and woollen uniforms in the tropical heat.

During his first week in the city he remembers how the Irish won over the hearts and minds of many of its citizens. 'A decision was taken by our commanding officer that we were going to give an exhibition of Irish dancing. So four dancers from our company did a fairy reel for the local chief and then handed him a bottle of Irish whiskey. That broke the tension. All the natives started coming up to our camp after that.

'They were very good to us. We utilised them; we got them to iron and wash our uniforms. We started to generate some income by our presence in the area as well as sharing our rations with many of them.'

This pattern of fraternisation was continued in the Lebanon where to this day local Shia women in Irish company areas take in uniforms to their homes to wash for the troops. Schools receive papers, pens, typewriters, notebooks, desks and chairs from Irish supplies. Orphanages receive financial support. Families are treated by Irish army medics. Seriously ill patients are taken to hospitals in Irish transport.

Conditions for frontline troops in the Congo were spartan, according to the men who fought there. Colum Deveney said the staple diet during the first few weeks in Elisabethville was powdered milk, spam and eggs along with 'dog biscuits' soaked in water.

He described the water as 'dire' pointing out that troops had to carry purification tablets with them all the time. But on Christmas Day 1961 there was a seasonal treat for the Irish contingent. The menu for 'A' company at the Tunnel, which was by this time under UN control, reflected the uneasy truce in the area.

It consisted of: 'Sniper soup. Turkey *à la* Tunnel. Cross "E" Ham. Roast and creamed potatoes *à la* shops. Purée of Peas *à la* Nobby Clarke. Cauliflower ears of Gendarmerie. Trifle Complacht "A". Elakat pudding. Tea and biscuits.' The toasts where made to the president and 'A' Company.

But even on Christmas Day there was work to be done in Elisabethville. Irish soldiers had to hold hard-won positions on the city's railway bridge. Comdt T.J. O'Donnell had a precarious Christmas morning. The Roscommon man had to pick up and dispose of an unexploded mortar bomb which was found in the grounds of the Irish headquarters in Elisabethville as his comrades prepared for festive celebrations.

On St Stephen's Day two Dubliners, John Moffat and John Robinson, were captured by Katangan forces. Both men spent nearly a month in captivity with thirteen other UN troops in a Katanganese prison at Kipushi, near the Rhodesian border. Freed on the day the 36th battalion held an open-air Mass, review and parade in Elisabethville to commemorate the Irish dead, they said they had been treated well during their imprisonment. This came as a great surprise to the battalion given the Katangans' previous record against UN troops.

By February 1962 the United Nations had 16,581 soldiers stationed in the Congo. The Irish contingent was 727, consisting of 695 troops and 32 staff. India's contribution of 5,826 was the largest and other major units were from Ethiopia, 3,057; Nigeria, 1,686; and Malaya, 1,471. In all, twenty countries contributed to the UN force. When the 36th and 37th battalions were rotating that year almost 2,000 Irish troops alone were stationed in the Congo, the highest ever concentration of the country's armed forces on foreign soil.

By April 1962 Tshombe declared openly that he was prepared to abandon sovereignty of the breakaway area. The UN campaign was a success rare in modern times. It had resisted colonial and tribal pressures. Aside from the military struggle, it had scored a victory on the diplomatic battlefield as well. Chief protagonist in this struggle was Dr Conor Cruise O'Brien who openly accused the British, French and Rhodesian governments of supporting the Katangan rebels.

The foreign powers, particularly the white minority-ruled Rhodesian government, had been actively encouraging Tshombe. O'Brien claimed white mercenaries and the expatriate communities in the Congo armed and trained Tshombe's irregulars. He also accused members of the British establishment, including press baron Lord Beaverbrook and the then prime minister, Harold Macmillan, of secretly backing the breakaway Katangan regime.

O'Brien's charges against Britain led eventually to his resignation from the post. It also caused a diplomatic flutter between Dublin and London as the Lemass government attempted to distance itself from O'Brien's comments.

On 10 December 1961 a fellow Irishman came to Dr O'Brien's rescue. The UN force commander during this period was Irish General Sean McKeown. He acknowledged in a statement to the UN that foreign mercenaries funded by overseas powers with financial interests in Katanga were encouraging the rebellion against the new government in Leopoldville. General McKeown's statement was a godsend. O'Brien described it as the turning point in the whole history of the Congo operation. The charges of covert support for Katanga by the old colonial powers such as Britain and France could no longer be ignored.

Among the mercenaries fighting against Irish troops during the Battle of the Tunnel was the infamous Dubliner ex-Captain Mad Mike Hoare. By mid-December there had been a decisive shift in British policy towards the Congo. Less than a week after General McKeown's statement both the British and more importantly the United States governments declared openly in favour of the UN force. The US administration urged President Tshombe on 15 December to call a ceasefire. His regime was by now well and truly isolated.

On the battlefield itself Elisabethville finally fell to UN forces on the night of 18 December 1961, although the fighting dragged on until 1962. While the Congo did not break up, thanks to the UN's sacrifices, it was to be led or rather misled for the next thirty-odd years by several dictators. Now known as Zaire, the central African country was bled dry particularly by the despotic rule of Joseph Mobutu who ruthlessly suppressed all opposition to his regime. Ironically as resistance to his corrupt dictatorship gathered momentum in early 1993, foreign troops including the Belgians and French, were back in the country protecting their expatriate population and attempting to impose a new order on the former colony.

For Irishmen like CQMS Jim Clarke the mission in the African bush more than 30 years ago was well worthwhile and benefited Irish troops in new peacekeeping zones such as Lebanon.

'I was very very proud to be Irish in the Congo,' he reflected. 'They set out to achieve their task and were wholly successful despite the things working against them. The Irish soldier gained a lot of international credibility in the Congo and our sacrifices were not in vain.'

Of the twenty-six Irish soldiers killed in the Congo the first man to die was 43-year-old Felix Grant of the 33rd Irish battalion who died after an operation. The last was Comdt Thomas McMahon, a 47-year-old serving at the United Nations headquarters at Leopoldville. He died on 28 September 1963 of natural causes.

After the Congo the United Nations blue berets were sent to police a number of hot spots where the cold war had been fought out by the allies of the two superpowers, the United States and the former Soviet Union. The UN was also dispatched to monitor border disputes and national and ethnic boundaries from Cambodia to Costa Rica.

A further eleven Irish soldiers lost their lives serving in various missions excluding Lebanon since 1960. The highest death toll outside the Congo and Lebanon was in Cyprus where nine Irish berets died exclusively in accidents and of natural causes.

One important lesson was learned from the Congo mission. The first force commander of UN troops in south Lebanon, the Ghanaian General Emmanuel Erskine, has pointed out that there is a misconception in the world that peacekeepers are forbidden to use force. The bloody battles of the Congo, where the UN used heavy armour, mortars and jet fighters, proved that blue beret soldiers can xperience which was to enable them to appreciate the political omplexities of the region when deployed in Lebanon in 1978.

The UN's role during hostilities between Arab states and Israel was to be a reactive one, to move and stabilise the politico-military situation after the wars of 1956, 1967 and 1973 were officially over. The standard weapon in the hands of UN forces during this period from the 1956 Suez crisis to Yom Kippur was moral force rather than tanks and guns. One example illustrates this important difference between peacekeeping and ordinary soldiering.

On 11 November 1973 the Israeli Defence Forces (IDF) were engaged in a potentially explosive situation in the Sinai desert with Finnish troops serving in United Nations Emergency Force II whose brief was to keep the warring parties apart. The IDF had attempted to occupy a UNEF observation post, which the Finns saw as a clear violation of the ceasefire line in the desert.

Heavily outgunned and outnumbered the Finns were ordered by their commanding officer to put all their weapons down. Then to the astonishment of the Israelis the Finns started marching unarmed *en masse* towards the advancing IDF armour. Fearing the risk of mowing down unarmed blue berets the IDF commander ordered his men to retreat.

In this incident at least moral force had won through. The Finns' willingness to put themselves directly in the line of advancing tanks and armoured personnel carriers to defend the UN mandate had stopped the Israelis literally in their tracks.

Today Finland still sends a battalion every six months to the peacekeeping zone in Lebanon. The country's troops are much admired by their Irish counterparts who speak very highly of Finnbatt which is stationed in one of the most dangerous parts of south Lebanon.

But while UN missions have been hampered by great power politics and diplomatic machinations at headquarters in New York, the incident in the Sinai back in 1973 shows at least how completely different peacekeeping and normal soldiering can be and in many cases how the former can be just as dangerous as conventional combat.

In the last major all-out Arab onslaught on Israel, the Yom Kippur War in October 1973, Lt-Col Colm Mangan was stationed as an unarmed UNTSO observer on the Golan Heights, the strategic mountain plateau which was a battleground between the Syrians and the Israeli Defence Force.

Lt-Col Mangan, then a young captain, was marooned in an isolated UN observer post on the Golan as fierce tank battles raged between

fight under certain conditions to defend themselves a
Security Council's international mandate. Since the
ever, pro-active peacekeeping, or rather peace-enforc
been widely used by troops who were held back by the
conflict fought across the globe.

CQMS Clarke decided to volunteer for UN service five
the Congo. He served on a six-month tour with the 9th
Group in the UN buffer zone between the Greek and Turki
munities on the island. He was stationed in Xeros, a town huc
mountains in the north of the country. He described the t
relatively peaceful. His comrade in arms back in the Congo, C
Deveney, also volunteered for a mission with UNIFCYP (U)
Nations Interim Force Cyprus) in 1969. Colum said he spent mos
his time under canvas in a Greek-controlled area near the North
coast. His company's main task was to monitor the coastline for
possible Turkish invasion which finally occurred with an airborn
assault on the island five years later.

Most veterans recall a quiet mission in comparison with the
battles in the Congo bush. Colum Deveney remembers one night,
however, when he thought he was back in the Congo under fire.

'It was during the first or second week,' he said. 'We were all still
sleeping when we heard these huge explosions. They were coming
from the shoreline. At first our commanders thought it was a
seaborne invasion, that the Turks had finally hit the island. But
there was no one on the beach. The entire area was deserted.

'Then next day we discovered who was behind the explosions. It
turned out that a local Greek fisherman called Giorgio was using
dynamite to blow up fish while he was out with his boat on the sea.
And we thought it was an invasion!'

The main focus, however, for Irish peacekeepers over the years
leading up to Lebanon was a series of missions to separate Israeli and
Arab forces in the Middle East. Since Israel declared independence
from the British in 1948 the United Nations Treaty Supervision
Organisation has monitored the ceasefire agreements along the various
frontiers surrounding the Jewish state. After the Arab-Israeli war of
1973 the Irish infantry group stationed in Cyprus was transferred
along with several other international contingents to police the truce
between the warring parties in the Sinai desert. In many missions, Irish
forces leapfrogged from one land to the next whenever the UN Security Council called. Irish officers have worked in Jerusalem, Damascus,
Cairo, Amman and Beirut developing a depth of knowledge and

the two armies. He had been a platoon commander in Cyprus but confessed that the divided island was a paradise of peace compared to the Golan Heights.

One Irish UNTSO observer, Comdt Thomas Wickham, had already been shot dead in Syria in 1967. The dangers of being wedged between two mechanised armies battling over a small escarpment was all too obvious to Colm Mangan. But luck was on his side when the danger was greatest.

He recalled his narrow brush with death after returning from the UN's latest and most dangerous mission to date, the observer mission in the former Yugoslavia in 1991. 'Our UN post on the Golan was pretty basic. It was a portacabin with two beds, one for each observer. I remember it was towards the end of the Yom Kippur War and it was becoming apparent that Israel was winning.

'I was lying on a chair outside the post sun-bathing at around one in the afternoon. I also remember I was reading a book by Frank Harris called *My Life and Loves*.

'I noticed a tank moving towards the post. My UN colleague who was a Dutch officer called me into the post. I must have been in there one minute when both of us heard the thud of a tank round impacting on something outside.

'It was a tremendous explosion which shook the post. There was dirt and grit everywhere. I ran out from the shelter to see what happened. One tank round had passed through a jeep parked outside and blew the chair I was sitting in minutes before to bits. The round would have cut me in two.

'The Dutch officer calling me in probably saved my life. An incident like that certainly concentrates the mind. For the rest of the day we were stuck in our shelter because there was heavy shelling on the Golan between the IDF and the Syrians.'

Lt-Col Mangan was not the only member of his family to have had a lucky escape during the Yom Kippur War. His wife and one-year-old son Cian were based in Damascus in accommodation provided by the UN during his stint on the Golan. During an Israeli air strike on military installations on the outskirts of the Syrian capital, the sonic boom from one of the jets broke a window in the Mangans' flat.

'Cian was sleeping in his cot at the time and a window in his bedroom fell on top of him. The force of the sonic boom probably caused the window to shatter. Miraculously there was not a scratch on the child. He was not injured at all,' Colm Mangan said.

Cian, who is now a student at Trinity College Dublin, and his mother Margaret were evacuated after that incident from Damascus to a more peaceful Middle East setting—Beirut.

'Believe it or not but Beirut was an oasis of tranquillity in the region at that time. This you have to remember was before the civil war broke out in 1975. As the IDF threatened to push towards Damascus towards the end of the Yom Kippur War, the UN advised us to move to Beirut. Can you imagine that happening today?'

During the 1973 war Lt-Col Mangan and his UN colleagues were caught in the middle of air and artillery strikes. He reserves particular praise even today for the Syrian soldier who operated as a liaison officer with the UN even when the Israelis had recaptured the heights during the fighting.

Although the IDF never raided Mangan's observation post, the Syrian liaison officer stuck to his task which was to report to the UN on the general situation in our sector. The Syrian's single-minded dedication to the job, despite the dangers, impressed Mangan.

Yom Kippur was Lt-Col Mangan's baptism of fire in the highly charged atmosphere of the Middle East. He witnessed large-scale ferocious tank battles. During one battle he watched from afar with his high-powered binoculars as an entire Syrian tank crew scrambled out of their blazing machine.

'I said to myself, "Oh my God, this is not for real. What am I watching?" That was a terrible sight. Their tank had been blown to bits. I don't think there was ever any chance that they survived.'

On another occasion Colm had to give first aid to a badly wounded Syrian soldier who stumbled on his post. 'He collapsed in front of us and I noticed there was a huge rupture in his stomach. His intestines were hanging out and he looked to be in great pain.'

Mangan tied up the soldier's horrific wounds, dabbing anti-septic on them while his UN colleague radioed the Syrian army to come and evacuate the wounded man. Mangan often wonders if the Syrian ever survived. To this day all he knows is that he was still alive when the medics took him away.

After an arduous year on the Golan, Mangan went on to rise through the army ranks and eventually commanded the Irish battalion in Lebanon during the second Gulf war.

His UNTSO experience on the Golan again demonstrates the depth of knowledge Irish officers and men took with them to Lebanon from 1978. Many of them had already been to Beirut and the southern frontier with Israel on UN observer missions.

In fact Irish troops first set foot on Lebanese soil not in 1978 but twenty years before during another civil war that threatened to rend asunder the fragile political settlement that barely held the country together. Ireland had only joined the UN three years before.

Observer Group Lebanon was established by the UN after sectarian warfare broke out between pro-western Christian Maronite factions and the pro-Arab nationalists in the Moslem community. The then Maronite president of Lebanon, Camille Chamoun, called in the American marines to preserve the regime which kept the Christians on top.

Calling in a foreign power to help suppress a tidal wave of Arab nationalism that looked to Nasser's Egypt for inspiration fractured the national covenant in Lebanon which was to operate on a power-sharing basis giving proportional political rights to the country's various religious communities. US marines arrived on 14 July to shore up the Christian-dominated regime. On the same day the monarchy was overthrown by the nationalist Ba'ath Party in Iraq. Up to 17,000 American troops backed by the US 6th Fleet propped up the Chamoun government.

But by late July Washington had re-assessed its hand in the Lebanon and started to put pressure on Chamoun to compromise. The stage was set for a quick withdrawal. By 9 December the Americans were gone. After the marines pulled out, leaving a deep anti-western feeling among underprivileged Arab Moslems which was to bear fruit in the late 1970s and 1980s, the replacement of Chamoun by a Lebanese army commander, Fouad Chellab, stopped the country from going over the brink.

The gap left by the departure of the Marines was filled by United Nations observers called to police the peace, including half a dozen Irish officers. Despite the long-term damage done to the credibility of the Lebanese state, UNOGIL achieved some positive results. Their presence discouraged the United States from a long-term occupation of the country and facilitated the American withdrawal.

More than 100 military observers were sent on the mission from 21 states. Indeed, the mission still exists with unarmed UNTSO officers liaising with the various armies of occupation and militias operating on the country's frontiers.

A number of Irish UNTSO officers live in Nahariya, the Israeli northern border town, and commute every day across the heavily guarded border to the United Nations headquarters in the Lebanese village of Naquorra.

Although the ground had already been prepared for a more pro-tracted and vicious civil war between the various factions in Lebanon, which was less than two decades away, Irish officers writing home spoke about a country which appeared to be a haven of calm in the midst of a war-torn Middle East. Thus it remained for seventeen years. But when the peace was broken with the outbreak of the civil war in 1975, chaos quickly ensued.

In Lebanon in 1983 Jim Clarke, one of the veterans of the Battle of the Tunnel, was once more wearing a blue beret. He had been in Lebanon only a matter of weeks and was posted to the Irish battalion's transport headquarters in the Lebanese village of Total.

During his first day there, Clarke was told that he was replacing one Danny Mulcahy who had gone home to Ireland to run in a charity marathon for his home battalion. Clarke had known Danny Mulcahy before. As a teenager Danny had attended the first official presentation at the Curragh on 4 June 1968 of the Distinguished Service Medal which was posthumously awarded to his father, Sergeant Paddy Mulcahy, for his supreme sacrifice in the Congo. His father's example spurred Danny and his brother Paul to join the Defence Forces. Paul is also a sergeant with the Ordnance Corps in Dublin's Clancy barracks. Like their father, both men have seen overseas service in the cause of peace. Jim Clarke was stunned at his 'Total recall' in April 1983. Here he was in another UN mission more than two decades on, relieving the son of a man whose life he tried to save back in the Congo. The incident brought back a flood of memories about his first experience of battle in the African bush.

There has been an unbroken Irish link from the Congo to other UN overseas missions including Lebanon. At any given time since 1978 there are scores of officers and NCOs serving in south Lebanon who first saw action in the Congo, Cyprus, Sinai and other peacekeeping tours, men like Tom Sheehan, a sergeant who worked in the signals platoon with headquarters company with the 66th Irish battalion in Lebanon. He has served overseas more than fifteen times in 37 years of service with the Defence Forces. Jim Clarke, Tom Sheehan and many others embody that long and proud record of service.

JUST LIKE CONNEMARA

To the first Irish officers to arrive in the hills of south Lebanon their area of operations looked like Connemara. The topography was bleak, rugged and beautiful. Apart from a cloudless sky and blistering sunshine the advance party which arrived there on Saturday, 13 May 1978 might have imagined that they were in the west of Ireland.

South Lebanon, however, was in chaos after the Israeli Defence Forces had launched an invasion involving 7,000 troops. The IDF had punched through Palestinian military defences all the way to the Litani River more than twenty miles north of the frontier.

Irish officers in the advance party were taken aback by the devastation caused by the invasion. In a report back to army headquarters the reconnaissance team, consisting of one lieutenant-colonel and seven commandants, said: 'The initial view of the area of operations was daunting. Power lines were destroyed; there was little or no traffic moving and businesses, shops and whole communities were wrecked.'

At least two-thirds of the population, in the area the Irish were to take over, had fled north to escape the advancing Israeli army, heading to relatives and refugee camps in Sidon and Beirut. There had been 60,000 people in the southern city of Tyre before the invasion; after the IDF's self-proclaimed 'Operation Litani' there were only reported to be 3,000 Lebanese civilians left there.

The operation had been launched following a series of attacks by the Palestinian Liberation Organisation and its offshoots on towns and settlements in northern Israel. The latest of these attacks occurred on 11 March 1978 when a raiding party of eleven Palestinian fighters landed on a beach next to the Ma'agan Michael Nature Reserve.

The result of this landing from Lebanese soil was the death of 37 Israelis with 78 wounded on the arterial route between the country's

main port Haifa and Tel Aviv. All the Palestinian fighters also died in
what became known as the coastal road massacre.

Everyone in the region expected cross-border retaliation by the
IDF. Five days later came 'Operation Litani' which in turn was to
lead to the deployment of UN troops in south Lebanon. It also lead
to the permanent occupation by the IDF of a belt of land running
from the Mediterranean to Mount Hermon which was later to be
proclaimed as the 'security zone'.

UN staff officers nursed suspicions that the hidden agenda
behind 'Operation Litani' was not just to smash the PLO's infrastructure in south Lebanon. There were also fears that the Israelis
were staying put in the south to set up a long-term buffer zone on
Lebanese soil. That strategic agenda was to have deadly implications
for Irish and other UN soldiers attempting to fulfil the Security
Council's mandate.

The United Nations Security Council was convened after the
Israeli invasion to discuss the situation in the south. The product of
that meeting was the passing of Security Council motion 425 which
ordered the establishment of the United Nations Interim Force in
Lebanon (UNIFIL).

The key word in the new acronym was 'Interim'. It suggested
a temporary operation to stabilise the situation in Lebanon and
re-establish the authority of the Beirut government. Given that
UNIFIL is still in the south and is unable to deploy right up to the
1949 armistice line with Israel, the word 'Interim' seems highly
inappropriate. The legitimate Lebanese government does not have
any authority anywhere within the security zone. The mandate has
yet to be fully fulfilled.

After an estimated 2,000 Lebanese and Palestinian deaths and the
loss of 20 Israelis in the Litani operation the IDF had pushed the
frontier almost 20 kilometres north of the official border line.

The Security Council resolution gave UNIFIL a five point brief:
(a) to determine cessation of hostilities by Israel; (b) to confirm Israeli
withdrawal; (c) to restore international peace and security; (d) to
assist the Lebanese government to restore its authority in the area;
and (e) to establish and maintain itself in an area of operations to be
defined through negotiations with the parties.

UNIFIL's first force commander was the Ghanaian General
Emmanuel Erskine. He first consulted senior officers with UNTSO
including his successor in the Lebanese mission, the then Irish Lt-
Col William Callaghan.

Observer Group Lebanon, based at five crossing-points on the Israeli-Lebanese border, were also put on standby to help in setting up the UNIFIL mission.

The Irish government had offered to send a battalion of troops to the region. On 3 May UN headquarters in New York informed the government that an Irish battalion would be acceptable. The first main UNIFIL contingent to arrive was the French who touched down at Beirut international airport on 23 March. This was ironic given that France had been the most recent western power to rule Lebanon until the country gained its independence in 1943.

Other nations to send troops to the new mission were Norway, Senegal, Nigeria, Holland, Finland, Fiji, Nepal, Ghana, and even in the twilight years of the Shah's regime, a battalion from the Iranian army. The Iranians were pulled out of the Lebanon after the 1979 revolution which toppled the Shah and put Ayatollah Khomeini in power. That revolution also had a profound effect on Lebanon giving new hope to the underdogs of that country, the Shia Moslems.

A helicopter unit was supplied by the Italians while the Swedes took charge of the medical company. Some of these countries, particularly Holland and the Scandinavians had long-standing friendly relations with the Jewish people dating from the dark days of the Holocaust. The special relationship between Israel and these countries was, however, to be severely tested by the reality of the Israeli occupation in south Lebanon.

Once the UN accepted Ireland's offer army headquarters dispatched the eight-man reconnaissance party to the area of operations. The first Irishmen to survey what was to become the Irish battalion area were Lt-Col Louis Hogan, Comdt Jim Mortell, Comdt T. McNulty, Comdt T. Moriarty, Comdt Jim Burke, Comdt D. Swan, Comdt John Harold and Comdt B. O'Donovan.

They left Dublin on 12 May and flew to Lod airport, Tel Aviv, where they were met by Lt-Col Callaghan. After driving to UNTSO headquarters in Jerusalem the Irish party flew by helicopter to the Lebanese border town of Naquorra where they were briefed by UNIFIL command.

Prior to the Israeli invasion Naquorra, which is only three miles north of the frontier, had been under PLO control. After the IDF smashed through the border towards the Litani the Palestinian fighters retreated to Tyre. Lt-Gen. Erskine admitted that Naquorra was probably the worst place to locate the mission's headquarters. But he claimed there was no other suitable alternative at the time.

UNTSO observers had been stationed there before the invasion and were well plugged in to the United Nations intelligence network at its communications centre in Jerusalem. The Lebanese army barracks had been considered as an option but attacks by the PLO on the French battalion's Col Jean Salvan in which he was wounded, the murder of a French and a Senegalese soldier, and other incidents resulting in injuries exposed the dangers of deploying in the city.

Naquorra was the site of an old customs post between Palestine and Lebanon before 1948. It is a Christian village bounded on the east by ridges and on the west by the sea. The narrow strip of land running parallel to the town could easily be cut off by militias using the ridgeline to direct fire into the area below. It was as vulnerable as the posts manned by Irish and other troops inside the self-declared security zone.

The headquarters today resembles an international Olympic village. Over seventy Irish troops are stationed there along with a military police company. One section of the base is called Camp Tara. It is manned by Irish staff and is guarded by French troops. There is a small helicopter pad mainly used for air medical evacuations in the various battalion areas flown by Italian pilots. Every race and colour is represented, from Ghanaians to Nepalese. The latest nationality to join headquarters staff were the Poles who arrived in Naquorra in 1992 with a company of army medics.

There is a false sense of relaxation in Naquorra. Sitting on the porch of the officers mess overlooking the Mediterranean, with the Lebanese fishermen's boats bobbing in the water below the small drop to the narrow shoreline, you could easily be mistaken in thinking a tour in the UNIFIL headquarters would be peaceful. Indeed Irish troops in the hills even cruelly call Naquorra 'Disneyland'.

But as Irish troops discovered, danger to them in Naquorra lies to the east along the ridgeline now manned by the Christian militia which is supported and armed by Israel. Look east today and you get a sense of the encirclement which Irish and other UN soldiers face inside the enclave, with militia, mortar, artillery, tank and heavy machine-guns permanently trained on the small strip of land around the UN headquarters.

Travelling from the coast to the hills the advance party of officers' vehicles had to negotiate a tortuous route from Tyre to Quana which was later to become the headquarters of the Fijian battalion. The unit report for the 43rd Irish battalion noted that the advance party found the Shia town of Shaqra suitable for a rifle company to be based in while the largest town in the hills, Tibnin, would be a good place to station transport and armoured units.

In the village of Haris the officers reported that they received excellent co-operation from the muchktar (mayor) who provided them with the community hall as a base for the troops. The locals even provided a cool store in which to place arms and ammunition.

Preparations were laid down to accommodate the 658 men of all ranks. French engineers got to work building tented camps, supply stores and power lines. The camp the French built resembled something from a base camp for climbers ascending Mount Everest. The tents perched on high ground overlook the wadis (dried up river beds) and valleys that dominate the area.

By 25 May a larger advance party of troops had arrived from Ireland. Within hours they were stationed in Haris without any serious incident on the way from Israel. That was to come later. The unit report for that first evening in the Lebanon described how Irish troops were now cheek by jowl with the invading Israeli army poised to pull out of the hills.

'As darkness fell, guards were positioned and the advance party settled down to its first night in south Lebanon under the watchful gaze of Israeli forces on the lines of hills to the south.'

The main body of the 43rd battalion arrived in Lod airport on 7 June. They waited five trying hours in the blistering sun waiting for UN trucks to arrive to ferry them north.

Private Mick Dolan spent his first sleepless night in the Middle East lying in his army truck in a transit outside Tel Aviv. Worse was to come for the 24-year-old artillery gunner from Dublin's Inchicore. 'When we finally arrived in Lebanon itself I said "My God! What a kip!" It was like passing into another time zone when we crossed the border from Israel. There were massive craters in the roads, houses with hundreds of bullet holes and in the UN area itself lines upon lines of green canvas tents.'

Despite the scenes of devastation he witnessed, Private Dolan described his first experience of Lebanon as the most exciting in his 21-year military career. 'I ended up in a tent at the village. Our accommodation was in fact shared by five soldiers. Headquarters company in Haris was very basic, a four-man tent which each of us shared. Most of the time was spent getting ammunition boxes and other supplies into our base in the village's community hall.

'There was one sergeant who had a very clever way of getting us to volunteer for that kind of duty. He would shout outside our tents

"Anyone for Volleyball?" When we came out hoping for a game, he had a pile of boxes for us to load into the hall or a truck. He conned us.'

As pathfinders in the battalion area, Private Dolan and his comrades spent most of their time digging trenches, building air raid bunkers, constructing latrines and taking down and relocating tents.

In the first few weeks and months of the tour, troops lived on pack rations such as powdered egg, milk and canned potatoes. 'We used to get these "baby biscuits" in our packs. They weren't that popular so most of the lads threw them out of the back of jeeps and trucks to local kids in the villages.'

Comdt Johnny McMahon remembers that the first troops were baking under the sun on Tel Aviv's tarmac because they were wearing winter combat kit from Ireland. Echoes of the Congo all over again!

They were taken from Ireland to Israel on DC-10 transport planes loaded down with equipment including some weapons.

Comdt Johnny McMahon, then a young captain destined to take charge of a platoon in Shaqra, said tempers were so flared due to the delay in Tel Aviv that a French officer behind the wheel in one of the UN transport vehicles actually got out of his cab and roughed up a fellow national outside Haifa over a row about his driving.

When his platoon finally reached south Lebanon the Co. Clare man then had to endure an attack from one of the soldiers' most niggling enemies in the hills—mosquitoes. During his first night he slept in his camp bed without any net because the UN had not issued any. The next day he woke up covered in mosquito bites on his left arm. He was eventually posted to the hamlet of Mahaibeb near Shaqra village where his platoon spent their six-month tour under canvas in six tents. One of the main problems with the makeshift accommodation, he recalls, was that the locals kept pilfering any canvas sheeting they could lay their hands on.

'I remember one very amusing incident when the women of the area came to steal some of our canvas one Sunday morning. The entire platoon had gone to Mass and the locals obviously thought we would all be away from the perimeter of the camp.

'We had no proper latrine; our toilets were simply covered over by a huge canvas sheet. In the middle of the Sunday service I heard these screams. When we went outside to investigate I noticed someone had tried to rip the canvas sheet off the toilet. Unfortunately for the women one of our guys had been going to the loo at the time.

'These women were roaring and shouting at him and us. They were really upset even though they had gone to lift the canvas off the latrine. It was as if it was our fault.'

But Comdt McMahon said if that was not enough the local muchktar arrived later that afternoon to complain to him about his soldiers' behaviour.

'He even accused the lad in the toilet of exposing himself to the women. He was very angry about the allegations. Eventually we managed to calm him down. But that incident shows what Lebanon can be like. Even though the soldier in question was totally innocent it was he who was to blame in the eyes of the local population, not the women sent out to steal our sheets.'

He describes the 43rd battalion's tour of duty as 'extremely busy, working all day, every day for six months'. Indeed it was not until half way through the tour that he and his platoon got 50-hour leave passes. There was also no extended leave which allows troops to go on a prolonged holiday in the region or even return to Ireland for a fortnight.

He and his men slept in camp beds all the time. Water had to be boiled constantly and access to it was sometimes denied by the IDF. Their main water supply came from a source in Metullah on the international frontier.

Water became so critical on the summer tour that the Irish battalion placed sentries with instructions to allow troops to use water only for drinking purposes.

The decision to guard water tanks may have seemed over the top but there were other considerations besides running short of water. The French battalion had to send 90 soldiers home during the first deployment because they contracted hepatitis from contaminated water. No such fate befell a single Irish soldier.

Irish standards of hygiene were regarded as the highest in the entire UN force. During the 43rd battalion's tour there was a constant search for water sources in the area. The battalion initially used a water source from Jwyya. Irish engineers even diverted it to Tibnin hospital. But water in the Middle East is tied up with politics. The man who rented the water source to the Irish battalion began to cut back on the supply. It emerged that he had been warned by the PLO who were active in the area not to supply the UN.

The first checkpoint Johnny McMahon ordered his platoon to establish in the company area was at Al Journ. This was the place where the 34th Irish soldier serving with UNIFIL died on 15 October 1992. Corporal Peter Ward was shot dead at the crossroads when Irish troops attempted to search Hizbollah guerillas returning from an attack against the IDF and their allies.

Comdt McMahon went back to Lebanon and served at Naquorra in 1985. Five years later he was chosen by the UN to work in one of the two largest Palestinian refugee camps in Beirut.

Back in June 1978 another militia group in the area was preventing Irish troops from carrying out the task laid down for them by the UN. An early indication of future relations between the Irish and the Christian militia group in the south led by Major Saad Haddad occurred on 9 June. When an Irish patrol reached Saff Al Hawa they were flagged down. One of the Christian gunmen told them: 'I have orders from my general not to allow you south of this place again.' When asked why, he replied: 'This is the Lebanon. We are the army of Lebanon and you are the PLO.'

Under the terms of the Security Council resolution the IDF was meant to withdraw from Lebanon on Tuesday 13 June. On the day of the final pull-out UNIFIL officers sought the leaders of the Christian militia or so-called South Lebanon Army, Majors Haddad and Sami Chidiac.

UNIFIL's official task was to deploy right up to the 1949 armistice line between Israel and Lebanon. It became evident, however, from that first meeting with Haddad and his Israeli masters that the blue berets were not going to gain access to the frontier.

A meeting finally took place between UNIFIL officers and the SLA leadership at Haddad's headquarters in Marajayoun. The UN were told Saff Al Hawa marked the northern limit to the Christian enclave and that this would be under the control of the SLA militia.

According to the Irish unit diary tempers flared during the meeting and there was 'much shouting and brandishing of weapons'. But UNIFIL's efforts were not totally in vain. The mission managed to get the SLA to agree to allow UN troops to set up some posts inside the enclave but none on the border with Israel itself.

The agreement on a limited number of posts inside Haddad's territory was however a double-edged sword for UN troops. Irish soldiers labelled the positions 'hostage posts'. UNIFIL had a presence in a part of Lebanon annexed illegally by Israel via its SLA surrogates. The problem was that these posts were isolated and surrounded by heavily armed SLA compounds and could be cut off at will from the main battalion areas. What was worse, UNIFIL's own headquarters was and still is inside the SLA's area and could also be surrounded and bombarded by the militia group at any time.

It was not surprising therefore that the first shots directed at Irish troops in the mission came from the SLA. On 23 June Lt Liam

Costello was ordered to occupy the village of Rashaf with two French-made Panhard armoured personnel carriers. At 8.00 p.m. the armoured patrol came under fire. Up to 100 rounds of machine-gun fire strafed the ground close to where both Panhards were parked.

The aim of the attack, Irish officers believed, was to force them out of the strategic village of At Tiri which UNIFIL occupied at the edge of the enclave. The SLA's deadly intent to flush Irish blue berets out of the village was made even clearer when posts in At Tiri came under direct fire up to 27 June. The battalion suffered no casualties in either village but the stage was set for a larger and more significant confrontation in At Tiri which will be dealt with in detail in the next chapter.

By the beginning of July the 43rd battalion wondered if the enclave occupied by the Israelis and patrolled by the SLA was becoming a 'no man's land' for UNIFIL. The talking, of course, continued. Meetings were set up between Lt-Col Eric Guerin, the Irish c/o, and Haddad on 6 July at the Lebanon-Israel border gate in Metullah. The parleying seemed futile given that on the very day Guerin eyeballed with Haddad, an Irish patrol from 'B' company was fired on by the SLA. Up to 30 rounds of heavy machine-gun fire were directed at the patrol which was forced off the road south of Bayt Yahoun village but again there were no casualties.

Despite the hassle and continual threats from Haddad's militia, the Irish achieved one notable goal by the end of July. The population in the Irish area of operations had shot back up to 75 per cent of what it had been prior to the Israeli invasion. The deployment of UN troops and co-operation with local Shia Moslem leaders persuaded people from the area to return to their homes.

There were other signs that some semblance of normality was returning to the area. During the invasion south Lebanon's main orphanage in Jwyya had been closed down on the order of local PLO commanders. By early July it had reopened in Tibnin thanks to the joint efforts of Irish and Dutch troops.

Tibnin is the largest town in the Irishbatt area with primary and secondary schools, a police station and a hospital. The population of the town is approximately 8,000, the vast majority of whom are Shia Moslems, although there is a small Melkite Christian community.

There are fourteen centres of habitation in the area which has an overall population of about 30,000 which rises in summer months to more than 40,000 due to Lebanese migrant workers returning home from the Gulf States, West Africa and the United States.

It was a meeting with one of these returning migrants back in July 1990 that gave me a personal insight into the way the Shia population sees the outside world. Every evening around 7.00 p.m. local vendors arrive to sell coffee and fruit juice outside the Irish battalion headquarters, Camp Shamrock, on the outskirts of Tibnin village.

An Irish officer, Comdt Connie Ryan from Tipperary, invited me to meet some of the locals who ritually walk up to the camp in the early evening to chat with friends and eye up the local girls who by the codes of strict sexual division saunter on the other side of the road. We sat down outside a small caravan owned by a local businessman called Ali Saad. As we sipped the scalding hot sticky black liquid I was introduced to several of the young men who had returned from oil company contract work in Bahrain.

One of them called Paul Kattoura continued to eye me slyly while I chatted to his friends about the political situation in their country and the fall-out from the Gulf War. All of them had excellent English.

At that time the official Lebanese army had surrounded the last remnants of Palestinian guerilla fighters in Tyre with tanks and artillery. I asked Paul what he thought of the army's action in Tyre. He told me he supported the operation and asked how I would like it if foreigners occupied my homeland. Before I had a chance to tell him that Ireland had a long history of colonial occupation, he suddenly said: 'Why are you shaking? Are you frightened? Are you a spy?' I remember I was wearing a short-sleeved army shirt and the biting wind off the southern hills chilled my bones. But he continued to stare at the wallet I held in my hand from which I had produced American dollars to pay for the coffees.

I panicked. Before entering Lebanon via Israel I had been advised to report to the IDF press office in Jerusalem. In a dank high-rise building a beautiful young female soldier had issued me with a laminated press card which she told me I needed to cross the frontier.

It said 'State of Israel' on the front with my press picture. Anyone who spotted it at first glance could have mistaken it for an Israeli citizen's identity card. It had jutted out of one of the pockets of my wallet when I went to pay for the coffees.

Had this young Lebanese seen the card? Did he think I was an Israeli spy? I never found out but after that incident I decided to keep very close to my army escorts at all times for the remainder of the trip.

Paul kept looking at me as I ignored his outburst, laughing with a slightly cynical snigger while I turned to the others in an embarrassingly obvious attempt to change the subject. His inquiries, however, revealed the suspicions deeply embedded in the psyche of south Lebanon's Shia community. Physically isolated in the hills, part of a sect frowned upon by the mainstream Sunni Moslem community, excluded from political power and at the sharp end of foreign invasions, their hostility and mistrust of the outside world crystallised in the stormy atmosphere of the post-war Middle East.

The Shia were the underdogs of Lebanese society, as they were throughout the Arab world. In the mid-nineteenth century the British traveller and writer David Urquhart visited the southern hills and described the population as oppressed people living in squalid conditions. They survived as small peasant farmers raising crops such as tobacco, cereals and vegetables. Although by the 1980s a larger population than both the Maronite Christians and the Sunni Moslems, the Shia held only nineteen seats in the Lebanese national assembly while the Christians had 30. Gerrymandering was not something exclusive to places like Northern Ireland; it was still alive and well in Lebanon in the early 1980s.

The struggle between west and east, Christianity and Islam, has been fought in the hills of south Lebanon for centuries. The remains of the Crusader castle perched on a hill above Tibnin is a monument to that history.

It was built in 1107 by the French Crusader Hugo de Omer during the European Christian states' push to recapture the Holy Land from the Moslems. Tibnin was selected as a site because the hill dominated the surrounding countryside and helped the Crusaders control the routes to Tyre.

Saladin, the great Moslem leader, captured the castle from the French in 1187. It became a focal point during this epoch for battles between the rival religious armies. The castle was destroyed and rebuilt several times over the centuries. It was sacked by Napoleon's army on their way to conquer Syria in 1804. French pro-Nazi Vichy forces were stationed there in 1940. A year later a British army battalion arrived and held the castle until Lebanon gained its independence in 1943. The first Irish soldiers in the area held their medal parade in the grounds of the castle on 12 October 1978.

But the legacy of foreign invasions cannot just be seen in the stones of Tibnin castle. The eyes and hair of some of today's inhabitants show the stamp of an alien presence in the hills. One of the most unusual sights for a first-time visitor to the Irish battalion area is the number of local people with blue eyes and blonde or red hair. It is clear that the crusading armies of western Europe fraternised with local women, something which would be completely taboo among the Shia population today.

Another undercurrent running through Shia culture is the exaltation of martyrdom. Given the 'blood sacrifice' culture which has permeated political life in Ireland since the Easter Rising, it is perhaps easier for the Irish than most foreigners to understand the cult of the martyr among Shia Moslems.

Posters are stuck on the walls of villages depicting the death of the Shia's hero, Immam Hussein, who was murdered by his enemies in Karbala (now in modern Iraq). The death of the Prophet Mohammed's grandson is complemented by the depiction of modern Shia martyrs carrying Kalashnikov rifles and RPG rocket launchers who fell in the struggle against the Israelis or their SLA allies. One of the fallen fighters called Tawoos looked like the all-American killing machine Rambo with his RPG rocket launchers, red headband and crisscrossed bullet belts strapped over a bare chest rippling with muscles. The posters bear an uncanny resemblance, at least in style, to republican murals on Belfast's Falls Road.

The Shia are sometimes portrayed in the western media as cutthroat fanatics obsessed with theological dogma. When you meet them on their home territory you soon discover the other side of the story. In south Lebanon they are a friendly if indeed somewhat suspicious people. They hold education in high esteem. They are well travelled. The Lebanese, like the Irish, are scattered across the globe. And they are finally people who want justice for their community after centuries of exclusion and denial.

One of the most uncanny scenes I witnessed occurred during a walk around Tibnin with a patrol early one evening in July 1991. A young boy of about 12 or 13 whooshed by us on a skateboard down the narrow slope towards the centre of the town. He wore a Hot Tuna yellow surf wear T-shirt and long black and orange baggy shorts.

After bringing the skateboard to a halt he met up with some friends at the corner of a garage and they started talking. They spoke in American accents. I was astounded. What on earth were American school kids doing in the hills of southern Lebanon? Comdt Ryan explained that many Lebanese, including Amal leader Nabbi Berri, a native of Tibnin, emigrated to the United States. They set up businesses in cities like Detroit and Chicago. These children in the Californian beach gear were the sons and daughters of migrants. They had been born in the United States but had come to the old country for their summer holidays. And like many Irish people who had left for the United States some of the Lebanese-Americans had returned home for good.

Irish troops appear to understand the Shia's concerns better than most. By and large the main Shia military and political organisation in the south, Amal—meaning hope—supported UNIFIL's presence. Amal wanted Israel out of Lebanon and an end to the PLO's domination of the south. The PLO and its offshoot factions were as much opposed to the UN's presence as the Israelis and their surrogates.

One of the main objectives UNIFIL had was to restore the authority of the Beirut government. The test of this authority would be whether or not the official Lebanese army could deploy in the south. The Irish unit history notes that there was 'joy in Tibnin' when the news broke on 31 July 1979 that the Lebanese army was heading south to re-establish the government's authority in the area. The Irish Troops' task was to help the Lebanese military to set up positions across the region. But as Irish officers noted with hindsight, the joy in Tibnin was short lived.

Seven hundred Lebanese troops moved south but were stopped at Kaukaba by heavily armed SLA forces. In a brief clash one soldier from the official Lebanese army was shot dead and nine others wounded. UNIFIL was put on maximum alert. The Lebanese army eventually pulled back along the Bekaa valley near to Syrian military contingents and reduced its strength to about 200 men of all ranks by 8 August. The deployment of Lebanese troops would have been a direct challenge to Saad Haddad's authority in the south—which his IDF masters wanted desperately to preserve.

The 43rd battalion suffered its first casualty in Lebanon not at the hands of any warring party but in a road accident. Private Finbarr Moon from Cork, who served at home with the 4th Infantry battalion, was killed in a crash in Brashit.

Throughout the summer there had been a spate of shooting and shelling either at or close to Irish positions. These incidents resulted in a meeting with the group behind the vast majority of the attacks—the SLA. On 12 July Irish officers attended their first ever meeting with SLA Major Sami Chidiac. He was described in the minutes of the meeting taken by Irish officers as 'tall, handsome and bearded, and bore a strong resemblance to Fidel Castro'.

During what was regarded as a cordial meeting with the French-educated SLA commander, the Irish expressed their concern over the amount of shootings and shelling incidents in the battalion area. In reply Chidiac promised to issue instructions to SLA compounds to stop shooting at Irish positions. But he cautioned against Irish hopes of complete peace with his militia. He ended the meeting by admitting that many of his men were ill-disciplined and badly trained.

'You have seen my soldiers. Many are very young and with limited training. I cannot control all their actions . . . . There I have done my best. I hope it works', Chidiac concluded.

Comdt McMahon acknowledged that Chidiac appeared to have better control over his forces compared to other SLA commanders. 'I met him on several occasions because of the hassle we had with his men at Saff Al Hawa checkpoint. Most of the SLA were just local warlords. They were ill-disciplined. Chidiac was quite OK but that didn't mean very much to us.'

Comdt McMahon described his soldiers as mainly very young kids barely out of their teens. 'There was one fella at Saff Al Hawa checkpoint who I'm convinced was mentally disturbed. If he happened to be manning the checkpoint there was hassle. He would cock his gun and fire a few shots in the air to show off. It was always tense if we passed by while he was on duty.'

The slight agreement with Chidiac brought a period of relative calm over the battalion area over the next few weeks, at least for Irish soldiers. The blood-letting between the Lebanese continued. On 5 August an Irish foot patrol found the bodies of two shepherds in fields outside Tibnin. The victims were a 12-year-old boy and a 40-year-old man. They had both been shot through the chest and the neck. Inquiries by the battalion discovered that Haddad's men had been responsible for the killings.

On the same day as the negotiations with Chidiac, a large contingent of UNIFIL troops was abducted in Tyre. They included one of the Irish battalion's chaplains, Fr Kelly. After negotiations with the Lebanese authorities in the city and the PLO all of the blue berets were released.

By early autumn the Irish were under fire again. The informal truce hammered out between Major Chidiac and Irish officers was over. A post at At Tiri village came under heavy machine-gun fire on 3 October. One soldier was injured when concrete splinters cut into his flesh after his post was riddled with bullets. Once again the SLA was behind the attack.

Haddad's men came close to killing their first Irish soldier on 25 October when SLA men tried to break into a B company post near Ras. Three SLA men who, according to Irish soldiers guarding the post, appeared to be intoxicated were denied entry.

A fight broke out and one of the SLA man stabbed Private Phillip Gallagher. After fighting off the militia men, Corporal Noel Mullins then radioed for help and administered first aid to his comrade who had been wounded in the stomach. For his bravery and level-headedness at the post Corporal Mullins received the Distinguished Service Medal.

As Irish engineers prepared the next battalion for the winter ahead the SLA fired nine 120 mm mortar rounds into Haddathah. Minutes later headquarters company received a message from the SLA claiming the attack was all a mistake.

At the end of October and early November the first Irish troop deployment had completed its tour of duty and started to return home. During one trip from the hills to Naquorra and the Israeli border on 20 November trucks carrying members of the 43rd battalion met an incoming party of troops from the 44th battalion heading towards the area of operations. As the two sets of troops passed by each other on the Burma Road a single voice rang out from a truck containing 43rd battalion soldiers.

The soldier shouted to his comrades going the other way: 'There's the 44th battalion lads. Welcome to the Lebanon. Six months' hard labour—be my guest.'

Major Haddad had a different kind of welcome for the new Irish contingent. An advance party of officers from the 44th had arrived a few days before to accept the handover from the pathfinders of the 43rd. After Mass on Sunday morning in Camp Shamrock, officers in both battalions retired to the mess to toast the new arrivals and celebrate the 43rd's departure. As they lifted their glasses SLA shells started to fall on Tibnin just down the road from the Irish headquarters.

THREE
VICTORY AT AT TIRI

On Palm Sunday, 31 March 1980 Lt Tom Aherne was manning the Irish checkpoint in At Tiri at the edge of the enclave. To his astonishment he was informed by one of his men that a group of Israeli officers wanted to see him. The group included an IDF brigadier-general and several majors and captains who stood at the outskirts of the village. At the time Lt Aherne did not realise the significance of the visit.

'They said they wanted to go into the village to talk to the muchktar. But I refused them entry. That was my brief as platoon commander there.'

Denying the IDF brass entry seemed to put their noses out of joint. Lt Aherne remembers a brief exchange between him and an Israeli general. 'The Israeli general turned to me and said, "This is not your country." So I replied to him, "Since when was this Israel?" After that they left the scene.'

One week later, on Easter Sunday, the IDF's surrogate force, the so-called south Lebanon army, opted for forcible entry into At Tiri. They brought with them a half-track armoured personnel carrier and two land rovers. By the time events unfolded that evening Irishbatt, along with other UNIFIL units, were at war. Irishmen, along with their comrades from other countries in the 6,000-strong international peacekeeping force, were to lose their lives in the battle to keep the United Nations mandate alive.

Since the very first day Irish troops set foot in south Lebanon the village had been a focal point for confrontation between the UN and the SLA. As the 43rd battalion's unit report noted, At Tiri found itself in a 'no man's land' between the Irish area of operations and Haddad's self-declared Christian enclave.

As early as 22 June 1978 the SLA raided the Moslem village, looting houses, burning one home down and threatening the population. After that incident soldiers from 'B' company drawn from the Southern Command at home were ordered to set up a presence in At Tiri following an appeal by the muchktar and other leaders. The very next day the Irish battalion's chief bomb disposal officer destroyed 50 cluster grenades which Haddad's men had left in the village.

Over the next two tours of duty the SLA harassed and threatened Irish troops as well as locals in At Tiri. On 27 June 1978 the SLA fired up to twelve shots at an Irish post. No one was injured in this attack. Throughout that first summer the SLA continued to call on the Irish to leave At Tiri. One soldier was wounded by concrete splinters on 3 October when the SLA fired on his post with a heavy machine-gun.

By December 1979 the SLA went so far as to kidnap the village's muchktar and held him for several weeks. As late as 5 March 1980 Irish soldiers stopped five youths, one armed with a rifle, known to be members of Haddad's militia, from entering At Tiri. This incident brought a tirade of abuse on Irishbatt from Major Haddad on his radio station 'Voice of Hope'. He accused UNIFIL of allowing the PLO to infiltrate through the force's lines to attack his enclave and Israel proper. And he continued to call for the Irish to leave At Tiri.

Why were Haddad and his Israeli masters so obsessed with At Tiri? In order to answer that it is important first to explain the origins of his militia and its role in south Lebanon. Ever since the 1950s Israel's political leaders dreamed of an ally in the Lebanese army who would help secure the Jewish state's northern border.

Major Saad Haddad was a regular officer in the Lebanese army in the south when the civil war erupted between Moslem and Christian forces in 1975. He was cut off from his headquarters in Beirut when hostilities broke out. By the time blue beret officers including future UNIFIL force commander Gen. Erskine arrived in Lebanon in 1976 Major Haddad, a member of the Greek Catholic Church from Marajayoun, took charge of a Christian militia in the south. According to General Erskine, Haddad's new force received all the military hardware they needed from the IDF.

As part of the IDF's military strategy heavily armed compounds manned mainly by SLA personnel started to sprout up along the ridgelines of the Christian enclave. From a distance today they look like warts on the landscape. Closer up they resemble the shape of a Christmas pudding, huge earth-mound constructions built originally by Israeli army engineers.

Most of the compounds contain one main battle tank, normally an antiquated World War II Sherman donated by the IDF. The bases' mortars and artillery also come from Israel. Even the olive green uniforms the SLA now wear are supplied from south of the Lebanese border. Perched on high ground, their role was and still is to dominate the area and intimidate the local population below in the Shia villages with artillery, mortar and heavy machine-gun fire.

The compounds were designed to be Israel's first line of defence against attacks on Israel itself mounted by the PLO or Lebanese Moslem forces. Sorties by Palestinians or the Lebanese Islamic resistance into either Israel or the enclave normally result in the compounds firing into villages and valleys below, with civilians as well as fighters being caught up in the barrage.

The SLA eventually swelled to a force of around 2,000 strong, of whom 80 per cent were Christian, while the remainder were Shia Moslems or members of the Druze sect. Such is the distrust of the Shia members of the SLA that Israeli military minders do not allow the Moslems to man any of the artillery pieces, mortars or tanks in their compounds. According to Irish defence forces' briefings to troops in Lebanon SLA officers are exclusively Christian.

Irish troops themselves were caught between a rock and a hard place. If they prevented PLO or Lebanese resistance fighters from entering the UNIFIL area and attacking the Israelis or their allies, the Irish risked being branded as pro-Israel. And if they blocked IDF and SLA attempts to extend the 'security zone' and depopulate the area, they were accused of having PLO sympathies.

UNIFIL's relations with the IDF and SLA deteriorated to such an extent that as early as 24 April 1978 Haddad's militia organised a mob which attacked General Erskine at a meeting with the major himself at Metullah, Israel. The general had gone to the border town to negotiate with Haddad to secure the release of three Dutch soldiers who had been abducted by the SLA.

Erskine was beaten by an angry crowd of men and women. They knocked off his beret and tore off his badges of rank during the fracas. The Ghanaian general described the incident as 'the most serious humiliation of my life'. He managed eventually to secure the Dutchmen's release but the attack on the regional representative of the United Nations Security Council showed the extent to which Haddad's SLA held the UNIFIL mission and the 'force of international opinion' in contempt.

By the time the 46th Irish battalion reached Lebanon UNIFIL was living under the ominous shadow of the SLA. By early October 1979 Irish headquarters had identified several SLA members who were harassing the UN. The battalion singled out one Ibrahim Kahil for particular attention. He was behind a series of hijackings of UN vehicles near the village of Blida.

Many of the clashes between Irish soldiers and the SLA had their roots in local disputes as much as the wider political and military situation. Kahil was angered at the Irish after he was involved in a road accident with one of the battalion's trucks on 1 October. He demanded compensation for damage to his car. UNIFIL insisted he caused the accident. When his claim failed the hijacking started. On Christmas Day, for instance, he stole an Irish jeep near Blida. His comrades in the SLA relayed a message to Irish headquarters that they could not control him.

Even language itself was at war in south Lebanon. By 1979 the Irish battalion no longer referred to Haddad's militia as the south Lebanon army. The UN could never recognise Haddad's forces as a legitimate army. The official Lebanese army regarded the renegade major as a traitor. The Beirut government demanded he stand trial for treachery. Even the leader of the Christian Phalange movement in east Beirut, Bashir Gemayel, refused to ally himself openly with Haddad even though Gemayel colluded with the Israelis right up to his assassination in 1982.

Instead of the SLA, UNIFIL invented a new acronym for his rag-bag gang, the De Facto Forces (DFF). On the opposing side were the PLO, its various splinter factions and the Lebanese National Movement comprising the mainstream Shia organisations, the Communist Party, Arab nationalist groups and Islamic fundamentalists. They were perhaps too neatly categorised by UNIFIL as 'Armed Elements' (AEs).

The Israeli-declared security zone became the 'Israeli Controlled Area'. UN troops had to be as diplomatic with language as they were with the physical operation of the mission at checkpoints, patrols and observation posts. From 1978 until the Battle of At Tiri and beyond, the promises from the DFF's masters, the Israelis, that Haddad's men would stop putting UN soldiers' lives at risk, were broken. In October 1979 the then Irish Minister for Defence met with Israel's Minister of Defence, Ezer Weizmann, in Jerusalem to seek assurances that there would be no more attacks on UNIFIL positions by the IDF or DFF.

Such assurances on the diplomatic field meant nothing on the ground in Lebanon. Attacks, threats and harassment of Irish personnel continued into the beginning of a new decade. But compared to the three previous tours the 46th's stint had been a relatively peaceful one.

Tom Aherne's main memory of his first tour of Lebanon prior to the events of April 1980 was that it had been an exceptionally cold winter in the hills. The temperature can fall in the Irish battalion area to just below zero in the months between December and mid-March. As well as the cold, troops have to cope with the mud which forms into a thick red gunge clogging up roads and paths during the rains. One corporal whose last winter was during the Gulf War in 1991 summed up the weather in the Irish zone: 'In the winter you can't move your vehicle for the red mud and in the summer the mud turns to dust which blinds you when the wind blows in your face.'

Aherne, who is now a captain and a very able former press officer at army headquarters in Dublin, was in charge of a platoon of men from his home battalion, the 1st Infantry, normally based in Galway. He described the winter of 1979–80 as 'quite appalling'. Apart from living under canvas tents in the wet and cold, however, it had been a relatively quiet tour for his platoon in At Tiri.

'It had been a miserable winter and we were hoping the weather would improve by March. The locals had told us that once March came it would brighten up. But during the first week of that month, I woke up in my tent and went outside to discover it was snowing. I felt quite sick at the sight of it. We were all hoping for sunshine and instead we got snow.'

In the outpost at At Tiri every day was the same, according to Aherne, even Easter Sunday when the infamous battle for the village began.

On the surface at least At Tiri seemed to have no military or strategic importance. It was a peaceful Shia Moslem village with a few thousand inhabitants. The Irish presence in a large house at the centre of the village had brought back some stability to At Tiri. A brand new school had opened and refugees who fled north after the first Israeli invasion in 1978 had returned to their homes.

Haddad's attempt to burst into the village that Easter Sunday morning and set up a presence there was part of a bigger game plan. Irish officers at the battalion headquarters realised that the real prize the DFF and IDF were after was in fact Hill 880. The village was to be used as a springboard to capture the strategic hilltop occupied by Irish troops.

Hill 880 was the dominating feature over the Irish battalion area. Controlling it would have given the DFF a commanding view of the main supply routes and roads of the Irish zone. In June 1992 I visited an Irish platoon at the hilltop post commanded by Mayo man Lt Joe Cully. From the top of his bunker there was a panoramic view of the entire area of operations. It was a clear day and you could see the snow-capped peak of Mount Hermon on the Golan Heights and to the west the Mediterranean. Capturing the high ground has been part of the DFF and IDF strategy in the hills. An hour on Hill 880 leaves you convinced that both forces would dearly love to control that position. Facing Hill 880, slightly below the Irish base, is a DFF compound with its artillery and heavy machine-guns trained permanently on the post.

The strategic significance of Hill 880 was first recognised by the commanding officer of the 46th battalion, Kerry man Lt-Col Jack Kissane. His vision in realising what the DFF and their IDF bosses were up to at At Tiri won the praise of General Erskine. Erskine points out that it was Kissane who ordered the hill to be occupied seven weeks before hostilities broke out at At Tiri. The Ghanaian general believes that the entire Irish area of operations would have been put in danger had UNIFIL lost Hill 880. The DFF constantly patrolled past the Irish checkpoint outside At Tiri. They would drive close to the position before veering left away from the village towards Saff Al Hawa. But at 4 o'clock on Easter Sunday afternoon a DFF half-track armoured personnel carrier and two jeeps drove straight through the checkpoint towards the village.

'I remember earlier in the day we had been playing soccer with the locals. There was also a battalion sports day being held at head-quarters in Total. Some of the lads in my platoon were also in bed resting after coming off night shift,' Captain Aherne recalled.

On hearing that the DFF had entered the village he roused his troops from their beds and ordered the platoon to block the dirt track leading up to Hill 880. The Irish commander also reinforced the checkpoint at the other end of the village. Reinforcements were called from C company's reserve under the orders of its commanding officer Comdt Dave Taylor.

With the track to Hill 880 cut off and the Irish checkpoint now reinforced with extra troops, the DFF inside At Tiri were effectively trapped. They decided to occupy the building known to Irish soldiers as the 'outhouse' to the right of the checkpoint. The DFF insisted they wanted to set up a post in the village. This was immediately refused when the two sides met on Sunday evening.

The following morning the DFF opened fire on Irish positions. It was during this attack that the Irish army lost its first man in action in Lebanon. Private Stephen Griffin was wounded in the head after the DFF started firing indiscriminately. He had been part of a machine-gunner group which occupied a position 300 metres away from post 615-A. After being wounded his comrades called for a medi-evacuation team to come into the village to rescue him. They had to crawl the entire route to get to the young Galway man. The DFF even fired on the evacuation team as it took Private Griffin away.

The 21-year-old army engineer had been part of the battalion's mobile reserve (BMR) which was dispatched from headquarters company in Tibnin to reinforce the position at At Tiri. He was immediately evacuated by helicopter to Naquorra and then to Ram-bam hospital in Haifa, Israel, where he died nine days later.

During the attack in which Private Griffin died, Captain Kevin Heery had a narrow escape when his re-supply vehicle was hit by DFF small arms fire. In the first 48 hours of the battle Irish and other UN troops who helped reinforce the position did not return any fire. It was only after Private Griffin's shooting that the decision was taken to shoot back.

Captain Aherne stressed that every step towards escalating the conflict between Irishbatt and the DFF was taken by Haddad's men only. 'They [the DFF] kept forcing the issue. In every incident, even Private Griffin's death, Irish troops never fired back even though our lads were under severe provocation. When we did hit back it was a controlled response.'

On the same day as Private Griffin was killed troops in 'hostage posts' within the enclave were seized and brought to a safe house in Saff Al Hawa. As plans were drawn up throughout the night of the 7th, Captain Aherne remembers that he and his troops prepared for a 'voyage into the unknown'.

'We didn't know where it was going to end. There was just a feeling of great tension although there was also a determination to get on with the job we were supposed to do.'

By Tuesday morning the DFF had moved to within 200 metres of the Irish house. As Haddad's men advanced, fire was then returned by the Irish. Acting on Comdt Dave Taylor's order for 'controlled' small arms fire, the platoon opened up with their FN rifles. The advance on the house was repelled.

The tide began to turn in Irishbatt's favour further that evening when UNIFIL and OGL representatives managed to secure the release of all nine Irish soldiers abducted from their posts in the enclave. The first three who were released from Saff Al Hawa were examined by battalion medical officers and were judged to be in good shape. OGL observers then went about securing the release of their six comrades still in captivity.

The following day Irish troops noticed that four Israeli M113 armoured personnel carriers and five half-tracks arrived with 80 men in the nearby village of Kunin. Despite the presence of Israeli armour nearby, the situation in At Tiri was relatively peaceful on 9 April.

The 'Battle' of At Tiri is perhaps a misnomer. It was not a typical military confrontation between two sides who only come in contact with each other in one murderous moment on the battlefield. The situation in the village was bizarre. There were periods of calm after short fire fights. Each side then re-supplied while their commanders met and negotiated. On several occasions throughout the week Major Haddad himself passed by troops with his entourage on his way to the southern edge of the town to meet his own men! The only way through to his fighters was via Irish positions.

Captain Aherne said that while Haddad was allowed through, his transport was not. Haddad even had the gall to converse with Irish soldiers while passing by with his escort, which Irish officers were convinced included an Israeli military agent.

'We believed one of those who were with him was IDF or Shin Bet [Israeli Secret Service]. This guy was an Israeli OK. I remember during one of Haddad's strolls past our position he put his arm around one of the lads and said, "Very good Irish." But the Irish soldier shook off his embrace. One of Haddad's aides turned to the lad and said, "You cannot do that to Major Haddad." The DFF man then got a smack in the face from our lad. He was a private called McManus from Donegal. He took no nonsense from the DFF,' said Captain Aherne.

The decision was taken over Thursday evening/Friday morning that the next time Haddad would not be allowed into the village. So next day when Haddad arrived down he was denied entry. According to one of his officers, Haddad was reported to be 'very upset'. Irish soldiers at the scene were told by the same DFF officer that 'this would be a bad day for the Irish'.

On the same day as Haddad's minor humiliation, the DFF almost killed Lt-Col Kissane, UNIFIL's second-in-command, the Norwegian Brigadier Ole Nielsen, the force's press officer Timur Goksel, its chief political adviser James Holger and UN chief logistics officer Colonel Jean Apied. They opened fire with a heavy machine-gun on the UN team as it made its way to At Tiri. Irish and Senegalese troops returned covering fire for the party.

There were further exchanges between UN troops and the DFF throughout that day. During one fire fight Fijian soldier Private Seveti Sovonaivalu was wounded in the head. He died the next day. DFF men also incited young men and women to throw stones at Irish troops. The tactic was continued the next day when Irish officers noticed buses arriving on the outskirts of At Tiri. Scores of children disgorged from the vehicles and marched towards the Irish and other UN positions in the village.

Captain Aherne said the children ranged from eight years of age up to about fifteen. Facing the Irish checkpoint at the southern cross-roads, they started throwing stones and setting tyres alight. The DFF then opened fire again with small arms and the pubescent rioters had become a human shield for the militia. The Irish then returned fire.

UNIFIL commanders had finalised plans to retake the village. It was to be a two-pronged attack from the checkpoint and the house in the village itself. The centrepiece of the offensive was to take out the half-track which the DFF had parked there six days before.

Private T.C. Martin from Clondalkin, Dublin, should have been celebrating his 22nd birthday. It should have been a double celebration on 12 April, for he was due to go home eight days later. Instead he found himself driving a light tank heading towards the DFF half-track which UNIFIL ordered to be destroyed. It was his first tour of Lebanon with the Eastern Command's 'A' company. Now a sergeant, he recalled his first experience of a real-life battle to me twelve years later during his latest tour in Lebanon with the 71st battalion.

We met in the Irish reconnaissance company headquarters just above Camp Shamrock on 6 June 1992. As we spoke during a birth-day party in the soldiers' mess, a battle was raging just a couple of kilometres away between the DFF and the Iranian-backed Hizbollah. Sergeant Martin sipped a bottle of weak Lebanese beer and recounted the central role he and the officer he shared the tank with, Lt Johnny Molloy, played in the battle for At Tiri.

'It got so rough that day I never thought I would get home at all. I drove the tank from the hill towards the half-track in the village.

As we drove through the village I saw the DFF firing at the feet of this group of kids. The DFF got them to roll burning tyres down towards our tank. I couldn't believe it was happening.

'Then the DFF started firing at my tank. I remember that the noise of the bullets striking the armour sounded like a bell being rung. From the fire and the shooting it started to get very smoky inside the tank. In order to cool down I poured a bottle of water over my head.

'I have to admit I was very afraid and wanted to go home but once our tank blew up the half-track a big cheer went up. We were isolated at the end of the village where the DFF APC was. But a Dutch armoured personnel went behind us to give cover.'

Lt Molloy also in the AML 90 opened fire, directing four tank rounds into the half-track. Although destroyed, the explosions claimed no DFF casualties. The Irish had waited until there was no one inside the vehicle before finally giving the order to blow it up. A heavy machine-gun position was also attacked by Irish troops. It was during this fire fight that a DFF man was killed and two others taken prisoner. The death of one of Haddad's men left the militia with a thirst for revenge which was brutally exacted on three Irish soldiers six days later.

Sergeant Martin savoured the brief triumph over Haddad's forces when, according to General Erskine, UNIFIL finally showed its teeth. 'The driver in the Dutch APC, I remember, was called Mario. When we hit the half-track he stood up in the APC and gave a clenched fist salute in the air. We equipped ourselves very well, especially Lt Molloy. I felt very confident in the tank with him. He was a good officer.'

On the same evening, as Sergeant Martin recollected his experiences about At Tiri on his latest tour of Lebanon, Lt Molloy was watching a battle raging between the DFF and Hizbollah fighters across the wadis above the village of Brashit. He stood on top of the house occupied by the Irish reconnaissance company north of Camp Shamrock observing the fire fight through his night-sight binoculars. The whole scene looked like a spectacular fireworks display. Pink and Orange flares lit up the entire area which minutes before had been in almost complete darkness. Brashit compound was clearly visible with the naked eye as red pulses of light shot out from the earth mound.

'You've got to remember that for every burst of light coming out of the compound there are perhaps six to seven rounds of heavy machine-gun ammunition being fired. I wouldn't like to be in those wadis tonight,' Lt Molloy said whilst taking a break from his observation duties to sip from a cup of tea he brought with him on to the roof.

From the wadis below you could make out flashes of white light winking every few seconds. The light was from the muzzles of rifles and rocket-propelled grenades being fired by Hizbollah fighters towards the DFF base above. Below the Irish house, some young privates, all from Cork city, were elbowing each other out of the way to take pictures with their cameras of the ensuing battle three kilometres away. The white light flashing from their Instamatics seemed uncannily similar to the lights pulsating at short intervals in the wadis near Brashit.

In contrast to the excited young soldiers watching their first battle in Lebanon, Lt Molloy appeared relatively indifferent to the show put on by the DFF and Hizbollah. The scene was even more absurd when the NCOs and privates in Recce company's mess started to sing 'Happy Birthday to You' in honour of one of Sergeant Martin's comrades. But then Lt Molloy spotted the first Irish Sisu armoured personnel carrier driving to the aid of villagers and Irish troops holed up in Brashit. The orange light on the white six-wheel APC marked out the Irish vehicle for the combatants outside the village. 'There's our lads now. They're going to Brashit. It must be over now. I hope they'll be safe.'

The Irish medics called into At Tiri during the 1980 battle recalled treating a Fijian soldier who had been hit by a stray bullet. Joe Munnelly, from Belmullet, Co. Mayo, said it was the worst task he ever had to perform in Lebanon. The 33-year-old medical orderly noticed that parts of the Fijian's skull and brains were inside his helmet after being wounded when a DFF man shot him. 'There was too much damage,' Joe said. 'One of his Fijian comrades kept asking me how his mate was going to be. I knew he was a gonner. I just did the best I could but the Fijian eventually died. It was a horrible sight and one I wish I could forget.'

Corporal Munnelly, who recollected his experience in At Tiri during a tour with the 71st battalion in 1992, had been part of the UNIFIL pathfinders fourteen years before. He served on four tours of duty with 'C' company. The blood and death at At Tiri did not put him off returning. 'My business is saving lives and getting as far away as possible from paperwork. That's what is great about coming out to Lebanon. It's not just a job for me. It's not just about the money.'

As the half-track burst into flames the Irish and other UN troops including Fijians and Ghanaians seized other DFF positions. T.C.

Martin had promised himself before the battle that if he got home in one piece he would light a holy candle at his parish church in thanksgiving for surviving the confrontation. In fact he lit nine candles in gratitude a month later on the day he arrived back in Dublin.

The terrified villagers who remained in At Tiri celebrated the UN's victory too. They came out of cellars and back rooms to greet the blue berets once the DFF had been finally flushed out of the village. Captain Aherne said it was uplifting to see the faces of happy villagers who were pleased that their home had not been taken over by the DFF and the Israelis.

'The villagers were aware that the IDF and the DFF had depopulated other small towns and villages in the enclave, mainly Shia Moslem ones. Driving the DFF out left us with a good feeling too. Looking back I suppose we demonstrated our resolve to do our job regardless of what the DFF or IDF wanted. As soldiers it was a good feeling.'

Travelling through At Tiri today, however, it is tempting to conclude that UNIFIL's victory there back in April 1980 was for nothing. The village is now a virtual ghost town with a population down from several thousand to about just over 100 people.

Driving through it in an Irish APC back in June 1992 I was struck by the fact that the only inhabitants left there are elderly men and women. It reminds you of the town in the Disney classic *Chitty Chitty Bang Bang* which contained no children because they had been rounded up by the ruler's henchmen and hidden away from sight. The only child we saw during our visit to At Tiri was a young girl who ran down the main street southwards towards her home. Only when she reached her door did she look back at the vehicle behind her. Noticing it was a UN APC, she smiled up at us and waved, relieved no doubt that it had not been the DFF or the Israelis.

Across the road from her home was a rusting playground with a broken swing close to the old school building. The desolation at the scene spoke volumes about the policy of depopulation in south Lebanon initiated by the IDF and their allies. At Tiri is a sad forgotten place but with one important difference to other villages from which terrified inhabitants fled after the second Israeli invasion in 1982: the UN still has a presence there.

In the opposite direction from the young girl's home is the house where Irish troops made their base back in 1978. Troops at the post serving with the 71st battalion claimed that the DFF never come into the village although they will venture to the edge of At Tiri past Irish

checkpoints. Corporal Michael Dempsey from Newbridge, Co.
Kildare has spent three of his four Lebanon tours at At Tiri.

He preferred to be posted in the most southerly Irish post inside
the 'security zone' because troops are allowed to become 'more independent'. The 28-year-old corporal expressed sympathy for the
remaining residents of the village. 'This is a very sad place,' he reflected as we stood on the roof looking towards Hill 880 and the DFF
compound facing it. 'There used to be a lot of people here. I feel very
sorry for those left behind. They're mainly the old, handicapped and
sick who've nowhere else to go. We do the best we can giving out rice,
cooking oil and food.'

Soldiers based at At Tiri also revealed that the only remaining
young man in the village is so terrified of being seized by the DFF
that he dresses as a woman when walking outside his home. Such is
the paranoia in the place.

The Irish troops work on guard duty and patrols at 12-hour
intervals. The remainder of the day is taken up with sleeping and
exercise. The 71st battalion even managed to build a weight training
circuit for themselves at the house.

The eleven men at the house including one officer, three NCOs
and seven privates stress that the DFF still don't come into the
village. And glancing out towards Hill 880 you realise the significance of this. Had Haddad captured At Tiri twelve years before
and then annexed the Hill, there would be more villages in the same
situation or worse than At Tiri is today.

While At Tiri resembles a ghost town, holding it in April 1980
gave the mission some credibility and resolve. And although it is
easy to point out UNIFIL's obvious impotence in the face of IDF
might and DFF menace, General Emmanuel Erskine points out that
it is hard to imagine the American-sponsored multinational force
that operated in Beirut two years later handling At Tiri in the
unified and co-ordinated way UNIFIL managed to do.

The Americans, the French, Italians and British limped away
from Beirut with their tails between their legs after the series of
suicide-bomb attacks on the multinational force. UNIFIL and the
Irish are at least still in At Tiri.

Erskine paid the highest compliment to Irishbatt commander Lt-
Col Kissane on a visit to Ireland in June 1986. During a reception at
the officers mess in McKee barracks, he spoke about Kissane's role at
At Tiri. The Ghanaian general told his guests, who included the then
GOC Lt-General Tadgh O'Neill that without Kissane's foresight

Private Hugh Doherty, who was killed with Private Kevin Joyce

Mohammed Bazi (*left*) photographed following the death of his brother at the Battle of At Tiri. His brother's picture is held by one of the mourning women

An Irish checkpoint inside the security zone. A South Lebanon army post can be clearly seen just down the road

Private Michael McAleavey being led away from his court martial at the Curragh, having been sentenced to life with penal servitude (Austin Finn, *Irish Press*)

An Israeli patrol passing through the Irishbatt area during the 1982 invasion of Lebanon

Tibnin Bridge

An abandoned village in the enclave following the Israeli invasion of 1982

Market day in Tibnin

Brashit camp

The mosque at Brashit destroyed by SLA shellfire

A Sisu armoured personnel carrier on the road to Hill 880 inside the Israeli security zone. The two soldiers are Privates Tony McCarthy and Paul Doolin, both from Cork (AIRMAN JOHN DALY)

Well wrapped up against the harsh Lebanese winter, Private Francis Mooney from Dublin takes up checkpoint duty at Al Journ, the village where Corporal Peter Ward was shot dead by the Hizbollah (AIRMAN JOHN DALY)

Lebanese landscape showing the snow capped Mount Hermon in the background (AIRMAN JOHN DALY)

The village of At Tiri where Irishbatt fought a series of running battles with the SLA (AIRMAN JOHN DALY)

in taking over Hill 880, UNIFIL's credibility would have been shattered.

One of the most important innovations UNIFIL used at At Tiri was the Force Mobile Reserve (FMR). It was established as a multi-national company strong force which would travel to flashpoints around the south. As well as providing back-up for UN troops under fire, the FMR has another, perhaps even more important political and diplomatic role. If the IDF or DFF attacked one of the battalions, this would undoubtedly cause the nation concerned to issue formal diplomatic protests to Jerusalem. But if the FMR was attacked during a major confrontation with the IDF/DFF or indeed any of the armed elements in the region, those behind such attacks faced the wrath of up to five to six countries. Firing at, wounding or killing members of the FMR brought down the diplomatic wrath of a whole host of countries, some of whom had long-standing relations with Israel and Lebanon.

On the ground in south Lebanon back in April 1980, however, Haddad's militia had little concern for the 'force of international opinion'. Haddad himself singled out the Irish in particular during several chilling messages to UNIFIL headquarters in Naquorra after his defeat on Saturday, 12 April.

In one message directed at Irishbatt, he raged: 'Because Irish soldiers opened fire on children and women at At Tiri and your soldiers' barbarian behaviour, I want to inform you from this day on, I am *not* responsible for the safety of the UNIFIL soldiers, nor for the acts of revenge that will be carried out against you.'

And in a second communiqué to Naquorra, Haddad even mentioned the troubles in Northern Ireland in a verbal onslaught on Irish troops. 'At Tiri village is Lebanese and so are its inhabitants. The meeting between the Lebanese forces and the Lebanese inhabitants of that village has been arranged. *No* foreign forces will prevent such meetings henceforth in the whole of Lebanon. In any case, if Irishbatt dislike the situation and they are interested in combat, it is suggested they go and participate in their fight in Belfast. After they liberate Belfast, we shall find another mission to keep them busy. In any case, not in the Middle East.'

While the DFF commander claimed to speak on behalf of the Moslems of At Tiri even his Israeli masters knew different. After the second IDF invasion in 1982 one Israeli adviser admitted that Haddad's militia was 'unacceptable' to the Shia majority in south Lebanon as a whole. A senior Israeli academic who also advised his army on Arab affairs in south Lebanon, Clinton Bailey, observed that Shia members of the DFF were 'looked upon as the dregs of Shia society' by their own people.

Haddad's ignorance of the Irish Defence Forces' role at home was amusing and bizarre but his truculent broadsides against the 46th battalion also had a more sinister twist. His verbal attacks on Irishbatt fanned the flames of hatred and revenge which had tragic consequences within less than a week of UNIFIL's victory at At Tiri when two Irish soldiers were murdered at the hands of Haddad's men.

Irish officers still believe to this day that Haddad and his Israeli masters made one serious miscalculation during the struggle for At Tiri. 'The greatest mistake the DFF made was that they attacked our troops or even opened fire. If the DFF had just sat there and done nothing they would still be in the village today.'

On the road south through the near deserted village twelve years after the battle, troops pointed to a poignant piece of graffiti on the wall. Painted in white was a heart with an arrow through it and the word LOVE written in English and Arabic.

FOUR 'SULHA'

John O'Mahony kept staring at the photograph of the man who tried to kill him. Over and over again as he sipped his gin and tonic the big red-headed Kerryman kept saying: 'Yes, it's him alright. That's definitely him. I could never forget that face.'

We met inside the bar at Barry's hotel in Dublin on election night, 25 November 1992. The rest of the hotel's clientele were glued to the television set blaring out the gains and losses from constituencies around Ireland. But John was not interested in the election for the 27th Dail. His thoughts were firmly fixed on the incident almost thirteen years before which dramatically changed his life.

He was visibly taken aback by the sight of the man who murdered his comrades, Privates Tom Barrett and Derek Smallhorne. The face of the 38-year-old father of five started to turn crimson as he stared at the picture. The man in the photograph which I had placed on the table had shot him and murdered the other two soldiers in the notorious 'Enclave Killings' in south Lebanon on 18 April 1980.

The picture itself shows a man on the extreme left dressed in black. He is standing with his hands behind his back, his eyes fixed firmly on the ground. He has a moustache and a little nick of white hair in the middle of a slicked back black mane. To his right are three women also in black weeping as they lean against a wall. One of them carries a framed picture of a young man in his early teens with a premature pimp-like moustache just above his upper lip. The young man was in fact the brother of the other standing beside his mourning relatives.

Over a week before the younger man was shot dead in a gun battle between Irish troops and the DFF during the struggle for At Tiri. Pointing to the man in black, John said: 'That's Bazi alright. I can still see him now the very last time we met when I was carried wounded into a car. He had a contented look on his face. He knew he got his revenge.'

Revenge or 'Sulha' is like an article of faith in the Arab world. It is no surprise that the philosophy of an eye for an eye and a tooth for a tooth originated in this part of the planet. A modern illustration of it is the reaction of former Lebanese President Suleiman Franjieh, a Christian who blamed rival Phalangist leader Bashir Gemayel for the murder of his son Tony, his daughter-in-law and grandchildren at their home on 13 June 1978. On hearing that Bashir had been blown to bits by a massive bomb in Beirut four years later, Franjieh was still disappointed. Because the Syrians had killed Bashir, he would now be denied his own revenge against the Gemayels for the murder of his son. It was revenge that led Mohammed Bazi to murder two of John O'Mahony's comrades in cold blood and leave him for dead in a bombed out school in the village of Ras on 18 April 1980.

But the revenge was not just personal. Saad Haddad's defeat at the hands of Irish troops in At Tiri left a thirst for settling scores within the ranks of his ill-disciplined militia. The DFF first wreaked vengeance on UNIFIL on 12 April when the militia attacked Naquorra. For just over four and a half hours Haddad's men fired their mortars, artillery, tanks, machine-guns and small arms at the headquarters. Outgoing telephone lines were cut while the barrage went on. Helicopters used to evacuate Lebanese civilians as well as UN personnel in medical emergencies were destroyed in the attack from the eastern ridge overlooking the HQ.

Even General Erskine, the UNIFIL force commander, narrowly escaped injury when his quarters were hit by mortar and machine-gun fire. The general attempted to contact the IDF liaison officer, Lt-Col Gary Gal, during the attack. But Gal could not be found.

The camp only had a small defence platoon consisting of Ghanaian infantrymen and French engineers. They fought back with machine-guns and rifles. They were not, however, allowed to use the 120 mm mortars at UNIFIL's disposal for fear that the rounds might hit the nearby Christian village and injure or kill civilians.

The hospital to which John O'Mahony was taken after being shot also had to be evacuated for a short time during the barrage. UNIFIL suffered no fatalities in the revenge attack but it did show how exposed Naquorra was to Haddad's militia. Disneyland could quickly change into a deadly firing range. As a result of the attack that Saturday UNIFIL formed a special defence unit consisting of French infantry troops. There were other ways open for the UN to protect their forces in the HQ. The key defence was the use of international political pressure on Israel to rein in their DFF puppets.

John O'Mahony, from just outside Killarney, joined the regular army in 1970 at the height of the Northern crisis. Prior to that he had spent several years in the FCA from the age of 16. He was determined to carve out a career for himself in the military. He volunteered for overseas duty and served in the UN force in Cyprus in the mid-1970s, a tour which he described as 'quieter and happier than the Lebanon'. His dedication to the army was so strong that even after the trauma of April 1980 he offered to go back to south Lebanon and serve another tour of duty.

But on his first and last tour of Lebanon John ended up as a stores driver based alternately at Haddathah and Al Sultaniyah with the southern command's 'B' company. Twice weekly he had to drive into Haddad's enclave to re-supply isolated Irish posts. 'There was a lot of hassle from the Christian villages such as Blida. Sometimes kids as young as 14 or 15 would lift their rifles and point them at you when you drove by them. You could see the twisted hatred in the kids' faces. They had obviously been hyped up by the adults,' John said.

Before that fateful afternoon John had several clashes with Bazi who was known to UNIFIL as a section leader in Haddad's militia. 'We were called out one day to the "Black Hole" post to re-supply them with water. In the end we spent four days at the water tower because the DFF was firing at anything that moved on the road. But at least at that time we were accompanied by an APC. On another occasion Bazi and his men stopped our convoy just inside the enclave outside Blida. They said they were looking for water. But we were under orders not to give them anything and we didn't oblige. One week later he spotted us again outside Blida and flagged down our convoy. He and his men managed to disarm us, seizing our FN rifles and stealing our lorry. He even took some dollars off me.'

Irish troops had been bracing themselves for some form of revenge attack after the DFF defeat at At Tiri. What was and still is inexplicable was why the UNIFIL command allowed Irish soldiers to drive virtually unprotected into the enclave only days after the DFF lost one of their men in a clash with Irishbatt.

What was even more bizarre was why these soldiers were put into the hands of the very DFF officer who predicted revenge against the Irish only days before at At Tiri. Abu Iskander was regarded by UNIFIL as a Lebanese operative for Shin Bet, the Israeli's intelligence agency in the country. On 12 April he arrived at Beit Yahoun and issued a threat to the Irish.

He warned that if any DFF man or civilian was injured or killed at At Tiri he would take 'appropriate revenge' against nine Irish soldiers who had been kidnapped by the militia during the struggle for the village.

Yet John O'Mahony, Tom Barrett and Derek Smallhorne were placed in Iskander's hands when they crossed into the enclave shortly after noon on 18 April. Their task was to help evacuate four Irish posts within the so-called security zone. They were accompanied by two unarmed UN officers from Observer Group Lebanon, Major Harry Klein of the US army and French Captain Patrick Vincent. They were part of the OGL's trouble-shooting Team Zulu which investigated cases of harassment and attacks against UN personnel in south Lebanon. Along with the two OGL officers were the American Associated Press reporter Steve Hindy and Lebanese photographer Zavan Vartam.

'It was like putting naked men into a lion's cage,' John recalled bitterly. 'We had no real protection. We should have been given proper cover that day. They should have seen it coming.'

A company sergeant told Private O'Mahony he would he going behind the lines that afternoon. 'I had a fair idea what it was like out there but I could do nothing about it. Orders were orders. Then I travelled to the transport platoon in Total to pick up Tom Barrett. As we drove out of Total I noticed he was trying to write a note to his wife. I asked him what he was doing and he said, "I don't think I am going to come back from this." I tried to reassure him but in the end his words were prophetic.'

Fate worked to save the life of another Irish soldier that day. Up until Derek Smallhorne told him he was driving into the enclave, Private Francis McGarry, from Drimnagh in Dublin, believed he was marked down for the mission. Private McGarry, who knew Small-horne well from their time together in the Supply and Transport corps, admits today that he could have been killed instead of his comrade.

'It always comes back to me,' Private McGarry said. 'I was initially asked to go along with the other two lads into the enclave that day. But Derek came into the base and said, "No, I am going on this job." So that was the last of it. When I heard what happened to him and the other lads I was shattered. I kept thinking, "That could have been me." I remember after the murders I vowed never to go back to Lebanon. But eventually I served again.'

As the convoy made its way behind the lines, O'Mahony was driving a soft-skinned American jeep with the two UN observers. Tom Barrett drove the second jeep and Derek Smallhorne was behind them in the white lorry with UN markings painted on the side in black.

They had been told they would meet Abu Iskander at Beit Yahoun. But the DFF/Shin Bet operative never turned up at the checkpoint. The convoy drove on under Major Klein's orders towards Saff Al Hawa where the DFF checkpoint was manned by only one militia man. The previous Sunday the position was bristling with armed DFF and backed up by a half-track APC with its .55 heavy machine-gun trained on every Irish vehicle passing in and out of the area.

As the three Irish vehicles approached the T-junction outside Saff Al Hawa John noticed a blue Peugeot car speeding by the convoy. He recognised Bazi in the front passenger seat. John started to wonder what was going on. The Peugeot sped across a dirt track behind the UN convoy. It was then met by a group of young men on the road close to the village of Ras. They were armed with Kalashnikov rifles.

When the convoy halted they were surrounded and ordered out of their vehicles. The Irish trio only had one FN rifle and a Gustav sub-machine-gun to defend themselves. They were heavily outnumbered and outgunned.

'They took us and put us in a truck commandeered by a DFF man. It's hard to remember what I felt like at that moment. I knew something serious was going to happen but you don't really have time to think too much. I just hoped we would be released into the UN's hands soon,' John recalled.

O'Mahony, Barrett and Smallhorne, along with the two OGL observers and the journalists, were taken to the old bombed-out school in Ras. Ironically when UNIFIL was first set up, the future force commander Lt-General Bill Callaghan had suggested that the school be used to house Irish soldiers as an observation post. In the end UNIFIL failed to establish a presence in the village.

According to the OGL report after the killings, the Irish drivers were 'very nervous and in a panicky state'. As for Bazi, the OGL officers noticed that he was a man of about thirty-five and appeared to be in charge of the DFF group.

At first they were led into the school toilets at gunpoint. Steve Hindy recalls talking to Barrett and Smallhorne as they relieved themselves in one of the broken latrines.

'I remember saying to the two Irish soldiers, "Look, don't worry. This kind of thing happens a lot." We were all terrified. Then I heard Harry Klein arguing with one of the Lebanese. The SLA men started to ask our nationalities. He wanted to know the Irish,' Hindy said.

It was at this point that John O'Mahony claims he saw an Israeli officer with the DFF inside the school. 'I had seen him before many times while driving into the enclave. He was short and stocky. Even in the school he was wearing an IDF uniform with Hebrew markings on it.'

John was adamant that an Israeli was present during their detention. I asked him five separate times about the IDF officer who UNIFIL believe was the Shin Bet handler for DFF men in the area. 'I am certain he was an Israeli. I saw him before. That's what I told the court of inquiry after Barrett and Smallhorne were murdered.'

This is where John O'Mahony and Steve Hindy's stories diverge. When pressed about the possible presence of an IDF officer in the school, Hindy replied: 'I don't think he was Israeli. He was working for the General Security Services (Shin Bet). But I think he was Lebanese.'

But John O'Mahony was sure the mystery man was an Israeli officer. Veteran Middle East reporter Robert Fisk has also made the same allegation, claiming the IDF man's cover name was Abu Shawki although his real name has never been disclosed. Fisk alleges he came across the same man in a dingy hotel in Tyre five years later and questioned him about the double murder .

While the terrified soldiers and civilians waited to learn of their fate in the school, Bazi suddenly appeared. 'He started to shout at us and pulled up his army uniform to reveal a black undershirt. I did not know what it meant but Tom Barrett did. Tom turned to me. He was shaking. He said something like "black is for death". Tom knew about these things. He had been in Lebanon before with the 44th battalion. Then Bazi pointed at me and said in English: "You, you are Irish." All of us had been disarmed by his men at this stage. Bazi picked up Tom Barrett's machine-gun and ordered us to go outside towards stairs leading to the basement.'

As the Irish trio were marched towards the first landing Bazi started to open fire with the Gustav wounding John and missing the other two. 'He hit me in the stomach and the ankle. As I was shot I keeled over and banged my elbow against the wall. Then he fired again and I was hit in the ankle.'

What was going on in John's mind during those terrifying moments? What did it feel like as the bullets ripped into his flesh? 'There are a million things going on in your mind when something like that happens. I think I might have said several prayers into myself. As for the sensation of being shot, it's a bit like getting an injection. Like an anaesthetic, it makes your body feel numb.'

While John lay wounded on the staircase, Barrett and Smallhorne bolted down the stairs and ran out of the school. When John looked up he saw that Bazi had been joined on the landing by the man he alleges was the Israeli officer. 'Bazi seemed to have gone off his head completely. I think the Israeli was even afraid of him. I could hear Major Harry Klein shouting at Bazi after this. The whole incident took only about two or three minutes but at the time it seemed like forever.'

It was now shortly before 1.30 p.m. The big Kerry man's last sighting of Barrett and Smallhorne was when they fled downstairs in a bid to escape Bazi and his henchmen. After that John remembers an eerie silence.

'It all went quiet so I got up and hobbled down the stairs. When I got to the bottom landing, I noticed there were people including some women sitting in the basement room. I collapsed against the wall but I was still conscious. There wasn't much blood so I reckoned I must have been bleeding internally. Then I bound my ankle tightly around the leg wound. I thought it would be better if the blood seeped out rather than inside.

'After a few minutes a young lad with a gun came out of the basement to look at me. I got up for a moment and then slumped back down again. For some reason I started to yell at him. He just went away but I didn't care at this stage what was happening. I kept yelling.'

The man alleged to be the Israeli officer came down to the basement where John was lying. The Irish private remembered that the man had his gun pointed and cocked at him. After a few seconds he went away and came back with Major Klein. 'Klein pulled me up and helped me get upstairs. I looked around but couldn't see the two lads anywhere. There was not a trace of them.'

When he was taken out of the school John looked around and saw Bazi staring at him. 'There was a contented look on his face as he walked towards me. I was being carried into a Mercedes which shortly afterwards took me to Beit Yahoun. That was the last time I saw Bazi's face until you showed me his picture. I will never forget that expression of his until the day I die.'

John O'Mahony had been fortunate not to die that day even though he believed he was going to be killed right up to the moment he was handed over to the Irish battalion area.

Barrett and Smallhorne were last seen being bundled into the blue Peugeot after being captured by young DFF fighters outside the school. Despite high level contacts between UNIFIL and IDF/DFF both soldiers were murdered. They were shot at point-blank range in the back of the head and their bodies dumped shortly after in an isolated spot close to Saff Al Hawa. It was not until 6.20 p.m. that officers from Observer Group Lebanon were taken to the area and shown the corpses.

One of the unanswered questions hanging over the tragedy was whether or not any of the victims had been sexually abused during their ordeal. This form of humiliation is nothing new in the Middle East. Steve Hindy recalled seeing John O'Mahony's pants down after he was rescued. When this ultra-sensitive question was put to John, he already seemed well prepared for it.

'I thought you would ask that. There have been lots of rumours. As far as I'm concerned there was none. No, believe me I would be man enough to admit it if there had been,' he replied.

The two OGL officers in the school started to argue with the young DFF fighters. One of Haddad's boy soldiers said he had been captured by the Irish during the Battle of At Tiri the previous week. Major Klein asked him if the Irish had treated him the same way they had with the three captured soldiers. He did not reply.

Then Captain Vincent asked him the same question in French. According to Team Zulu's report the DFF fighter pretended that he could not understand even though the previous Sunday he had spoken French to UN officers.

John O'Mahony meanwhile was transferred via Beit Yahoun into Irishbatt area and rushed to the UN helicopter pad inside the Norwegian logistics base facing Camp Shamrock.

'You're not going to believe what happened next,' John said. 'One of the soldiers who escorted me to the helipad was drinking a can of lemonade. When he saw me being laid out in the ambulance he took the can from his lips and tipped it against my stomach next to the wound. I don't know why he did this but I remember telling him that if he did it again I would kick his head through the window.'

Before being put into the helicopter John remembered being given a shot of morphine. His only other memory prior to waking up in hospital was being wheeled into the operating theatre at UN headquarters in Naquorra.

So concerned was the UN for John's safety in Naquorra that armed guards were placed around the hospital. They were there not just to keep out the pack of reporters that had descended on the camp but to ward off DFF agents under orders to silence the key witness to the enclave killings.

It is well known among UN officers that many of the Christian Arabs working inside Naquorra camp are DFF sympathisers. Many have relatives in the militia.

John did not learn about his two comrades' fate until hours after he came round from his operation. 'Comdt Quigley came to see me and I asked about the two lads. When he told me I felt terrible. I kept seeing Bazi's face as the commandant relayed to me what happened to Barrett and Smallhorne. I still think about those lads every day. They are always in my thoughts. I never really got over it 100 per cent. Maybe I never will.'

The officers investigating the double murder were told that Bazi had killed the Irish soldiers in revenge for the death of his brother at At Tiri. Abu Iskander confirmed to UN officers that Bazi was a soldier in Haddad's army. Troops with the 46th and 47th battalions were put on alert after the double killing. Checkpoints and OPs were issued with photographs of Bazi. Irish soldiers were ordered to arrest him on the spot if he passed through their area. In the weeks following the Barrett and Smallhorne murders there were several false alarms in the Irishbatt area regarding Bazi. Gunner Eddie Johnston, from Kildare, who arrived only a fortnight after the killings, remembered receiving an alert call that Bazi had been spotted at Tibnin bridge. He recalled that in the troops' eagerness to be the first to arrest the suspect every jeep, truck and APC rushed to the bridge. They were disappointed. The man stopped in a car at the checkpoint turned out to be someone else.

Bazi was never arrested or tried for the killings. Indeed the Israelis spirited him away from the area and arranged a safe passage for him to the United States. He spent several years living among the Lebanese expatriate community in Detroit. But UNIFIL has confirmed that he has since returned to south Lebanon.

Steve Hindy learned that the Irishmen were murdered after he returned to Beirut that evening. 'I was just stunned by the news but my journalistic instincts told me to get this story down on paper. So I went to work and filed the story to New York. At least it got highlighted around the world.'

Hindy described his friend and photographer Zavan Vartam as a 'man without fear'. But after the incident at Ras the photo-journalist did not venture out again into Haddad's enclave. 'It took a lot out of me too,' Hindy confessed. 'It's not something I could forget in a hurry.' The AP reporter eventually left journalism altogether and set up a brewery with a business partner in Brooklyn, New York.

John O'Mahony is still furious that the man who murdered his comrades and attempted to kill him was never brought to justice. 'No one should get away with murder. It was cold-blooded murder and he should still face trial.'

It is doubtful, however, that Bazi will ever stand trial. After all who would try him in the absence of a proper judicial system in south Lebanon where the legitimate Beirut government cannot exercise its authority?

UNIFIL could hardly have arrested him even if they could have. That would have meant building prison camps in the area, a move way beyond the mandate given to the mission by the Security Council. Who would have tried Bazi? Who would recognise the court? It is a cruel fact of life in south Lebanon that murderers often get away with this crime when there is a legal vacuum in the country. Revenge was also out of the question because it would start another never-ending spiral of tit-for-tat killings between the DFF and UNIFIL. Irish soldiers had to bite their lips very hard and grin and bear such trials.

What if John O'Mahony ever came across Bazi again? 'That's hard to tell but I think time will eventually catch up with him. Justice will be done, hopefully.'

As a result of the killings, the eleven contributing countries to UNIFIL held an emergency summit in Dublin the following month. They had met to protest about the murders and thrash out ways of strengthening the peacekeeping force. General Erskine believed Israel was embarrassed to the extent that the IDF took direct charge of Haddad's forces. But UNIFIL's main objective, to fulfil Security Council Resolution 425, was frustrated. The IDF still held on to the enclave via its puppet Haddad.

Irish diplomats operating out of Beirut made high-level contact with the various Christian militias in the city to ask them to exert influence on Haddad's forces. The small Irish diplomatic community had extensive contacts with all the various factions in Beirut at the time including Phalangist leader Bashir Gemayel and former Lebanese President Camille Chamoun. Although Haddad's DFF was technically on the same side as the Christian forces in the north the renegade major was regarded as a pariah even by his nominal allies. Haddad and his men were dancing to Jerusalem's different tune.

Anger in Dublin over the killings spilled out into the capital's streets. Workers in markets around the city refused to handle Israeli goods in protest at the murders of Barrett and Smallhorne.

John O'Mahony is not just bitter about a killer escaping justice. He is also angry at the officers who sent him into the enclave on that fateful day. He feels they should have been given better armed protection including an armoured convoy. Despite this John desperately wanted to remain within the army's ranks after he was flown home to Ireland still tied to a stretcher.

'I was boarded out of the army on medical grounds in October 1983. I really wanted to stay in despite what happened. Shortly before I had to leave the army I had a medical examination. The doctor gave me a clean bill of health but the military authorities still said I was medically unfit to serve. I still believe to this day the real reason I was boarded out was because I took a court action against the army. I was one of the first people who brought my commanding officers up to court.'

John finally settled his action with the army out of court on 7 November 1989. The state accepted liability within a day of the case opening in Dublin's High Court. He told the court that he suffered from depression and abdomen and ankle injuries. He received substantial compensation from the military. John still has his UN service medal which he keeps at his home in Knockeenahone with pride. In many ways he is still an army man at heart.

Was it difficult to re-adopt to normal life after what happened? 'I was always by nature strong minded. I got back into things. I eventually got married to Mary and had five children.'

On the fourth finger of his left hand John was wearing a silver ring with the Star of David etched on the face. Inside the star there were Hebrew markings. The ring symbolises his capacity to forgive whilst not forgetting the violence inflicted on him.

'Oh, the ring,' he added, 'I bought that in Israel when I was given leave from Lebanon. I enjoyed Israel and met some nice people there. The ring reminds me of happier times in the Middle East.'

Extra security precautions were put in place following the double-murder. Armoured escorts were beefed up and smaller convoys were taken via helicopter to Naquorra. There were of course other dangers besides the ever-present DFF threat to Irish troops in south Lebanon. The 47th battalion lost two men in two separate road accidents during the tour. Congo veteran Sergeant Edward Yeats was killed after his APC overturned when it hit a large boulder on the road to a post known as the 'The Black Hole' in the enclave on 31 May. Just under six months later Corporal Vincent Duffy died after a traffic accident in the battalion area.

DFF threats to Irish personnel continued. The militia's 'Voice of Hope' radio station kept up the broadcasting barrage against the battalion. Its blood-curdling attacks on the airwaves meant the Irish were still a target despite the international outcry over Barrett and Smallhorne's murders.

Just six weeks after the killings, however, Irishbatt could have lost another group of soldiers but for the linguistic skills of a British civilian aid worker with the UN. Eddie Johnston had to escort a relief worker with UNICEF into Beit Yahoun village. The UNICEF volunteer's task was to come to the area to help reopen schools in the south on the orders of the Beirut government. He had a scheduled meeting with the head teacher at Beit Yahoun. Because they were entering the enclave, the Irish escort had to liaise with a DFF officer known as Major Hassrouni.

Eddie, now a barrister working in Dublin, remembers they were joined on the escort by a local interpreter. The meeting took place in the school house with the aid worker pressing the DFF to re-open the school for local children. During the discussion there was a prolonged conversation between the interpreter Irishbatt had sent in with the convoy and Major Hassrouni. Eddie said he started to get nervous as the DFF officer kept questioning the interpreter, pointing constantly at the Irish soldiers in the room. The young Irish gunner suspected something was wrong.

The aid worker suddenly turned to Eddie and whispered: 'I can understand Arabic fluently. The major is asking your friend how long you would be missed by your headquarters if his men abducted you and your comrades. The interpreter might set you up.'

Eddie alerted his comrades and they got up, weapons cocked, and left the room pointing out that the meeting was over and that they had to return to base. The group quickly made their apologies and drove off at high speed back to the nearest Irish position.

'I drove to our checkpoint down the road and told them what had happened in the village. Without the aid worker understanding Arabic I don't know what might have happened. The DFF was still baying for Irish blood at the time. We could have ended up like Barrett and Smallhorne.'

'RUBICON'

A black bearded Israeli gunner leapt out of the tank turret. Behind him was a huge convoy of armour pointing northwards towards Beirut. It was the second week of the IDF's second invasion of Lebanon which began on 6 June 1982, the 38th anniversary of the D-Day landings at Normandy.

Irish troops with the transport platoon in Total had lost count of the hundreds of 'Merkava' tanks, armoured personnel carriers, half-tracks, trucks and jeeps passing through the village. Sergeant Noel Leavey had grown tired of logging and photographing the bewildering number of armoured vehicles cruising past UN positions giving victory signs to Irish troops as they passed.

He was stunned, however, when he heard a tank gunner shout out in a thick Ulster accent to the Irishmen perched on a roof above the village shops: 'How are Northern Ireland doin' in the World Cup, lads?'

Sergeant Leavey listened in disbelief as the IDF soldier kept inquiring about Billy Bingham's team's preparations for the 1982 World Cup in Spain. 'He said he was from Northern Ireland,' Noel recalled. 'He moved to Israel after meeting and marrying an Israeli girl while on holiday out there. After a year living in Israel he was obliged to do his military service and ended up in Lebanon. All he was worried about was how Northern Ireland was doing. He was afraid he would miss the matches on television. Then he simply waved up to me, wished us all the best and got back into the Merkava. I never saw him again but it shows you it really is a small world.'

Sergeant Leavey spent most of June and July on the garage roof monitoring the incoming Israeli army. 'I saw them rolling through Total. It was unbelievable, an absolutely awesome sight. The odd tank would stop and the gunner would chat to our lads at the checkpoint.

'I remember one incident during the first week of the invasion when an Israeli soldier jumped out of a tank and walked into one of the locals' shops facing the garage. It gave us a bit of a laugh. A few days before the owner, Muhammed, had been cursing the Israelis and calling them all kinds of things. But when the first Israelis walked into his shop he was all over them, trying to get them to buy things.'

The Israelis had in fact broadcast instructions to the local population in Arabic to hang out white flags in their villages. Some locals even went as far as to cut up white and blue ribbons in order to make Israeli flags for the incoming invaders .

On Day One of the invasion Irish transport drivers listened to the BBC World Service on their radios as the announcer said that a new ceasefire had been drawn up between the Israelis and their adversaries. While the ceasefire announcement was being read out, an air battle was taking place over Jwyya village with Israeli jets blasting Syrian Mig 21 fighters out of the sky. As water trucks carrying supplies hurried back into the Irish battalion area, the roads east of Tyre were being clogged up with cars, trucks and buses heading north with scores of wounded Palestinian fighters inside. The reports had been wrong. The war was on.

Irish officers based at Naquorra had been expecting some kind of Israeli military incursion north of the enclave months before the actual invasion. One Irish intelligence officer said he was tempted to give up counting the number of times the unmanned hi-tech 'drone aircraft' had flown over UNIFIL's area. The spy-in-the-sky aircraft were designed by the Israeli air force to fly over enemy territory and photograph the terrain below. They were used prior to 6 June to photograph PLO positions across the south giving them an accurate picture of the forces they would face.

On the eve of the invasion and particularly in its first hours Irish signal troops noticed the frequent use of the codeword 'Rubicon' when they listened into the IDF radio networks. It was in fact the signal for the invasion. Unknown to Irish troops, UNIFIL in general, the local population and even most of the IDF soldiers, the hidden agenda of the second Lebanon invasion was an ill-fated attempt to establish a small 'empire' north of Israel.

Irish soldiers heard 'Rubicon' so many times during those first few days that signalmen at the listening post in Daynar Ntar named a local dog that they had adopted as Rubicon Major. The post itself was the same place where Private Kevin Joyce was seized from just over a year before and Hugh Doherty was shot dead by Palestinian fighters. UN intelligence indicates that Joyce may still have been alive and in the hands of his Palestinian captors prior to the Israeli invasion.

The post had been attacked before 'Rubicon' on 26 May when PLO fighters fired 100 rounds of small arms fire at the Irish position and an APC parked outside it. A lethal cocktail of political mis-adventure by the Israeli government, sporadic PLO rocket attacks on Israel's northern border and the attempted assassination in London of the Israeli ambassador propelled the Middle East towards war. The shooting in London gave the architects of the invasion the green light to push forward. The invasion was given the name 'Operation Peace for Galilee'. It was officially meant to push the PLO out of the south and impose a new 40 kilometre line of defence north to protect Israel. But the main master planner of the project, Defence Minister Ariel Sharon, had grander designs in mind. Sharon wanted to impose a pro-Israeli government on Lebanon led by Christian Phalangists which would agree to a peace treaty with Israel on Jerusalem's terms, making it the only other Arab nation apart from Egypt to sign an accord with the Israelis.

He attempted to strengthen co-operation with the United States and drag it into the quagmire with Israel. He believed he could final-ly destroy the PLO once and for all while inflicting a debilitating military blow against Syria, thus reducing Damascus' influence on Lebanon. Victory in Lebanon would ensure that Israel was master over the region and give it final control over the occupied territories of the West Bank and Gaza Strip.

Like many other grand politico-military designs, 'Operation Peace for Galilee' plunged both countries into disaster. Key ministers in the Israeli cabinet were deceived by Sharon. The head of the Mossad, Israel's renowned intelligence service, opposed the war. Israel's Lebanese allies, the Phalangists, and Haddad's DFF were unreliable and carried out acts of sectarian slaughter against Palestinian refugees, the most notorious of which was the Sabra and Chatila massacres of 17 September 1982 in which hundreds, perhaps thousands, of civilians died. Five hundred Israelis also lost their lives in the country's first defeat since the foundation of the state. Deaths among the Lebanese ran into the thousands.

Irish and other UN troops were impotent in the face of the IDF's firepower. On the day before the invasion the IDF received per-mission to ignore UNIFIL's presence in the south and simply drive straight past them. The Israeli general staff had initially been told to skirt past the UNIFIL zone but this would have put IDF troops at a disadvantage. The best way to cross over the Litani River, beyond the point they had reached in 1978, meant that the IDF had to cut through the UN area. In the end the Israelis chose what looked on paper to be the easier option. The United Nations 'force of international opinion' seemed lost on them.

The IDF swept through UNIFIL's area along three axes—up the coast road past Naquorra, a right hook movement into Fijibatt at Jwyya and across the narrow eastern end of the 'security zone' from northern Galilee.

Irish company areas reported sighting huge troop and armoured movements on the day the invasion started. At 2.00 p.m. soldiers with 'A' company told headquarters that a large IDF column had gone through their checkpoint at Al Sultaniyah. The convoy included 115 tanks along with APCs, half-tracks and trucks. The next day 'C' company informed headquarters in Camp Shamrock that another IDF column passed through an Irish weapons platoon, Beit Yahoun. It took several hours to pass by. Noel Leavey counted at least 150 vehicles going through Total that day including huge tank transporters and water lorries.

Several days later during a trip to bring water supplies to the Force Mobile Reserve at Quana he witnessed an aerial battle between Israeli and Syrian jets. 'I looked up from my cab and saw these two jets over Tyre. They were involved in a dogfight. One of the planes suddenly burst into flames and started to fall out of the sky. It was weird watching it happen.'

The Israelis poured so much armour into Lebanon that they forgot to bring some basic repair equipment with them. Gunner Eddie Johnston was actually stopped by a group of IDF soldiers as he returned with water in his truck from a waterhole near Jwyya several days after the invasion started.

Eddie pulled up beside the Israeli encampment and noticed that an IDF jeep was lying kinked to one side of the road after it had sustained a puncture. The 19-year-old gunner believed he was about to be hassled by the IDF soldiers. As Johnston stopped his truck and started to quote the UN mandate to him, the Israeli asked in English if he could borrow his jack to take off the punctured wheel. Johnston was astounded. Here was one of the mightiest and most battle hardened armies in the world going into a hostile foreign country without a ready supply of wheel jacks. The Kildare man refused the Israeli's request, reminding him that his army's presence was a violation of international law, and drove on back to Total village.

Whilst UNIFIL could do little to halt the IDF advance, the force was under orders not to allow the DFF to gain access through the area under the Israelis' military umbrella. The Irish unit report however confesses that it was extremely difficult at times to distinguish between the IDF and Haddad's militia. For a start there was a lack of uniformity with IDF identity cards when they bothered to show them at UN checkpoints. Secondly the DFF's olive green uniforms were almost the same as IDF fatigues even down to the Hebrew markings sewn onto the material. 'C' company came to the conclusion that the only safe way of telling the IDF and their surrogates apart was by their weapons. The IDF standard issue infantry rifle was the Galil, a gun modelled on the Soviet-made Kalashnikov. Haddad's militia on the other hand mainly used Kalashnikovs which had been captured from the PLO and their Lebanese leftist and Moslem enemies.

Every Irish soldier is briefed before and while out in Lebanon on the arsenals of the region's warring parties. In the Defence Forces, *Handbook on Lebanon* photographs and technical details are printed to help troops find out what they are up against and how to distinguish between one faction and another.

As the Israelis sped towards Beirut, they tried to impose a new authority in the south particularly among the Shia population. Over the months of July and August new militia groups mushroomed in villages within the Irishbatt area and the general UNIFIL zone. The Israelis were trying to establish a client administration in the south which would prevent the PLO and their allies from returning.

During the summer the UN had to invent another acronym— 'Lebanese Armed and Uniformed by Israel'. The Israelis invented more fanciful names for these gangs such as 'The Forces of Kerbala' or 'The Partisans of the Army'. Even language was at war again in south Lebanon.

The new Israeli-created militias in the Shia villages of the south were designed to replace Moslem organisations such as Amal, which, although under orders not to oppose the IDF in the area, refused to collaborate with the army of occupation. Indeed by the time the IDF reached the edge of Beirut on 12 June, Amal fighters from the city's Shia Moslem areas had engaged in bloody clashes with the Israelis. As one American observer of events in Lebanon correctly pointed out, no credible Moslem political organisation or leader could openly embrace the Israelis or their puppet Saad Haddad. The Shia in the south had accepted the Israelis' presence in the early days of the invasion but only reluctantly.

Attempts by the IDF and Shin Bet to build an alternative to Amal was the most pressing problem Irish soldiers faced during the summer. By August 'A' company reported that the IDF tried to establish a proxy militia in Dyar Ntar but were unable to recruit anyone from the village at all.

Irish troops had some success in stopping Israeli-sponsored gangs patrolling through the 'B' company area particularly in Haddathah village. Their comrades in 'C' company managed to identify the main leader of an LAUI operating from Brashit.

Irish intelligence discovered that one Hussein Abdul Nabi was the leader of a small band of armed men who terrorised locals living in the village. Nabi, a native of Brashit, was eventually allowed to patrol through his birthplace on his own with a gun in his hip holster. Officers with 'C' company were unimpressed by his swagger noting that 'he used his new authority to drink Arak (a milky white Lebanese spirit) until the small hours in the Mingy shop beside the commanding officers' house'.

According to the Company's report Hussein Abdul Nabi answered to a Shin Bet officer called 'Captain Dani' (a.k.a. Abu Amour). The report also noted that the main man operating for the DFF in their area was still Abu Iskander, Haddad's henchman who issued bellicose threats to Irish troops at the Battle of At Tiri and the contact who never turned up on the day of the Barrett and Smallhorne murders.

A secret UNIFIL intelligence briefing also written shortly after the Israeli invasion profiles the role of Hussein Abdul Nabi. It discloses that he was paid 700 Lebanese pounds per month by the IDF and had murdered several villagers in Brashit. Nabi, the briefing reveals, also ran a protection racket in the area imposing a 'tax' on 350 households. Most significant of all was his bid to set up a pro-Israeli village committee in Brashit.

The secret report by Irish UN officers found that Nabi drew up the nominations for the committee himself. It would rival and eventually replace the officially recognised council in Brashit. One of his stated aims was to establish an 'Israeli liaison office' in the village.

Aware of his plans Irish troops successfully halted his activities. Nabi was physically prevented from controlling the village with his hired men. Here in Brashit Irishbatt managed at least to support the authority of the officially recognised local committee. Elsewhere they had limited success. Beit Yahoun now had to pay 'taxes' to

Major Haddad's militia after the DFF managed to carve out and consolidate another slice of the UNIFIL area under Irish control.

Another agent run by Captain Dani of whom the Irish were aware was Haydar Dayk from the village of Jwyya. According to the UNIFIL report he previously infiltrated the PLO for the Israelis. Irish officers noted that Dayk had a severe alcohol problem. Was he the man who UN intelligence officers believe seized Kevin Joyce a year before in Dyar Ntar? The problem with identifying anyone in Lebanon is the commonplace names used by the local population. Dayk led the so-called 'Forces of Kerbala' and wore a uniform originally given to him by the PLO. When I pressed a former senior UN intelligence officer about Dayk he seemed convinced that he was not the same man involved in the Joyce kidnap.

The locals were reluctant to see Irishbatt leave the hills throughout the summer as the IDF besieged Beirut, expelling the PLO from the capital, smashing Syrian military resistance and trying to force a pro-Israeli government on the country.

The elderly mayor or muchktar of Tibnin was sure of one thing throughout that turbulent summer—UNIFIL and specifically the Irish should stay in south Lebanon. On 17 September hundreds of Palestinian men, women and children were massacred by Lebanese Christian Phalangists in the Sabra and Shatila refugee camps in west Beirut. The slaughter occurred under the gaze of IDF soldiers. Rumours spread throughout the south that Haddad's men had participated in the killings. Speculation about possible DFF involvement at Sabra and Shatila spread paranoia among the Shia population in the Irish controlled area. Tibnin's muchktar, Abbas Fawaz, pointed out to visiting journalists that south Lebanon had been relatively peaceful over the summer. But if the Irish departed 'the big problems will start again like before 1978'. Irishbatt was in fact an oasis of peace during the period up to Israel's withdrawal from Beirut.

The population of the Shia south actually increased as refugees left the devastation of Beirut to return to their families in the UNIFIL area. Haddathah village, for instance, doubled in size within a month of the Israeli invasion. This was the opposite of what happened in the first Israeli invasion in 1978 when the population of the south fled to Beirut to escape the fighting.

Refugees from the 1982 invasion were given camp beds, blankets, food and fuel by the Irish who made life in the hills a little more bearable for terrified civilians fleeing Beirut which was now under a merciless siege.

As well as preventing Hussein Abdul Nabi's gang taking over Bras-hit, Irish soldiers shored up normal life by reopening the village's schools and patrolling the nearby wadis during the day to protect local farmers in their fields. One visible effect of the invasion was to reduce traffic on the roads which were only used by UNIFIL and IDF vehicles. This had one positive spin-off—the number of road accidents sharply decreased.

Construction work started up again after June as sand lorries started to rumble along the narrow roads every day. The relative calm in the battalion area gave Irish soldiers time to build new quarters, including an officers' mess with colonial-style wicker chairs and crossed hurley sticks over the door. This marked the establishment proper of Camp Shamrock as it is known today—a mini Irish village of white and blue painted Nissen huts on the edge of Tibnin. The calm in the Irish area even allowed the recently formed 51st battalion's pipe and drum band to perform in the villages. On one parade through Brashit the band members believed they were under attack when local shopkeepers started throwing things at them. At first they thought the locals were hurling potato skins as a mark of disapproval. It was only when one of them looked down and saw sweets scattered over the street that they discovered it was a friendly gesture.

Support for the Irish presence in Tibnin and other Shia villages in the absence of an overall political settlement in Lebanon seems quite genuine even eleven years after the invasion. A persistent rumour that runs rife throughout the area is of an imminent Irish pull-out. The recurrent rumour surfaced during a meeting the author had with an Irish officer and a young but rising influential Amal commander in Tulin village on 4 June 1992.

During an interview about Amal's strategy in the face of the growing Hizbollah threat in the area, Abu Gawas, a representative from the Council of the South, the effective voice of the new Lebanese government in the region, kept asking if Irish troops were about to leave his country. Asked what would happen if Irishbatt left the area he replied: 'There would be a great revolution. The people I represent want UNIFIL to stay. Amal supports UNIFIL's presence and the relationship between us is good.'

Back in June 1982 the Irish presence in the hills of the south seemed in some doubt. Even the 51st battalion's commanding officer Lt-Col Michael F. Minehane admitted that the IDF invasion 'raised doubts in our minds as to the role of UNIFIL in our new circumstances'. The Irish c/o, who went on to command UN forces in Cyprus ten years later, stressed that UNIFIL was not redundant.

Speaking in Tibnin after the Sabra and Shatila massacres, he said: 'There are nine villages here with a population of 20,000 in the Irish battalion's area. The vacuum would be filled by some other forces. The Haddad irregulars had attempted to come into the Irish area in the wake of the Israeli invasion. We prevented them from coming in.'

But by 16 October the entire Nepalese battalion had pulled out and returned home. Diplomatic pressure too was mounting on Ireland to change completely the entire UNIFIL mission. A secret internal UNIFIL staff paper written by an Irish officer revealed that the United States wanted the 6,000-strong peacekeeping force out of south Lebanon.

On 29 September the IDF finally withdrew from Beirut and were replaced by an American-led Multinational Force (MNF). The MNF consisted of 1,500 American troops along with smaller French, Italian and British contingents. Behind the deployment was the goal of establishing a pro-Israeli government in Lebanon, namely that of Christian Phalange leader Amin Gemayel.

According to the internal UNIFIL report the plan for UN forces was drawn up by President Ronald Reagan's Middle East envoy Phillip Habib and Belfast-born US General Pat Collins. Under the plan there would be no UNIFIL in the south; their place would probably be taken by the IDF and Lebanese forces friendly to Israel. The secret paper discloses that the United States wanted UNIFIL to set up a new base in the disputed Chouf mountains far north of the original peacekeeping zone. By late 1982 the plateau was a battleground between the Christian government's forces and the leftist Druze militia. The Irish government resisted the Americans' plan.

Commenting on American designs for UNIFIL the report said: 'It is becoming more evident that the central government of Amin Gemayel does *not* enjoy widespread approval or consent. The dispute in the Chouf is at the very heart of internal Lebanese politics. The enforcing of central Lebanese authority in these circumstances by UNIFIL would be partial in nature, political in function and entirely unacceptable in casualty costs.'

The author of the report adds that this was the Irish diplomatic position at the time. It is interesting to note that for all Washington's diplomatic and military influence in the Middle East, Irish officers on the ground had a clearer grasp of the realities of Lebanese affairs. Moving UNIFIL north to the Chouf would have been disastrous for the mission. It would have been seen by the Druze who lived in the mountains for centuries as a politically partial move against them in favour of the Christians. Indeed the Christian government eventually collapsed and its forces were routed by the Druze and their Moslem allies by the end of the following year.

Throughout the invasion and siege of Beirut it was remarkable that only one UN soldier, a Norwegian, lost his life in the opening shots of the fighting. Up to rotation time with the next battalion, the Irish contingent did not lose a single man. Indeed the only casualty during the early days of the Israeli invasion was a military police sergeant who had to be evacuated from Gallows Green camp north of Tibnin to Naquorra after being bitten by a snake.

There was, however, a close call between Irish and Israeli soldiers at Al Sultaniyah on 22 June. Irishbatt's engineering officer had been called in by 'A' company to help them construct new toilets for their tented camp. His job was to place explosive charges to blast holes in the ground. Just as he set off the explosions that afternoon an IDF armoured column was passing by the Irish position. On hearing the blast, young nervous Israeli conscripts leapt from their APCs and trucks and scattered in all directions. In the collective panic the IDF troops cocked their rifles and took up firing positions obviously under the belief that they were being attacked. It took careful and patient persuasion by Irishmen at the scene that the explosions had innocent origins. One shot fired, however, could have led to tragedy.

While the Irish battalion suffered no casualties over the summer, tragedy struck in Beirut when an officer with UNTSO was killed in a landmine explosion. Comdt Michael Nestor died after his and three other unarmed observers' vehicle ran over the mine on 26 September. The 36-year-old Dubliner had been in Beirut less than a week after the Sabra and Shatila massacre.

Comdt Nestor, Majors Randall Carson and Harley Warren (United States) and Finnish Captain Karl Lasonen had been travelling in an area 10 km east of Beirut when the blast occurred. Oddly, all four men shared the same quarters at UNTSO's camp in the Israeli border town, Nahariya. Another Irishman received a Military Medal for Gallantry that day for recovering the bodies of his four colleagues. Comdt Michael Lynch drove into dangerous and hostile territory to identify and take back his comrades' remains. On recommendation from General Erskine, Comdt Lynch was awarded the MMG for his courage.

Both Erskine and his successor as UNIFIL's new commander— Co. Cork man Lt-General William Callaghan—visited the families of the four officers at Nahariya. Erskine poignantly recalled that while talking to Comdt Nestor's widow, he remembered the day a month before the tragedy when he and her husband had lunch together at UNTSO's observation post in the Lebanese village of Khiam.

Comdt Nestor had been in the Middle East since May 1981 and was married with three children. He joined the army in 1964 following in the footsteps of his father. Ambrose Nestor actually served with the UN in Cyprus along with General Callaghan the very same year his son entered the Defence Forces.

In the course of every six-month tour in Lebanon troops are re-supplied by sea from the Irish Naval Service. Even with Beirut still at war in December 1982, Irish sailors arrived in the capital's harbour to deliver fresh supplies for their comrades in the 52nd battalion in the south.

Warrant Officer Michael Martin could not believe the sight he witnessed as the L.E. *Aoife* docked in Beirut harbour at the end of the week-long voyage from Ireland to Lebanon. 'There was still fighting going on in the city,' he said. 'We could see explosions going off. Beside us near the port were destroyed ships upturned in the water. At the first sight of Lebanon I thought it was like hell on earth. You could hear the mortars and the shell fire, see the smoke rising from the buildings. But then my feelings changed when I caught sight of smiling Irish faces waiting for us at the quay wall.'

Irish officers from UNTSO and troops with UNIFIL's transport platoon had come to the harbour to off-load the supplies for the battalion. Despite the continued fighting in the city, Michael decided to go ashore and explore Beirut. He ended up being driven around on his macabre tour by a senior UN officer. 'The first thing I noticed was that every road and street surface was peppered with gun and artillery round holes. In one street near the shore I noticed that a huge palm tree had been cut cleanly in half by what was probably heavy machine-gun fire. The tree seemed to say something about the place. Even with the destruction you could still see the former majesty of the city.'

One of his abiding memories of Beirut was the sight of the Holiday Inn in the eastern side of the city. Michael looked up and saw a huge gaping hole in the side of the hotel's seventh floor revealing the stairway and hall leading to the rooms.

What of the morale of his comrades stuck in Lebanon during such as testing time? How had the invasion and subsequent fighting affected them?

'They were glad to see people from home alright,' Michael said. 'On the ship we used to get daily news from Ireland over our network. So although the lads in south Lebanon got a smattering of news per week, the sailors would be really up to date. The lads on the quay were hungry for news. They were also hungry for home comforts. I remember Tayto crisps and bottled Guinness were very popular. We had boxes of the stuff to load off the *Aoife*. Generally the lads seemed in good form. I was surprised at how well they were coping.'

Partly as a result of learning about the conditions of troops in Lebanon Warrant Officer Martin helped form the Defence Forces' union PDFORRA which battles for better wages and conditions for members at home and abroad. One of the most controversial issues PDFORRA has raised in relation to service in Lebanon is the effects of being caught in a war zone on troops. Ten years after the Israeli invasion PDFORRA claimed soldiers returning from peacekeeping duty in Lebanon were suffering from Post Traumatic Stress Syndrome.

The union alleged that soldiers coming home found it difficult to re-adapt to normal life after being under fire in Lebanon. It accused the military authorities of ignoring the problem which PDFORRA said was widespread among Lebanon veterans. One of the by-products of the 1982 invasion was that Ireland's Defence Forces gleaned new information on coping with battlefield stress from one of the forces they faced in Lebanon—the Israelis.

During and after the invasion the Israelis developed techniques to counter the effects of being constantly shelled and fired on in the bloody conflict. The technique rejects the traditional forms of clinical 'white coat' treatment for soldiers suffering from combat stress. Instead of transferring a fighting man under visible signs of strain, the IDF kept him as close as possible to his unit or platoon.

The Irish Defence Forces' psychologist, Lt-Col Coleman Goggin, admitted that the Israeli theories developed from 1982 are now being seriously studied by the military authorities in Dublin up to and including the general staff.

The traditional medical approach to battlefield stress was practised at the beginning of World War II and continued right up to 1973 by the Israelis in the Yom Kippur War. This technique gives no responsibility to the patient for his recovery and tends to ignore forward treatment at the front and prevention of the next stage after combat stress—Post Traumatic Stress Disorder (PTSD).

As a result of the 1982 invasion Israel's Defence Forces became world leaders in coping with combat stress. In that conflict those soldiers transferred from the fighting zone were kept in army barracks rather than medical centres where they were subjected to a military fitness regime as part of their therapy. Recent studies by IDF psychologists show that frontline treatment of troops under strain successfully returned more than 70 per cent of Israeli soldiers to the battle zone within three days. It is worth pointing out that the Israelis carried out thorough research about the problem of battlefield fatigue whilst in Lebanon. The IDF actually treated and chronicled all known cases of delayed Combat Stress Reaction during the campaign. It is also interesting to note that the Israeli studies of their troops found that there was no specific personality that was prone either to cracking up on the battlefield or displaying great acts of heroism. No one could predict therefore who was going to be a victim of Combat Stress Reaction.

The central idea behind the theory developed in the aftermath of the invasion was that the military should encourage a 'bonding relationship' between members of a unit in order to support those under stress, whether due to combat or personal problems. Soldiers are encouraged to build up a support network for each other to help cope when attacked or firing close at their posts. The key to success for the IDF, at least in this field, was not to treat the soldier as a potential hospital case in the initial stages of combat stress. Through comradeship and group loyalty the Israeli soldier was encouraged back either to the front or at the very least to stay in his unit at battalion or brigade headquarters.

Even before Irish troops touch down on Lebanese soil the army at home prepares them for what it is really like to be the target of bombs and bullets from an enemy force. Every soldier going out to Lebanon is subjected to 'battle inoculation'.

Several weeks prior to their departure the next batch of peace-keepers are taken to the Glen of Imaal for the training exercise. Up to 120 soldiers at a time are marched across a firing range into a huge trench. After several minutes resting on pile bursting hard planks the barrage begins.

Even with ear plugs you can hear the constant crackle of machine-gun fire as bullets whizz over your head and the dull thud of the bombs exploding on each side of the trench. But the worst sensation is the violent sickening vibration which shakes your bones. Every few seconds your entire body feels as if a huge weight is pressing down on it. The ground shock leaves you feeling that a gigantic invisible hand is punching your stomach, knocking the wind out of you.

The air reeks of cordite, petrol and smoke while you are constantly showered with dirt, grass and top soil. The only thing you can see outside the trench is the plumes of black smoke shooting up overhead. This 15-minute ordeal is meant to give the soldier a taste of what it can really be like being under fire in Lebanon.

The exercise even starts with a realistic scenario. The firing begins when a huge explosion goes off in the distance. This is meant to be a roadside bomb planted by Palestinians or Lebanese resistance fighters near an Israeli position or a DFF compound. For about 30 seconds there is an uneasy silence and then all hell breaks loose. The main barrage overhead and outside the trench signifies the retaliation fire from the IDF/DFF. And of course the Irish are in the middle.

Despite being in the middle of a renewed and vicious war in 1982 between the IDF and the Palestinians, by the end of the 51st battalion's tour of duty officers and men alike took pride in the fact that the Irish contingent had not lost a single soldier.

Casualties had been expected as a result of troops caught in crossfire between the Israelis and their enemies. What stunned the soldiers, both those returning home and their replacements from the 52nd battalion, was that the worst loss of Irish lives occurred in one incident in Lebanon which was caused by the actions of one of their own men. And no amount of 'battle inoculation' or psychological support could have prevented what was about to happen at Tibnin bridge.

TERROR AT TIBNIN BRIDGE

As Private Michael McAleavey waited in Dublin airport for the plane to Beirut on the night of 21 October 1982 he had something to show his friends from the 2nd infantry battalion who were there to say goodbye. The Belfast man produced a red and black Nazi armband from his kit bag.

It seemed a dangerous and provocative symbol to be taking to Lebanon. The UNIFIL zone was, after all, swarming with Israeli troops many of whose relatives and family friends had perished in Hitler's Holocaust. But according to those who knew him, this was a typical stunt by McAleavey. The 21-year-old soldier known as 'Mackers' to his friends was a raker who loved stirring things up in his home unit at Dublin's Cathal Brugha barracks. No one took his swastika waving display seriously. They were not aware, however, that his far right anti-Semitic views would lead to disaster less than a week later.

On the plane with him to Beirut was fellow northerner Corporal Gregory Morrow. McAleavey and he had been friends at their barracks. The day before their flight Corporal Morrow got on the Belfast–Dublin train at Lurgan with his wife Collette. The couple joined McAleavey and shared a few beers on the journey to Dublin. McAleavey recalls that they had only one other fellow-traveller in their carriage—the former Mid-Ulster MP Bernadette McAliskey.

Unknown to Corporal Morrow his wife was pregnant. He was never to discover the good news. Within a matter of days of leaving for Lebanon he would be brutally slain along with two other Irish soldiers by the man he shared a drink with on the Dublin train.

McAleavey remembers that he had known Corporal Morrow well, since most of the northerners in the 2nd Infantry battalion stuck together socialising and supporting each other during their time at Cathal Brugha.

When the first contingent of troops for Irishbatt's 52nd battalion touched down at Beirut international airport in the early hours of 22 October Michael McAleavey pulled another stunt to impress his comrades. As he tramped onto the tarmac he fished out another emblem. The man from nationalist West Belfast waved the ultimate symbol of northern loyalism, the Red Hand of Ulster flag, in the air. Fellow troops laughed as he shouted out: 'We're here Northern Ireland.' It was another act of the maverick whose unorthodox views were alien to all the men he was serving alongside.

The new troops were delayed travelling to the UNIFIL zone for two hours by the IDF which blocked their route out of the airport. The Israelis were still surrounding west Beirut at the time. This made McAleavey very angry. It compounded his view that the Israelis were the aggressors in Lebanon and backed up the anti-Jewish bigotry he nursed from his schoolboy days.

By the time the 52nd battalion was allowed out of the airport it was dawn. Driving south from Beirut along the coast road the troops witnessed the results of Israel's invasion in June. Entire towns and villages were devastated. Buildings were reduced to rubble or shot to pieces. Terrified civilians were either too frightened to come outdoors or had fled the area. War debris was everywhere to be seen. The trail of destruction left by the advancing Israeli army fuelled McAleavey's hatred of the Jewish state.

His most vivid memory of those first few hours in Lebanon was the ordnance left by the IDF. 'The main thing I remember about that first day was seeing thousands of cans of 1.02 mm mortar shells scattered in fields and along the road we were travelling on. I had fired that type of mortar on heavy weapons training and I knew the kind of damage it could inflict. I tried to imagine what it must have been like for the civilians on the receiving end of that. It made me angry and resentful that the Israelis had got away with this.'

He finally arrived at Al Sultaniyah village which was then the headquarters of Eastern Command's 'A' company. While there he experienced another example of Israeli power. As he was being briefed on the Irish area of operations an Israeli jet streaked overhead breaking the sonic boom and almost shattering the windows of the Nissen hut he was in.

During his first night in the hills McAleavey said he found it impossible to sleep due to the heat. He kept waking up in the middle of the night and pulling back his mosquito net. Despite complaining to officers about the heat he claimed he was never given the chance to acclimatise.

McAleavey's first duty in south Lebanon was a menial one which he rather enjoyed. Someone at the Dyar Ntar post where Kevin Joyce had been seized and Hugh Doherty murdered 19 months before, had painted a huge Star of David on the wall. The symbol was a red rag to an anti-Semite like McAleavey. He decided to erase the Jewish star. He detailed two local Shia Moslem boys to carry out the task. They were given a tin of duty black paint from Irish army stores for the job. As well as painting over the Star of David the boys left a message for the 52nd battalion. The boys' prank tickled McAleavey. From Arabic it translated as: 'Irish Go Home.'

Ironically the Belfast man's next task which led to him murdering three comrades should never have happened. He was never detailed for checkpoint duty at Tibnin bridge. A Corporal Johnson at Al Sultaniyah asked McAleavey to swop duties with him. Johnson had been marked up for the bridge. Instead, McAleavey, known to be a dedicated military man, agreed to take over. He went to Tibnin bridge around 2 o'clock in the afternoon of 27 October along with Corporal Morrow, Private Peter Burke and Private Thomas Murphy.

Tibnin bridge is one of the most strategically important checkpoints in the entire UNIFIL area. Roads emanating from the bridge lead out to Tyre city in the west and Tibnin to the north. Israeli military traffic passing from the security zone into UNIFIL en route to Beirut had to pass the bridge over a dried up river bed. Overlooking the bridge on a steep incline is a machine-gun post. Below is a bunker from which Irish troops monitored vehicles passing through. It is one of the bleakest, most isolated spots in south Lebanon and is cut off from most of the major UNIFIL camps and outposts in the region.

The four men's task that fateful night was to stop vehicles, check for identification and if necessary search cars, lorries and military transport going through their checkpoint. For most of the day there had been few vehicles travelling along the bridge. McAleavey said there were also no arguments or ill feeling between him and his three colleagues that day. Relations with Corporal Morrow, who was in command of the checkpoint, were 'very friendly'.

Around 8.00 p.m. the post reported a vehicle approaching the bridge. It was a jeep with Israeli military markings. Corporal Morrow stood on the road and flagged it down with the aid of a torch. McAleavey went over and covered Morrow with his FN rifle. The other two privates remained in the bunker. The Lurgan man shouted over to McAleavey that the occupants were Israelis and that there were two men in the jeep. They were suspected Shin Bet agents. When Morrow asked the driver for his identification he simply pulled open his jacket and displayed his insignia. The Israeli said that that was all he needed to show in order to identify himself.

McAleavey had his first face to face encounter with the IDF. He refused to accept the driver's explanation. He pointed his rifle straight at the window and reminded the Israeli that his corporal wanted to see identification. The man said he did not carry any ID and that he should not have even been stopped. The Belfast man went into a fit of rage. 'I told him he was at a UN checkpoint and that if I wanted to stop him he would be stopped. He got out of the car and grabbed the front of my rifle. I pulled the rifle back and said I would knock his fucking head off.'

The Israeli turned his back on McAleavey and started to talk to his colleagues in the car in Hebrew. Then the Irish private couldn't help himself. He taunted the Israeli with a stream of anti-Semitic abuse calling the driver a 'dirty Jew boy'.

Corporal Morrow realised the situation was now getting out of hand. He decided to break up the confrontation. He simply waved the jeep through the checkpoint. McAleavey was furious. He saw the corporal's action as another sop to Israeli power.

Morrow then chastised McAleavey about his ill-disciplined remarks telling him it was a 'fucking stupid thing to do' given the circumstances. McAleavey though was unrepentant. He taunted the corporal about the fact that he had forgotten his Gustav submachine-gun and had to borrow another from a colleague before taking charge at the bridge. He criticised Morrow's command calling him a 'stupid bastard' for letting the Israelis through. Even a child of three would have remembered to have taken his own personal weapon on duty with him, McAleavey jibed.

Morrow hit back. He started to taunt McAleavey about him begging to be taken to Lebanon with the 52nd. He said the Belfast man was only a sub going on the tour because another soldier had backed out at the last moment. Private Murphy then came out of the bunker and joined in the barrage against McAleavey, slagging him that he wouldn't be seen dead beside him on parade.

The corporal then decided enough was enough. He ordered McAleavey to take up the position at the machine-gun post and to carry ammunition boxes over to it. In a typical outburst of insubordination McAleavey refused to go over advising Morrow to get 'one of your cronies' to do the task. Then the Belfast man walked away. At that moment something snapped. He remembered the mad moments next which led to murder.

Turning around with his rifle in hand he put on the firing mechanism to automatic and opened up on the three men. 'I started spraying and just held my finger on the trigger. I remember the rifle jamming up or I may have changed mags. But I just cocked it and opened up again. I then remember running in and out of the bunker beside them and mopping up. That last thing I remember was shooting Corporal Morrow who had gone around the side of the bunker.'

Recalling the killings just over 10 years later in Portlaoise maximum security prison, McAleavey estimated it took him around 15 seconds to kill all three men. He clinically described how he murdered them.

'I did exactly what I had been trained to do: to kill efficiently and without mercy. It was a mad outburst, I know, but at that moment I acted instinctively.'

He pleads now that he genuinely regrets what happened. The deaths were the result of a moment of sheer madness. He claims he never preplanned the murders. This does not however explain the way he 'mopped up' seeking out his quarry around the bunker in order to make sure each of them was dead. McAleavey said there was blood everywhere. It scarred the walls of the bunker. It lay all over the ground and on the dead men. What was going through his head at that time? How did he react to seeing three comrades lying dead as a result of his action? 'I suppose it was a feeling of disbelief. I didn't want to admit to what I had done and went into a kind of shock. I was simply bewildered.'

In the bunker Corporal Morrow (20) from Lurgan, Co. Armagh, Private Peter Burke (19) a single man from Suir Road, Kilmainham and Private Thomas Murphy (19) also single from Claremont Court, Glasnevin lay dead. Morrow and Murphy had been in Lebanon for only five days. Private Burke was due to return home a week after the shootings. The killings actually occurred only minutes after the first detachment of troops from the 51st battalion arrived back at Dublin airport.

Bewildered or not, McAleavey acted fast. He grabbed hold of the radio pack in the bunker and contacted battalion headquarters. Around 8.40 p.m. Corporal John O'Connor was manning the radio room in Camp Shamrock. He received a distress signal from Tibnin bridge. At first he couldn't make out what was being said. Then a person answered in a garbled voice: 'We've been hit.'

Corporal O'Connor alerted command and an armoured convoy was dispatched to the bridge to investigate. They arrived there at 8.45 p.m. Captain John Ryan and medical orderly Corporal Thomas Renwick travelled to Tibnin bridge in an ambulance. When they got there someone screamed at them to put their lights out. They went towards the bunker and found McAleavey inside muttering to himself. He was shaking violently. Captain Ryan tried to talk to him and calm him down. He told the private he would have to be taken to hospital. Then McAleavey started to speak. He blamed the Israelis for what had happened saying, 'The Yids did it.'

When he was helped out of the bunker McAleavey spotted two Lebanese civilians who had strayed into the area after the shooting. They had their hands up and were being laid on the ground to be searched. With his rifle still in his hand McAleavey charged towards the Lebanese. He jumped on top of them and started punching them in the back shouting: 'Bastards! bastards! They killed them.'

Further loss of life was only averted by the quick actions of two Irish soldiers at the scene. Sergeant Martin Leavy grabbed McAleavey's rifle barrel and pushed it into the air. After grappling with it for a few seconds the sergeant managed to take it from him. McAleavey then ran towards Comdt Thomas Hodson and tried to snatch a Gustav submachine-gun from the officer's hands. Fortunately Comdt Hodson prevented him from taking the weapon.

The theatrical performance had been for a reason. In blaming the Israelis and then the Lebanese for the killings McAleavey was acting like Lady Macbeth. He was trying to wash out the spot of guilt on his own hands by putting someone else in the frame. His story sounded convincing enough on paper. Other Irish troops like Doherty and Joyce had been killed at isolated outposts similar to Tibnin bridge. The Irish battalion was a target for several rival militia groups in south Lebanon. But even within minutes of arriving at the murder scene investigating officers found their first clues that would lead them to the real killer.

Private Alan Henry discovered empty cartridges of 7.62 ammunition. The spent rounds were the same as the type used in the FN rifle. He handed them over to Military Police Comdt Rory Campion. McAleavey even had an answer for this. He explained that he had fired off several rounds into the wadis after the shooting because he thought he saw some movements in the darkness and expected to come under fire again.

The most senior Irish military intelligence officer in Lebanon who happened to be at the bridge that evening said he had his suspicions within half an hour of arriving there.

'We knew there was no third party in the shooting. From the way it was executed and the bullets found at the scene suspicion fell on the survivor. The problem was cracking McAleavey down. His story seemed plausible. He turned out to be a tough nut to crack. What was worse was once we were sure it was him the authorities back in Dublin refused to believe our reports. They found it difficult to accept that one of our own had done it.'

McAleavey said he also believed that some officers suspected him within about an hour but they simply couldn't prove it. If however he was so remorseful about what he had done then why did he not just own up that same evening? He confesses that he should have told someone the same night. Had he done so he believes he would have been treated more sympathetically. He clings to the view that he simply cracked up and withdrew into a fantasy story about someone else committing the murder.

The carnage at the bridge sickened the soldiers who arrived there. Two bodies were lying at right angles to the front wall of the bunker. Corporal Joe Archibold said one of them was Private Burke who was lying on his back with his blood-stained gun on the right-hand side of his body pointing towards his feet. He had head injuries and powder marks under his chin. Corporal Archibold said he remembered seeing a lot of blood on the ground. Private Murphy was lying on Private Burke's left-hand side about three feet away. Private Murphy's head was within a few feet of the bunker wall.

A trail of blood led to the side of the bunker where Corporal Morrow lay dead. The Gustav submachine-gun he had borrowed was lying across his body and there was a lot of blood at the back of his skull. All three were put into body bags and transported the next morning to the American hospital in Beirut for examination.

McAleavey meanwhile was taken by ambulance to Camp Shamrock's medical centre. En route he continued to mumble about the 'bastards' who killed his comrades. He refused to be sedated or talk about what happened at the bridge. Officers noted that he had no lacerations, bruises or marks on his face. The only thing they noticed was that he was wild eyed.

The killings sent shockwaves through the battalion, UNIFIL and Ireland. Irish newspapers were full of speculative reports that a pro-

Israeli militia group had carried out the slaughter. Leader writers questioned if Irish involvement in the mission was worth it given the continued loss of life. Irishbatt's intelligence officer pointed out that no one at home ever imagined that 'one of our own' was responsible.

Over the next few weeks and months Michael McAleavey maintained his wall of silence. He was held in 'closed service duty' at Gallows Green Military Police headquarters. He continued to demand that he be allowed back to Al Sultaniyah. Had he been allowed to return to his comrades in 'A' company, he claims, it would have been easier for him to admit the terrible truth.

He was allowed a certain degree of freedom during his stay at the MP's camp. McAleavey was able to jog on the Tibnin run while under escort. He carried out clerical duties at Camp Shamrock and was able to walk over to the Mingy shop facing Gallows Green.

Most of his mates he met while on the Tibnin run, McAleavey claims, were sympathetic to him. They inquired after him and expressed sympathy about what happened at the bridge!

Military Police interrogators questioned him on several occasions about the killings. He frustrated their efforts to get to the truth. McAleavey maintained his story that the bunker had come under fire by armed elements in the wadis and that he had been in the bunker when his colleagues were slaughtered.

'The MPs treated me very badly. They threatened me and shouted a lot during our sessions together. They antagonised me so much I withdrew into myself and kept up the story.'

During his stay at Gallows Green McAleavey continued to defy his officers and breach military discipline. He was put on a charge for calling an NCO a 'Free State bastard'. And he was further disciplined for refusing to give the salute to Irish President Patrick Hillery during a pre-Christmas visit to Camp Shamrock.

The most serious incident of insubordination occurred two days after Christmas when McAleavey again confronted Israeli troops. A convoy of IDF conscripts stopped at Gallows Green and went into the shop facing the camp. McAleavey broke away from his escort and ran into the shop. While inside he started an argument with a group of Israelis hurling more anti-Semitic abuse at them. His escort quickly pulled him out of the shop before the confrontation turned nasty. Michael McAleavey just couldn't help himself. He started accusing them of killing his friends.

He confesses that during his stay at Gallows Green he did contemplate suicide. One day he stood on the roof of the camp and considered flinging himself off. But the sight of the sharp crags below put him off. By this time, he says, he was already half-dead. There was no easy way out for the Belfast man. His rifle had been confiscated from him the day after the Tibnin bridge killings for his own safety!

After nearly four months trying to break McAleavey down the army decided to switch tactics. The Gardai were finally called to Lebanon. McAleavey speaks in almost admiring tones about his civil interrogators. He felt they were true professionals who got to the truth within days of arriving in south Lebanon.

On 22 January Detective Inspector Patrick Culhane and Chief Superintendent Daniel Murphy interviewed McAleavey at Gallows Green. They quizzed him about his army career and family background. They showed him an album of photographs taken after the shooting. The album contained scenes which in McAleavey's words 'sickened me'. The wall of silence was crumbling. The detectives offered McAleavey tea and expressed sympathy for his plight. At 11.10 a.m. he agreed to make a statement about the killings. He concluded the statement at 12.30 p.m. McAleavey said it was the truth and he did not want to change it. He signed it and asked God to forgive him for what he had done.

After confessing to the killings he broke down and wept. The detectives offered him cigarettes and then a bowl of soup. One of them even put his arm around the killer. He was formally charged with murder.

The news that an Irish soldier had been charged with killing the men at Tibnin bridge was a devastating blow for the Defence Forces. It was the first time an Irish soldier had turned his gun on his comrades, although it is worth noting that a similar incident occurred when an Austrian UN soldier killed two of his colleagues in an isolated observation post on the Golan Heights. McAleavey's comrades back home in Cathal Brugha barracks were stunned. Brendan Hamill found it hard to believe. He had known McAleavey's eccentricities but never suspected anything else.

'When I heard the news I felt as if I had been shot. Greg Morrow and Mackers were in my unit. We all drank together. Everybody knew Mackers was a bit of a raker but never that mad as to kill one of his own mates. Then again how do you know if anyone is that mad?'

Brendan detected a degree of bitterness against northern soldiers following the news about McAleavey. He said there were times when he went to take a weapon out of the stores at Cathal Brugha colleagues would whisper behind his back: 'Don't look now lads. There's a northerner with a gun. He might end up killing us all'.

Two days after his confession Michael McAleavey was taken by armed escort from the battalion area to Beirut. Just like his journey south four months before, the convoy was delayed by IDF checkpoints for several hours. When they finally reached Beirut he was taken to the four-star Riviera hotel to be held overnight.

McAleavey said he remembered being handcuffed to the bed inside the plush hotel which was in what was left of the commercial heart of west Beirut. He recalls a bizarre incident the next morning when a waiter came into the room with breakfast for the prisoner. The waiter saw the Irish soldier chained to the bed. He put down the tray, muttered something in Arabic and ran out of the room with a terrified expression on his face. McAleavey said the MPs who escorted him to Beirut treated him with courtesy despite knowing what he was charged with. He met one of them five years later while in Mountjoy prison.

'I remember walking along the landing in the 'Joy one day and I spotted the MP. I strolled over to him and said, "Remember me?" He started to chat with me and asked me how things were going. He had left the army to join the prison service. I quipped that whatever you do in the army you'll always end up in prison one way or another.'

The following day the prisoner was taken onto a chartered flight to Dublin via Vienna. While on the plane an air stewardess offered McAleavey complimentary drinks from the bar. An MP handcuffed to him in the next seat refused on his behalf. It was at that moment, McAleavey said, that he finally realised what was happening to him. He felt he had finally come out of a daze. The fact that someone was now making decisions on his behalf, no matter how trivial, demonstrated his loss of freedom.

What lay behind the man charged with the triple murders? Here was a confused complex personality who had grown up in a culture of political violence and sectarian slaughter. Born in 1961 at Belfast City Hospital, Michael McAleavey spent his formative years in the period leading up to the outbreak of the Northern troubles. His family was forced to flee their home on the fringe of the loyalist Tiger Bay area of north Belfast. They moved to the relative safety of west Belfast.

Along with his father James and two sisters Michael lived in a terraced house in Rockville Street off the Falls Road. He attended St Kevin's primary school before going on to St Thomas' Secondary School on the Whiterock Road. Many of his school friends joined the Official and Provisional IRA and later the INLA. One of his closest friends was shot dead by loyalists as he stood on the junction of the Falls and Whiterock Roads in 1973.

Although he did enlist in the junior IRA for a few weeks Michael McAleavey eventually chose a more unconventional path compared to the ones take by his peers. He eventually joined the tiny neo-Nazi organisation, the National Socialist Irish Workers Party, which had post office box addresses in Dublin and Cork. The NSIWP later tried to recruit Irish UNIFIL veterans who had witnessed at first hand the devastation caused by Israeli power in Lebanon. The neo-Nazi group however failed to exploit the veterans' resentment against the IDF. Most serving and former soldiers ignored the NSIWP's rantings.

McAleavey explains his own involvement with the party as simple teenage rebellion against a school teacher at St Thomas', whom he loathed. Former Belfast city councillor for the ultra-leftist Peoples Democracy, Fergus O'Hare, claimed McAleavey tried to recruit fellow pupils into the NSIWP. O'Hare said he put up Nazi stickers and drew swastikas around the school as well as distributing NSIWP news sheet in west Belfast.

Michael McAleavey protests that he never took the NSIWP seriously. 'Look, the whole thing was a complete joke. O'Hare was always trying to ram his left-wing politics down our throats. Being a Nazi was a reaction to that, nothing more. It was two fingers to Fergus O'Hare. I am not a Nazi; I don't think I ever was.'

There was another side to Michael McAleavey besides his teenage flirtation with neo-Nazism. According to his father, Michael had varied musical tastes which ranged from classical to 1950s rock 'n roll. James McAleavey still keeps his son's classical tapes which include composers from Bach to Bartok. His son used to attend the Belfast rock 'n roll society disco twice a week at the Bailey bar, a sleazy pub frequented by teddy boys, rockabillies, punks and withered prostitutes in the city's dockland area.

He also enjoyed reading novels and books on philosophy and art. He was described as an apt pupil but only achieved three O levels. He left school in 1979 to work as a tool maker on a British government training scheme. Then out of the blue in early 1980 he applied to join the Irish army. He was leaving the troubles at home to find troubles of his own far away.

After working for a while as a clerical assistant in the heavily fortified Falls Road dole office he left to join the army enlisting at Aiken Barracks, Dundalk on 7 August 1980.

From his time however in basic military training he claimed he was unhappy and disillusioned with life in the Defence Forces. After a year he tried to buy himself out of the forces but could not afford it. His main reason for applying for Lebanon was that overseas duty would shorten the length of time he would have to serve in the army.

Despite being disgruntled he was regarded by both officers and men who served beside him as a dedicated soldier who always turned up for parade on time in prime condition. He was a fitness fanatic who spent his spare time hill walking and parachuting with a private air club. He was desperate to win his wings.

He was seconded for training with the elite Army Ranger Wing during Operation Foxtrot in the summer of 1981 and was also appointed to the battalion's police at the 2nd infantry's home barracks. He claims his Ranger's flash was ripped off his uniform after his trial by MPs when he was led out for waiting photographers hoping to get a snap of the triple killer. He alleges this was to avoid causing the army embarrassment because he had been selected for the forces' elite squad.

There were however some tell-tale signs about the darker side of his personality. Brendan Hamill, who now lives in Andersonstown, west Belfast, remembered the morbid pictures McAleavey used to pin over his bed in Cathal Brugha. Most of the men had pornographic pictures or football teams cellotaped to their walls. Michael McAleavey was different. Above his bed were the photographs of decapitated bodies unearthed during investigations into the El Salvadorean death squads!

His bizarre sense of humour was shared by one of the greatest mavericks ever to join the Irish Defence Forces. Billy Pollock came from Sandy Row, one of the most hardline loyalist areas in Belfast. Pollock became an outcast after informing his family he wanted to join the Irish army. He left the army after three years of service and went to England where he joined the Fascist National Front.

Brendan Hamill recalled how McAleavey and Pollock used to join them every Friday evening after work in the Lower Deck pub in Rathmines. One of their favourite stunts was to turn up drunk at the end of the evening and sing 'God Save the Queen' after the Irish national anthem was played at closing time. He incurred the wrath of his military superiors in November 1981 by going absent without leave for a week. He explains this was at the time of Ian Paisley's Third Force and the imminent threat of civil war in the North following the hunger strikes. McAleavey claims he was asked by the

Official IRA to train some of its members to protect areas such as Springhill from loyalist attacks. Senior figures from the dormant OIRA dismiss this as pure fantasy. One former OIRA commander said the Irish soldier would have been the last person they would have sought help from in the event of such a doomsday scenario.

While Michael McAleavey was held in custody in Ireland up until his trial began in June he claimed soldiers seeking revenge were trying to poison him. One month before his trial started he staged a hunger and thirst strike at the Curragh military hospital which lasted for a week. Outside cooks had to be brought into the camp to cook his food which he insisted was laced with poison.

His trial was held up because the Defence Act had to be amended to grant him the right to appeal his sentence. When it finally got under way at the Curragh there were harrowing moments for the dead men's relatives during the three-month trial. The mother of Private Peter Burke collapsed during testimony from a Swedish pathologist who examined the bodies after the shooting.

As well as the murdered men's relatives McAleavey's two sisters also attended the trial, travelling down from Belfast when they could.

During the court martial Corporal Morrow's widow gave birth to a daughter on 17 July. She revealed that she had got news that she was pregnant shortly after her husband went to Lebanon. She named the child Carrie because it came nearest to the name her father was best known as, Gary.

After almost four months the seven-man military jury headed by Judge Advocate Lt-Col Patrick Ghent found Michael McAleavey guilty of murder. He was given a mandatory life sentence with penal servitude. The following day he was discharged with ignominy from the Defence Forces.

Michael McAleavey stood impassive and frozen in the dock when the judge read out the sentence. He said he felt a strange relief when the court martial was finally over. 'I really did feel sorry for what I had done. All the pressure on me was lifted after the sentence. I said to myself, "Well, that's it. It's all over now." I was sorry in particular for Collette Morrow and her wee girl.' He had pleaded that at the time of the shooting he was temporarily insane. The killer claims he should have been charged with manslaughter because the murders were not premeditated. Temporary loss of sanity does not, however, explain his subsequent actions particularly the way he clung desperately to his alibi that a militia group killed the men. Whatever went through his mind in those murderous seconds at Tibnin bridge he seemed in control afterwards when questioned by investigating army officers. Whilst he had a short fuse he never flinched for almost four months.

Michael McAleavey became the Defence Forces' public enemy number one. In prison he was the repeated target of attacks by criminals who claimed to have connections with relatives in the Defence Forces. In one incident in Mountjoy jail in October 1985 he was badly injured after a vicious row with a member of a leading Dublin crime family. The former private was exchanging books in the prison library when he was confronted by the criminal. After the fracas he was rushed to the Mater hospital with a fractured skull and a broken left arm. It was his second beating in the same year at the prison.

He was constantly transferred between Limerick and Mountjoy jails before eventually ending up serving his sentence at Portlaoise. He is now held on the landing normally reserved for INLA prisoners. This is a supreme irony. The Irish soldier who joined a neo-Nazi organisation ended up alongside ultra-left republican terrorists such as Dominic McGlinchey and the so-called Border Fox, Dessie O'Hare.

In the flesh Michael McAleavey does not correspond to his monstrous media image. He cuts a sad if pathetic figure inside Portlaoise. He seems at times somewhat distant. When he talked his ice grey eyes searched the walls and ceilings of the pre-fab where we met in January 1993. There was something uncannily youthful about his face even though his hair is receding and there are streaks of grey at the sides of his head. The only sinister aspect of his physical appearance was a cynical smile he gives when questioned about his past.

Nevertheless he was outwardly very friendly if fatalistically cynical about an author's motive. He is on first-name terms with prison officers who call him 'Mick'. He has just completed an Open University arts degree and hopes to study for an M.A. He says he is happier at Portlaoise 'because the prison officers treat you like a human being'.

Michael McAleavey also reads everything he can about Lebanon. The country where his fate was tied up still fascinates him. He also likes to keep in touch with events in Northern Ireland even though he believes he will never see his home again.

At thirty-two, he believes his life is over. This is despite the fact that he could be due for temporary release depending on behaviour within less than seven years. His own view of the future is however quite chilling. 'I want you to put this on record. The way I feel at the moment I don't want to be released. After all what could I do on the outside. I would only be a burden to my family. There is nothing out there for me anymore. I'm better inside.'

Several months after the shooting Irish troops were replaced at the bridge by the Nigerian contingent of UNIFIL. The Africans however did not last long. They believed the spot was haunted. When McAleavey's former friend Corporal Brendan Hamill arrived in Lebanon for his second tour in October 1983 his first duty was to take over the bridge from the Nigerians. Despite the trauma of the last twelve months the Irish contingent was determined to continue its mission. It was business as usual at the bridge.

SEVEN THE BULL

Lt-General William Callaghan was sleeping in the bedroom of a plush hotel in Florence when word reached him that the Israelis were poised to invade. In the middle of the night a UNIFIL officer woke him up and told him that Israel's ambassador to London had been shot and wounded and that the IDF were massing their forces on the Lebanese border.

The new UNIFIL force commander had been in Florence to watch Italian helicopter pilots attached to the peacekeeping mission training in their home country. Callaghan, known affectionately to his troops as 'The Bull', had to rush to Rome and catch a flight to Beirut. Once back in the Lebanese capital on invasion day the general flew by helicopter along the coast to Naquorra.

From the day he arrived back on Lebanese soil to the triple murder at Tibnin bridge five months later Callaghan faced the greatest series of challenges he ever encountered in 48 years of service in the Defence Forces. Indeed his time of office as force commander for six years spanned most of the major incidents that affected Irishbatt from the kidnapping of Kevin Joyce to the Israeli withdrawal from nearly all of Lebanon in that country's first ever military defeat.

Several months before 6 June 1982 Callaghan had been confident that the Israelis were going to invade Lebanon. 'There was no doubt about that. There was going to be an invasion alright. You have to remember the IDF was pulling troops out of the Sinai desert in late 1981 when it was handed back to the Egyptians. It was obvious the Israeli military authorities were planning to switch their focus to their northern border.'

On meeting the Israeli general staff, Callaghan was simply told of the IDF's intention to invade. He is adamant that UNIFIL troops were not caught on the hop when the IDF finally swept into Lebanon. 'Our units were alerted to this. In the job I had you must prepare for every contingency. I was particularly ready for an invasion as early as 1981. It was not a matter of if they would invade, but when.'

The general still displays an acute awareness of the political and military situation in the Middle East. Part of the reason behind UNIFIL's original deployment in 1978, he believes, was the peace talks between Egypt and Israel. 'The reason for the speed with which UNIFIL was set up and sent to Lebanon was to allow Anwar Sadat to go to the Camp David peace talks. He could not have gone to the United States to meet Begin if the IDF had still been in Lebanon.'

Callaghan stresses still that he was realistic about UNIFIL's prospects. He pointed out that it was and is only a small piece in the overall Middle Eastern political and strategic jigsaw.

The general replaced Emmanuel Erskine as force commander on 15 February 1981. He was, however, no stranger to the Lebanese scene. For a short period in the early days of UNIFIL Callaghan was in fact the *de facto* commander of the mission while the UN waited to appoint an official commanding officer.

From 1972 he had been travelling to and fro from Israel and Lebanon on a regular basis as an officer with UNTSO based in Jerusalem. Probably more than any other Irish officer, William Callaghan embodies the strong link between previous UN missions and Ireland's involvement in its longest ever overseas commitment, Lebanon.

A native of Buttevant, Co. Cork, he joined the Defence Forces in 1939 as a cadet. After a course at the military college in the Curragh he signed up with the 10th infantry battalion which is now an FCA unit in the Southern Command.

Throughout the Emergency years he rose quickly up the ranks from 2nd lieutenant to captain. He said he learned a lot in time of war, experience which he put to later use in UN missions across the Middle East.

'The Emergency was a good time to be a soldier. It was a stable job and the ongoing situation made it very interesting and challenging. The military operation we launched then is very similar to what we are doing in the Lebanon. We did a lot of training exercises, took over houses and establishments and had the constant fear of invasion to spur us on.'

By the time Irish troops were being flown to the Congo, Callaghan had gained a commission as a commandant in the forces. He shares something similar with another UNIFIL veteran, CQMS Jim Clarke. Like Clarke, 'The Bull' also served under the UN flag for the first

time in the Congo during the infamous Battle of the Tunnel in
December 1961.

He commanded a company during that battle urging his NCOs
forward while under continuous automatic and mortar fire. 'A' company lost three men in the struggle to capture the Tunnel; Callaghan's
'B' company lost none. It was a remarkable feat at the time. Here was
a battalion with no previous experience of overseas service, exhausted
after three days' air travel, going into action almost immediately in a
tropical downpour. It was a proud moment in Callaghan's career.

In between further stints of UN service Callaghan took charge
of an FCA unit in Tipperary, a job he thoroughly enjoyed as he
raised and trained his own unit. He believes that working with part-
time soldiers, who were also of course civilians most of the time,
helped in his UN duties. It took him out of the rarefied camouflaged atmosphere of barracks life.

His next posting was in 1964 as company commander with the 40th
Irish battalion in Cyprus. While the Congo was more primitive, at
least Cyprus had a relatively good infrastructure built by the outgoing
colonial power—Britain. The mission was, however, 'very confusing'.
Callaghan's soldiers had to separate the warring Greek Cypriot and
Turkish communities in the island.

Ironically it was during this tour that Callaghan decided to take
leave to visit Lebanon on holiday. He spent several nights in Beirut.
He remembered that the Lebanese capital was then a 'buzzing lively
place with a lot going for it'. The general even took time to travel to
the Bekaa valley and see the ancient Roman temples of Baalbek. Very
few tourists would venture there today. The town is now one of the
main headquarters of the Iranian-backed Hizbollah and during the
1980s was home to a small contingent of Iranian revolutionary guards,
the Pasadran.

Many Irish soldiers chose to visit Beirut while on holiday leave
from Cyprus. The commanding officer of the 69th Irish battalion in
Lebanon, Lt-Col Frank Colclough, recalled visiting Beirut, like
General Callaghan, for a rest while on Cyprus. Today Irish troops
go in the opposite direction. Soldiers of all ranks take flights and
sailings to Cyprus for holidays and meet up with friends and family
from Ireland while on leave from Lebanon.

In total, the general served three tours of duty on Cyprus, returning
to the island a second time as second-in-command of the Irish contingent in 1967. From Cyprus Callaghan learned a valuable lesson
about the violation of UN mandates by one of the warring parties. In

1967 the Turks attempted to invade the island by sea. They were stopped off the coast only by the intervention of the US 6th fleet. The lesson was simple—only the involvement of one of the major political and military powers in the world could stop one of the parties to the UN signed agreement breaking the mandate set by the Security Council. In this case, the United States thwarted Turkey. In 1982 the United States failed to stop Israel violating the UN's mandate spelt out in Security Council resolution 425.

After Cyprus came further involvement in the Middle East mire with an appointment as a senior staff officer with UNTSO in Jerusalem. By 1979 Callaghan had become brigadier-general of the unarmed UN observer force travelling from Israel to Egypt, Jordan and Lebanon. With 300 officers from nineteen nations, including twenty Irishmen, under his command the general gleaned vital information and experience about the region.

He also witnessed one of the first real acts of *détente* between the superpowers after the Yom Kippur War. Following the October war, the former Soviet Union joined UNTSO. Callaghan took pleasure in commanding officers from the Soviet and American armies who served side by side on observation posts around the Israel, Syrian, Jordanian and Lebanese borders. There was something richly ironic about that, Callaghan remembers—a soldier from a small neutral nation commanding other soldiers from the world's two greatest powers.

For a few weeks prior to General Erskine's appointment, Callaghan took charge of setting up the area of operations to be controlled by UNIFIL. He described the early days of the mission as a 'human and logistical nightmare' as thousands of troops from nations as far flung as Fiji and Senegal arrived in south Lebanon.

'I knew Lebanon pretty well. From 1972 I had been travelling up to our UNTSO post at Khiam. You've got to remember that with many of the missions in the Middle East, one usually leads to another. That is, a new mission is usually established with help from another. Thus UNTSO, which included several Irish officers, helped put UNIFIL into place. That's the way peacekeeping has come to work.'

Having built up an extensive network of contacts with the warring parties in the region, Callaghan temporarily left the Middle East in 1979. He returned to Dublin as assistant chief of staff of the Irish army in June of that year before succeeding Major-General Patrick J. Carroll as adjutant-general.

Two years later 'The Bull' was back at the request of UNIFIL who appointed him force commander. He came to the job, he said, with a

pragmatic and realistic attitude. He had learnt while serving with
UNTSO about the realities of peacekeeping in the region.

Early on his appointment caused controversy. On 22 March 1981,
after just one month as force commander, high-ranking Israeli officers
demanded that Callaghan be replaced. 'The Bull' was bizarrely
accused by one Israeli source of 'trying to apply Belfast methods in
southern Lebanon'. The accusations were made over Israeli radio
stations after Callaghan issued a strong statement condemning
the DFF over the deaths of two Nigerian UNIFIL soldiers. They
had been killed in a mortar attack on their platoon headquarters.
Callaghan laid the blame squarely at the feet of Saad Haddad's forces.
The general made it clear to Haddad's Israeli backers that UNIFIL
troops would not be sitting ducks.

His firm stand on the killings and his desire to strengthen the
peacekeeping mission enraged Israeli commanders. One 'authoritative'
military source quoted on Israeli radio attacked Callaghan's stance.
'One of the problems is that the new UNIFIL commander lacks the
necessary qualifications to command such a touchy spot. He ignores
totally Israeli interest in the area and, more serious, has not the
slightest interest in Major Haddad and his people.'

This seemed to be an incredible accusation given O'Callaghan's
long-standing record of service in the region. Furthermore, many of
those 'authoritative military sources' from the IDF had no doubt met
the general on several occasions while he was with UNTSO and in the
early days of UNIFIL. Warning signs that Israel had further designs on
Lebanon also flashed up during broadsides against UNIFIL and
Callaghan. The IDF chief of staff Raphael Eitan predicted that if the
official Lebanese army deployed right up to the frontier 'the people of
southern Lebanon may well become refugees in Israel and the border
will once again become a jungle which the IDF will not tolerate'.

How did Callaghan feel at times like this? Did he not have to bite
his lip until it bled in order not to react to these well orchestrated jibes?
Was he ever tempted to fire a verbal broadside back at his accusers?

His reaction sums up the diplomatic qualities Irish peacekeepers
have learned to apply in missions like Lebanon. 'I never overreacted. I
am a pragmatic man. Certainly there were times when I could have
got annoyed at that but what was the point? I knew the IDF generals
well. I realised the way to handle them. Peacekeeping is about restraint
and patience; that's the way it has to be played.'

General Callaghan had one lucky escape from death in the early
days of his appointment. It happened one morning when he was
travelling to a Dutch battalion post to inspect a troop parade.

'There had been shooting on the road along which we were travelling,' he said. 'My escort stopped the jeep. We were sitting there for some minutes when I noticed someone walking up along the convoy on my side of the vehicle. I don't know where he came from but suddenly he looked in at me from outside the jeep. Then he produced a pistol from his trousers, cocked it and pointed it straight into my face. He looked extremely excited, as if he was out of control. I ordered my driver to put the boot down and I slammed over the window. We drove off leaving your man on the side of the road. I don't know who he was or which faction or militia group he belonged to. But there is one thing for sure. To this day I have no doubt that he would have fired and that would have been that. I hope he would have missed.'

The biggest crisis Callaghan had to deal with during his first few months was the Joyce kidnap and the killing of Hugh Doherty.

'Of course it was a shock to all of us. It's even more disconcerting when you can't account for one of your own soldiers. The operation to find out exactly what happened to Kevin Joyce still has to go on. It was an extremely difficult time for me, particularly because the lads were Irish. But the mission had to go on. That's the only way you can operate as a soldier—get on with the job in hand.'

The general stressed that time and time again he prepared for all kinds of events including kidnapping, murders and even invasions. The Middle East is, after all, a place which can change overnight. But despite being prepared mentally for the IDF invasion on 6 June 1982 he confesses he was still overawed by the amount of men and machines the Israelis put into action in Lebanon.

'The Israelis had a massive display of armour and fire power. They had total superiority, at least in the early days. We would have been insane to physically resist that power. In that situation we had no mandate to stand in their way. The UN did not give us it.'

From his office in Naquorra Callaghan could see the Israelis pushing north towards Tyre and eventually Beirut. In total it is estimated that the IDF may have put in excess of 50,000 troops into Lebanon. UNIFIL intelligence reckoned that they also had 1,800 tanks and 3,500 APCs in the field as well as complete control of the skies.

UNIFIL in contrast were only lightly armed, their heaviest weapon being the 120 mm mortar which was only used as a weapon of self-defence at the very last resort. IDF commanders had been told by their general staff simply to ignore UN lines. It looked on the surface that the Israelis had humiliated Callaghan's force.

'The Bull' however does not accept that thesis. He argued that UNIFIL equipped itself well in the face of the invading forces.

'UNIFIL's presence had one positive thing in its favour—we provided an international observation in the area at that time. Perhaps things would have been much worse had we not been there. My troops could provide the best and most objective (excluding journalists) reporting of the ongoing situation in the early days of the invasion.'

He described his meeting with Israeli generals in the first few days of the invasion as 'extremely tense'. During one discussion with IDF chief of staff Raphael Eitan, Callaghan raised the possible scenario of UN soldiers being killed by Israeli fire. Callaghan recalls distinctly a pervading silence over the meeting when that scenario was brought up. Eitan failed to reply to his question. The prediction came true within hours of the invasion when a Norwegian UN soldier was shot dead in crossfire between the IDF and Palestinian guerillas.

At least one contingent, the Fijians, used some imagination in interpreting their mandate. They sat down on the road holding up the Israeli advance for several hours. It is understood that General Callaghan did not reprimand them too severely.

Wasn't it now time for UNIFIL to give up? Surely the second invasion along with the inability to deploy right up to the international frontier finally exposed the mission as an embarrassing failure? What was the point of committing thousands of troops including 700 Irishmen to an area which the force no longer effectively controlled? As a peacekeeping mission, south Lebanon was a million miles away from the situation that prevailed 30 years earlier in the Congo.

Callaghan answers his critics by pointing out that a peacekeeping mission can only work effectively if the terms of the agreement have the consent of all the parties. Clearly with the Israelis it did not. The PLO too were unhappy with the UN presence in an area they once dominated. Haddad's militia also wanted the UN to go.

Moving to halt the Israeli invasion would have signalled a move away from conventional peacekeeping to peace enforcement. The latter could hardly be done without a mandate from New York and with only the light weapons at the force's disposal.

General Callaghan dealt only in realities. He appreciated each side's concerns and demands, realising from the start that the force under his command was in a no-win situation. 'The Palestinians felt they had the right, according to the Cairo convention, to attack Israel and thought the UN's role was to eject Israel from Lebanon. The Israelis on the other hand saw their northern settlements threatened and saw the UN's role as ejection of the Palestinians. And of course there was the world expectation that somehow

UNIFIL would solve the problems of south Lebanon, which of course it couldn't.'

By October at least one battalion under his command, the Nepalese, had left the region. It came as no surprise. The official line was that Nepbatt was going home to help in emergency relief efforts after a series of disastrous floods swept through their country on the roof of the world. Whatever the real reason for their departure, it was another blow to the forces' morale, although not a fatal one.

'As force commander, I realised I had to be ready for these kinds of things, especially when some of the soldiers under your command come from Third World countries. Famine, floods or political turmoil could easily erupt back at home. At a moment's notice they could be called back home. It's worth noting, though, that the Nepalese are back in south Lebanon again. That says something about their commitment to UNIFIL.'

What was it like commanding a multinational force whose personnel spoke a variety of languages, believed in different faiths and came from distinct political and social cultures? There were nations who were members of the North Atlantic Treaty Organisation. There were countries like Ireland who were neutral yet still within the western European community. There were others who were in the non-aligned camp like so many of the Arab states exercising power and influence on Lebanon.

'The Bull' had to employ all his powers and trawl from his long UN service to cope with such a challenge. He described the first two years in particular as a 24-hour job.

'You've got to remember there was no standardised training. Everyone had their own military traditions and operating procedures. Some, like the Nepalese, employed a very formalised British militaristic way of conduct. Others followed patterns closer to the Soviet army. One advantage for us Irish was that the standard language adopted by the mission was English.

'In many ways peacekeeping is more difficult than conventional warfare. You have to be subtle, tactful and above all else restrained in your actions. It's hard enough to get a single battalion to act this way. Imagine then how difficult it can be to keep 7,000 soldiers from all over the globe acting in this manner,' he reflected.

During his stay as force commander Callaghan became acquainted with some of the key players in Middle East politics. Of the Israeli generals he knew, he said he had a very good relationship with his IDF counterpart Ben Gal, the Israeli army's c/o for its northern command.

'I always tried to have a good working relationship with him. It was important never to slam any doors, especially where the IDF was concerned. If you are to stick to your mandate then you can't close the door on anyone. Even after the invasion I got on with Ben Gal very well. We had our arguments. But I was determined to keep the lines of communication open with him and the other IDF generals.'

His trips into south Lebanon and the Israeli-declared 'security zone' also brought him into contact with Major Haddad who was, Callaghan said, 'very unpredictable'. When he speaks of Haddad his tone is one of mild amusement. You can picture 'The Bull' still smiling over the table while Haddad went into one of his rages against UNIFIL and/or Irishbatt.

'Haddad could fly off the handle very easily,' Callaghan said. 'He was prone to make threatening statements all the time. Every time I met him over an incident he was always flanked by senior Israeli officers. You just had to sit back and listen to him and be patient.'

Callaghan had a working relationship with senior PLO commanders in his area including the organisation's chairman Yasser Arafat and Walid Khalil (a.k.a. Abu Jihad) who commanded the Palestinians' military wing. He would travel to Beirut prior to the invasion to meet the PLO bosses spending hours of negotiations over local clashes between Palestinian guerillas and UNIFIL soldiers.

He had several run-ins with Arafat personally who denounced UNIFIL's inability to stop the Israeli advance towards Beirut. Among the other leading figures he met in the region were Israeli Premier Menachem Begin and Lebanese Christian leader Bashir Gemayel. In these tense, often hostile meetings, Callaghan had to exercise his restraint. At times he found himself on the receiving end of verbal attacks, accused one day of being pro-PLO, the next pro-Israeli.

UNIFIL's future was in serious doubt during the summer of 1982. Callaghan nimbly avoids questions about whether he was aware of American designs to force the UN to set up in the Chouf mountains and allow Israel and its proxy forces to take over its peacekeeping zone in the south. He acknowledged that the Americans had an idea to extend their own multinational force in Beirut outwards to the rest of Lebanon. But these plans lay shattered in the ruins of the MNF bases blown to bits by suicide bombers in Beirut.

'I think the MNF is a good example of a peacekeeping force becoming involved in the battle. UNIFIL was never part of the battle. If we were seen to be taking sides we would have become an enemy to many Lebanese,' he reflected.

How did Irish troops cope with the stresses of invasion, occupation and the deaths at Tibnin bridge? General Callaghan believed his fellow countrymen gave a good account of themselves during this time. He offered some interesting reasons why Irish troops, in his eyes, make such good UN peacekeepers. He puts it down to three things: the school system, a strong sense of family and Ireland's neutrality.

'Our school and family systems produce caring and sensitive people. It stresses the worth of the individual as well as the drive for academic success. Families in Ireland bind together, they look after the weaker members in hard times. Irish soldiers are more inclined therefore to sympathise with the underdog. We are also a bit cunning. The Irishman is very reluctant to buy a pig in a poke. You need that kind of attitude when you're working in Lebanon.'

The general also believes Irish members of UNIFIL returned from Lebanon as better soldiers than they had been before their tour of duty. 'When Irish soldiers go to Lebanon they see a world far away from their own. All the things they take for granted at home are sometimes not available in Lebanon. Housing, education and health care are almost non-existent out there. Soldiers have to cope with that and help locals the best way they can. This makes the Irish troops who go out there to be better soldiers. They are more rounded and can handle people better.'

Operationally he feels Lebanon has been a 'wonderful training opportunity' for troops. They see how other armies operate and the sort of mistakes they make.

Irish troops have the distinct advantage of being part of the English-speaking world while remaining a neutral nation. 'A neutral country like Ireland would have a particular place in peacekeeping. In this part of the world we are seen only as peacemakers who attained freedom from a colonial situation.'

The general too had to maintain his own special form of 'neutrality' within UNIFIL. As commander of an international force he had to be careful about his own nationality. 'It is a bit of a disadvantage really having a force from your own country under your command. One has to be more neutral, and I certainly can't appear to favour Ireland more than any other country,' he told reporters while still in Lebanon in January 1985.

Callaghan and his troops needed all the patience and tact they had while the situation in the south deteriorated as the Israelis attempted to impose their surrogate forces on the local population. And as the IDF's master plan in Lebanon fell apart UNIFIL troops watched as the Israeli military slowly retreated towards its self-declared security zone.

In the first month of 1983 UNIFIL was facing massive harassment from Israeli forces and their allies. The Israeli authorities, for instance, refused UN helicopters permission to fly out of Naquorra on twenty-five occasions. General Callaghan had been scheduled to fly out on two of these flights. A third was for the transfer of the body of a Finnish soldier.

As the IDF retreated it faced new foes behind it in the south from renascent Shia guerilla movements, the main one of which was Amal which supported UNIFIL's presence in the region. The other rising Lebanese resistance organisation was the pro-Iranian Hizbollah which had a less than benign view of UN soldiers in their homeland.

In response to increasing attacks by the Shia resistance on Israeli soldiers, the IDF applied an 'Iron Fist' policy punishing villages it believed were harbouring Lebanese fighters.

Irish and other UN troops did their best to minimise the horrors of the Israeli retreat—the country's first defeat in modern history. Reflecting on the Israelis' objectives in Lebanon, General Callaghan claims they failed on all counts.

Irish troops physically put themselves in front of Israeli soldiers who raided villages and threatened to blow up houses, schools and community centres in retaliation for attacks on IDF and DFF patrols in the south. Irish troops even resorted to fist fights with the IDF in order to prevent the Israelis from harassing villagers under UN protection.

'They [the IDF] came into Lebanon in 1982 allegedly to stop attacks on Israel's northern settlements. While they swept the PLO out of the south for a while, their policies created a new anti-Israeli movement which attacked the IDF more successfully than the PLO had. The IDF enraged and alienated the local population. Their designs for Lebanon failed once Amin Gemayel went to Syria to sign a pact with Damascus in 1984. The Israelis did not achieve their objectives. I think it was a fairly humbling experience for Israel after all its previous victories in the Middle East.'

The Irish general and his troops watched as the feared IDF, which had strutted so confidently into Lebanon two years before, retreated with its tail between its legs. Irish and other UN soldiers were left to police the chaos left in the wake of the Israelis' withdrawal.

By 1985 the IDF had withdrawn from most of Lebanon except the so-called 'security zone' which was like a militarised south Armagh magnified a thousand times.

The Israeli invasion of 1982 clearly threw into question UNIFIL's credibility as the international force was swept aside by the IDF. By the time Callaghan departed as force commander in 1986 the Israelis still occupied the narrow 10 km-wide security belt of Lebanese territory. Its Lebanese surrogates, the DFF and other forces, continued to stalk the south harassing and harming villages and UN soldiers alike.

Callaghan, however, cites one simple statistic which he feels is a real index of his troops' achievements during that time. 'When I first worked with UNIFIL as acting commander in 1978 there were only 20,000 people left in the south following the first Israeli invasion. But by the time I left there were 250,000 back living in the region. There was a massive building programme going on. This was very obvious at the end of my posting every time I took a helicopter flight over the area. From the helicopter you could see new houses radiating out from UN positions. The roads got better. Water supplies came back to normal. Schools, orphanages and hospitals started to reopen.'

The Irish general who rose through the Defence Forces ranks had reached the pinnacle of his military career as force commander in Lebanon. In recognition of his role in peacekeeping, Lt-General William Callaghan received accolades from home and abroad.

After leaving UNIFIL at the end of 1986, satisfied that his soldiers had done their best, the general spent another year in Jerusalem with UNTSO. When he finally left the Middle East on 1987 General Callaghan was granted special permission to don his uniform for the last time. He was welcomed home by the former Minister for Energy and Communications, Ray Burke, who represented the Minister for Defence, Lt-Col Vincent Savino (another Lebanon veteran who served with Callaghan) and GOC Eastern Command Brigadier-General Patrick Monahan.

Thirteen former Irishbatt commanders who also served with him in Lebanon were there to greet him at Dublin airport along with his wife Hilary, son Declan and daughters, Marie, Fiona and Clare. He then inspected a guard of honour from his former unit, the 2nd Infantry Battalion to the accompaniment of the Army No. 1 band. It was a fitting salute to a man who had served Ireland well in the cause of peace at home and abroad. The very next day Callaghan retired from the Defence Forces.

Even at 71 Callaghan's physical appearance justifies his nickname. He is a big boned hearty looking man. His face shows no signs of the strain and stresses he endured while commanding the UN force at its most critical juncture.

EIGHT EARLYBIRD

In south Lebanon everything is not what it seems to be. An Irish soldier's friend today could be his enemy tomorrow. A local known to be in one militia group could turn up in the ranks of another. A well-travelled route regarded as safe territory may easily turn into a killing zone.

The largest Shia Moslem militia in the Irish battalion's area, Amal, is normally pro-UNIFIL. Amal commanders have openly demanded that Irish troops remain in the region to protect their people. Soldiers of all ranks are often on first-name terms with Amal militia men from local villages. Despite this spirit of co-operation it was a master bomb maker serving in Amal who targeted Irish troops in an attack which claimed the life of a young Co. Galway man in 1986.

By the mid-1980s the roadside bomb had become a regular weapon in the arsenal of renascent Shia Moslem militia groups in their war against the Israelis. It posed a deadly threat to Irish troops caught in the middle. Huge bombs packed into cars and trucks were left on isolated roads in the south and detonated when IDF or DFF patrols went past. Amal and the more militant pro-Iranian Hizbollah were inflicting huge casualties on the Israelis. Coupled with suicide bomb attacks on Israeli positions throughout the south, the mainly Shia resistance campaign using the roadside bomb and the hit and run guerilla style sorties were taking a heavy toll of Israeli life. The IDF's response to mounting attacks was a policy of the 'iron fist' which in reality meant massive retaliation on Shia villages.

Irish soldiers as always were in an impossible position. They tried to stop the IDF depopulating villages and seizing prisoners at will. They physically stood in front of Israeli armour and fought with their bare fists at checkpoints to prevent the IDF entering UNIFIL-controlled areas.

In one incident in the summer of 1984, for instance, Irish soldiers tried to stop an Israeli column crossing Tibnin bridge. In response to this an IDF officer walked up to an Irish lieutenant and slapped him in the face. As well as these random humiliations and hassles there was also the constant threat that troops could be killed or wounded in IDF retaliatory attacks on the Shia.

But the Irish battalion was also required to prevent Islamic resistance attacks on the Israelis. This angered Shia Moslem fighters who wanted the Irish out of the way in order to engage their IDF/DFF enemies. The battalion came under severe pressure in the mid- to late 1980s as the Moslem resistance to Israeli occupation intensified.

Irish troops were at the sharp end of the UNIFIL mission. Most of the main targets for resistance attacks on Israeli and DFF positions were stationed at the edge of the Irishbatt area. In fact the only other part of the UN zone that witnessed attacks of this nature was at one DFF compound in the Finnish battalion area. The rest were almost exclusively in Irishbatt's domain. The terrain was also the best suited for guerilla attacks anywhere in south Lebanon. Shallow wadis with gentle slopes leading up to the compounds proved to be perfect infiltration routes for Amal, Islamic Resistance and Hizbollah to launch their sorties against the Israeli enemy and its surrogates. The IDF even admitted to Irish officers that their men were sitting on the most dangerous terrain in south Lebanon.

One of Amal and Hizbollah's main targets was (and still is) the DFF compound facing the Irish post on Hill 880. Irish troops had, however, defused several roadside bombs and booby traps in the way of a DFF patrol which used the same route as the Irish every day. The man who designed these bombs decided to teach Irishbatt engineers a lesson.

Lt Aengus Murphy was a quiet spoken 25-year-old officer attached to the 59th battalion. On the morning of 21 August 1986 he started the long trek to Hill 880 in search of explosive devices.

The young platoon commander led his patrol on foot along the At Tiri–Haddathah road close to the hill. He was accompanied by Gunner Liam Molloy (20) from Nurney, Co. Kildare and Private Colm Moore (20) from Carlow town. Behind them was an Irish armoured personnel carrier with a two-man crew inside. As the patrol walked past the hill around 7 a.m. there was a huge explosion. A bomb containing 150 lb of explosive mix and a 120 mm mortar round was detonated from a firing point nearby. Lt Murphy took the full force of the blast. Gunner Molloy suffered eye injuries and was temporarily blinded. Private Moore was wounded in the leg.

Troops perched on Hill 880 immediately ran to their comrades' aid. But it was too late for Lt Murphy. He was killed almost instantly in the explosion. Molloy and Moore were evacuated by helicopter to the Swedish medical centre at Naquorra.

Lt Murphy was the first Irish officer to be killed serving with UNIFIL. He was due to have taken two weeks' leave in Cyprus where he had planned to meet his fiancée Martina Rhatigan for a holiday. He was a prominent Gaelic footballer with the Tuam All-Stars club.

With club and college experience under his belt, he then captained the Galway under-21 side for two years in succession and won an All-Ireland medal with the junior side. He turned his back, however, on further football glory to pursue an army career following in the footsteps of his father, the former c/o of Western Command, Brigadier General Kevin Murphy.

Lt Murphy joined the Defence Forces as a cadet in November 1979 and was commissioned in 1981. He served in McDonagh barracks in the Curragh and the Army Apprentice School at Devoy barracks, Naas.

In targeting Lt Murphy and his comrades, Shia Moslem fighters were sending a clear warning to the Irish battalion. 'If you interfere with our war against the Israelis and their allies then you will be killed. Don't get in our way.'

Perhaps the greatest frustration Irish troops have to deal with in south Lebanon is knowing who killed their comrades while at the same time being in no position to do anything about it. Within a few minutes of the explosion on Hill 880 Irish officers were aware that Amal's top bomber had been responsible for the explosion that killed Aengus Murphy. In fact they caught the bomber red handed!

The killer, known to the battalion as Jeywad Casfi, came from Brashit and had previously been on speaking terms with Irish troops in the village. He was arrested just yards from Hill 880 shortly after the bomb went off. Casfi and another local man were actually found with bomb-making material, including a command wire, close to where the bomb went off.

Irishbatt had been aware that Casfi and his comrades were behind a series of explosions in the Haddathah-At Tiri area prior to Lt Murphy's murder. Just 24 hours before the killing Irish troops reported that another similar bomb had exploded on the road between the two villages. Despite this intelligence and the fact that they caught Casfi in the act, the bomber was handed over to the Lebanese police.

The battalion had no choice. UNIFIL after all was trying to impose the Beirut government's authority on the south. All criminal matters connected with Lebanese citizens had to be dealt with by the country's civil power.

It was a real measure of the impotence of the Lebanese authorities that within a matter of days Casfi was handed back to his own militia group, Amal. He and the other man arrested on Hill 880 simply disappeared for a while despite protests from Irish politicians. As with others suspected of murdering Irish troops, the killers got off scot free.

Lebanon was however a land without a proper judicial system. Justice in Lebanon came in the form of a mock trial and summary execution. The 'lucky' prisoners received a bullet in the back of the head. Other unfortunates suffered torture, mutilation, rape and beatings in slow, cruel deaths. UNIFIL had neither the power nor the political mandate to prosecute the culprits. And in a land of shifting alliances and fickle agreements, Irish soldiers had to live and work side by side with Amal in the Shia Moslem heartlands.

Casfi's luck ran out towards the end of 1989. Israeli Shin Bet agents seized him in a raid on south Lebanon on 15 December. He was snatched and, the UN believed, taken to a prison across the border. He has not been seen or heard of since.

Irish troops with the 64th battalion had no cause for celebration however. They knew that Casfi had been lifted in their area and that it was the Irish who were going to get the flak from the master bomber's comrades. The resistance believed at the very least that Irishbatt had done nothing to stop the Israelis seizing their man. Some perhaps had darker but totally unfounded suspicions of collusion with the IDF.

It did not take long for Casfi's comrades to take revenge. Within hours of Casfi's abduction three Irishmen from Recce company were seized by a group of armed men at Tibnin bridge. After protracted negotiations with Amal's leadership the men were freed the next day. But the resistance fighters had neither forgiven nor forgotten the Irish.

During the winter of 1989 a huge landmine was placed on a road used daily by Irish troops driving water trucks to the village of Kabrika. Mercifully the device was found in time.

Just five months after Lt Murphy's murder, another Irish soldier was killed, this time at the hands of Amal's sworn enemy, the De

Facto Forces. Private William O'Brien had been on checkpoint duty at Brashit camp on 6 December when DFF gunmen opened fire. The 25-year-old Athlone man died instantly after being hit in the head by several rounds which riccoheted after machine-gun fire was directed at the checkpoint into the village. Once again doubts were raised back at home as to the future of the Irish battalion's involvement in UNIFIL. The then Defence Minister, Paddy O'Toole, said the country's role in Lebanon was being looked at very seriously. In the end the army and government held their nerve despite this latest tragedy. The mission continued.

This period proved to be one of the most dangerous and costly the Defence Forces ever faced abroad. Four weeks after Private O'Brien's death, Corporal Dermot McLoughlin was killed when a round from an Israeli Merkava tank landed in the Irish billet in Brashit.

Around 8.45 p.m. on 10 January 1987 a single tank round was fired into the base. The platoon commander immediately fired two red flares in the air to show that the position the Israeli tank gunners were firing at was a UN post. After the incident, Irishbatt's operations officer, Lt-Col Jim Harold pointed out that the UN flag was also flying from the base which was well lit up.

Despite this the Israeli gunners fired a further two rounds that evening, one of which killed Corporal McLoughlin. The Israeli barrage, which lasted eleven minutes, was also directed at the village. IDF officials later claimed Brashit was used as a jumping-off point for the Hizbollah who had killed six DFF men in an earlier attack on the compound overlooking the village. Corporal McLoughlin's death drew a storm of protest from the Irish government and UNIFIL force commander, Major-General Gustav Haegglund, who claimed the tank fire was totally unprovoked.

Less than a fortnight after the killing the IDF announced that it had disciplined two officers connected with Corporal McLoughlin's death. It was the first time the Israelis ever admitted responsibility for the death of UN soldiers in south Lebanon. The Israeli authorities even offered Corporal McLoughlin's widow Holly $50,000 in compensation. Mrs McLoughlin rejected the offer despite having to bring up five children on her own.

She said no amount of money could compensate her or the wives of other Irish soldiers killed in Lebanon. She called on the Israeli government to direct its army and their DFF allies to change their attitude towards UNIFIL troops. Speaking from her home in Cairns Drive, Sligo, Mrs McLoughlin declared: 'My husband looked forward to his tour of duty as a peacekeeper with UNIFIL. His only interest was to try to do some good. Out of respect for everything which Dermot meant to me and for every Irish soldier who has died in Lebanon I rejected this offer.'

After learning about her husband's death, she recalled her feelings when Dermot left his base at Finner Camp in October 1986 for Lebanon. 'I could not put into words what I feel about the Lebanon. It was something he wanted to do and I would not stand in his way. A friend told him he was tempting fate going there. But he said he could be killed crossing the street.'

Within a matter of months two Irish battalions had lost three men between them, one to the Shia Moslem resistance, one to the DFF and another to the Israelis. The Irish were being hit from all sides.

The death toll could even have been much higher. During the 61st battalion's tour the resistance targeted an Irish observation post containing eighteen soldiers. It was situated on top of a hill overlooking a deep wadi between Tibnin and Al Sultaniyah. From the house, Irish troops could observe the movements of resistance fighters infiltrating the route towards nearby IDF/DFF compounds.

A local man, friendly to the Irish battalion, was ordered to rig up the house with explosives. The intention was to blast the house into the wadis below killing anyone in it. It failed to go off and to this day senior Irish officers do not know why. For whatever reason a major tragedy had been averted.

The Irish area of operations contains miles of dirt-track, steep stony pathways and roads which snake across deep wadis and exposed hilltops. The terrain posed hidden dangers for Irish patrols. UN soldiers could easily become the unwitting victims of roadside bombs, mines or booby-traps intended for the Israelis or their allies.

An instance of this occurred on 17 November 1988 when 'A' company soldiers noticed a command wire leading from one UN post to another outside Haddathah. On further investigation the troops found a bomb just metres from a supply route normally used by Irish traffic.

Camp Shamrock was informed about the bomb and Irish headquarters immediately asked UNIFIL HQ to send in French engineers to defuse it. The Irish battalion's operations officer was told however by Naquorra that the French no longer carried out such tasks. The Irish would have to do the job themselves.

Commandant Ray Lane (then a captain) remembered that the bomb contained 20 kilos of TNT and was surrounded by nuts and bolts. His men then uncovered a secondary device nearby, buried in a wall. A pressure plate had been hidden in the ground which led to a projectile in the wall.

Both devices were dismantled by human hand that day. After that incident, Captain Lane said the Irish battalion learned a vital lesson. If it was to deal with bombs and mines on its own it would need specialist equipment including bomb disposal robots.

The 64th battalion's tour was an exceptionally bloody one. On 24 February 1989 Private Michael McNeela was shot and killed after the DFF opened fire with a heavy machine-gun at the Irish checkpoint in Haddathah. The Dundalk man, who served at home with the 27th Infantry battalion, was hit in the chest by a single round. Although army medics rushed to the scene Private McNeela was dead within minutes.

He had joined the Defence Forces in 1985 and served on his first tour of Lebanon two years later. The UN noted after the killing that since the beginning of December 1988 the same DFF compound from which the fatal shot was fired had attacked Irish positions on thirty-four separate occasions, including seven at the very spot where Private McNeela died.

Almost one month later a huge explosion on a road outside Brashit killed three Irish soldiers from the Western Command. The bomb on 21 March 1989 claimed the largest loss of Irish life in Lebanon since the shootings at Tibnin bridge.

Shortly before 7.30 a.m. Corporal Fintan Heneghan (28) along with Privates Thomas Walsh (30) and Mannix Armstrong (26) were travelling on a routine journey between the two Irish posts at either end of Brashit. As their car headed north along a dirt road there was a massive explosion. Two of the men died instantly; the third was dead before help could reach him. All three had only two weeks of their tour to complete.

Follow-up investigations found that the gang that planted the bomb had used at least more than one Soviet-made landmine which was surrounded with rocks and TNT. Judging by the size of the crater made in the road Irish engineers suspected that the culprits had used a TM46 landmine.

The device was no stranger to the Defence Forces. It had first turned up in Ireland in 1974 after army and Gardai intercepted the MV *Claudia* off the country's coast. The vessel had been carrying a huge arsenal of explosives and arms to the Provisional IRA. Included in the haul were firing pins for the TM46.

Two of the dead in the Brashit bombing, Mannix Armstrong and Thomas Walsh, were married. Private Armstrong came from Sligo town and his wife Grainne was pregnant with the couple's first child at the time of the tragedy. Private Armstrong came from a military family. His brother John served in the army as a corporal in the 28th Infantry battalion—Mannix's home unit.

Private Walsh lived in Tubbercurry, Co. Sligo with his wife Pauline and young daughters, Donna (6), Laura (4) and Paula (2). One of his brothers, Tony, served with him in 'C' company during the 64th battalion's tour of Lebanon.

Corporal Heneghan was a single man from Ballinrobe, Co. Mayo. He was the son of local Fianna Fail councillor, John Heneghan. His home unit was the 1st Infantry battalion based at Renmore barracks, Galway. He had served on three previous tours of Lebanon in 1982, 1986 and 1987.

After the Brashit bombing tragedy initial suspicions were raised that the DFF were responsible for placing the mine. The spot where the men died was less than a kilometre from a DFF compound and the Irish patrol's route could be observed from there on a daily basis.

The explosion, however, which left a 6 ft crater in the ground, was found to have been detonated from a firing point inside Brashit village. The village was at the centre of Shia resistance to the Israelis and the DFF. It was soon learned that Casfi's comrades had finally exacted their revenge. The Brashit bombing settled the score for the resistance fighters. Irish troops in the village were aware of a Believers Resistance unit, an off-shoot of Amal, operating there. Members of the cell had close ties with Casfi.

Amal's leadership in Beirut had actually signed an accord with UNIFIL several years before, pledging support for the UN soldiers on the ground. The Shia Moslem organisation even instructed its members to hand over heavy weapons at UN checkpoints and they were even issued with yellow identity cards.

The family of Amal's leader, Nabbi Berri, invited Irish troops into their home in Tibnin and were on first-name terms with many officers and men. Yet in the same area men nominally attached to Amal were putting Irish lives in danger and plotting murder against Irishbatt.

In response to the loss of life, UNIFIL allowed the Irish to draft into Lebanon a newly formed bomb search team that had seen action at home along the border with Northern Ireland. The battalion had its own Explosive Ordnance Disposal Team whose task was to defuse and destroy bombs. Selected soldiers were also trained on assault pioneer courses in order to clear conventional battlefields of mines and ordnance. One soldier selected for the course in 1981 was none other than Private Michael McAleavey.

Every Irish battalion up to the spring of 1987 had also deployed Explosive Ordnance Recognition teams (EOR). The essential difference between the new unit being set up and the old EOR was that the latter acted in a defensive mode. It cleared up confined areas around Irish posts, checkpoints and living quarters. The new unit had to be 'offensive'. It had to go out there and clear routes beyond Irish camps and bases.

The new units would cover wide areas outside Irish bases including wadis and narrow tracks travelled by troops. But it was clear after Brashit that the Irish contingent needed a specialised unit to seek out and isolate explosive devices in order to allow troops to carry out their duties safely on the ground. Irishbatt was allowed to draft in the new unit because its operational zone contained several hot spots of Moslem resistance against the Israelis and their allies. UNIFIL could not function with any credibility if Irish troops were unable to patrol freely in one of the most troubled zones under the mission's control.

The first ever Special Search Team (SST) was deployed along the border in late 1987 after it was introduced by army students returning from an international search course. At that stage it was confined to Engineer Units. But the SST was then extended to infantry battalions, particularly border units. Special training was carried out and hi-tech top-of-the-range equipment procured on the international arms market. After the Brashit bombing tragedy the Department of Defence decided to send an SST to Lebanon to prevent the type of incident that claimed the lives of Corporal Heneghan and Privates Thomas Walsh and Mannix Armstrong.

Captain Conor Furey from the Engineers Depot at the Curragh received only ten days' notice in May 1989 when he was ordered to train Irish troops in search and clearance techniques. He had already served with the SST unit in operations at home but never dreamt he would be jetting off to the Middle East to take on such a daunting task.

'The biggest problem was getting our stores together. I would like to have had more equipment and time to prepare but the need was urgent. When I got there I spent the first three days studying maps of the area under Irish control. The first aim I had was to determine the safest routes our lads could take out there.'

The equipment which was used at home to detect IRA and loyalist bombs is still regarded as among the most advanced in the world. It included the Vallon MI 1612 metal detector which uses integrated circuit technology. The Vallon is capable of detecting metallic objects

Lieutenant Niall McCarthy and Private Francis Powell in a Panhard armoured personnel carrier

In the outskirts of Tibnin

Commandant Connie Ryan (*left*) stands at Fish Junction

A local person delivering goods to a Mingy shop

Company Sergeant Peter Brogan in the village of Majdal Selim
with a group of local children (AIRMAN JOHN DALY)

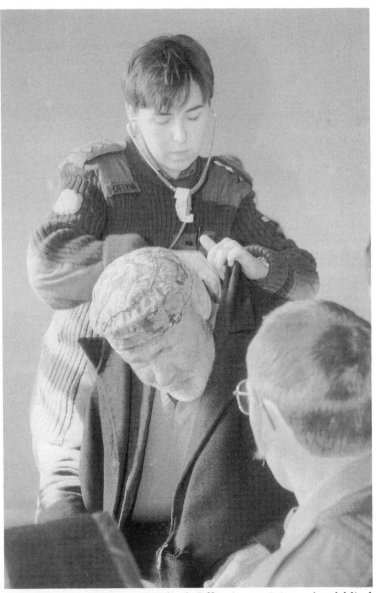

Captain Clare O'Flynn (Medical Officer) examining a local blind man at the At Tiri clinic

An Irish army bomb disposal officer returns from defusing a shell near Tibnin

An Irish UN observation post in the enclave

Airman Peter Cummins at post 615 in Majdal Selim

A goatherd tends his flock in the South Lebanon hills

A Sisu gunner (AIRMAN JOHN DALY)

The Imam Mussa Sadre, flanked by two photographs of Nabi Berri, leader of the Amal movement, looks down on two members of the 69th Irish Battalion at Al Journ

in the ground or in shallow water. The Irish also took with them an RDK device, which looks like a large car vacuum cleaner. The RDK is a highly sensitive detector which indicates surface-laid or lightly buried wires and cables which could be used to trigger bombs. A third device, the Ferex 4021, was procured to detect ferro-magnetic objects buried deeper in the earth. The rugged terrain of south Lebanon proved to be a tough testing ground for such equipment. Its use on a daily basis resulted in simple breakdowns and faults in internal circuitry.

Because this search equipment was limited, Irish engineers, in tandem with the Signals Platoon, modified and repaired it. Captain John O'Dea, an officer who served with the 66th battalion, pointed out that improvements invented by Irish troops were later adopted by the equipment's manufacturers. The improvements to bomb search devices also had a knock-on effect at home where new improved versions of the equipment are now used in the hunt for paramilitary explosives. The lessons of Lebanon are helping to save lives back in Ireland.

The Irish battalion also had its remote controlled bomb disposal robot, the Hobo, which can be activated from a range of 800 metres. It has three cameras and an expanding arm for lifting bombs. The robot is also mounted with a shotgun and water jet. The Hobo represents the sum total of the Irish armaments industry. The robot, which costs approximately £60,000, is manufactured in Cork by Kentree Ltd.

The Hobo has been able to crash through stone walls, cross small rivers, withstand explosions at point blank range, push a car and withstand flames. The success of the Hobo is reflected in the fact that it is now in service with armies in more than twenty countries worldwide.

A concept pioneered by Irish troops during the 65th battalion's tour was to train soldiers in each of the company areas in search and route clearance techniques.

When he arrived in Lebanon in early May 1989 Captain Furey dreamt up a plan which effectively shut down the number of roads Irish convoys could travel on. He drew up a 'danger colour scheme' mapping out areas of threat.

Red areas were roads and dirt tracks which were the most precarious. Captain Furey recommended that these should be out of bounds. Routes coloured in amber represented roads which, although posing dangers, could be travelled in emergencies. Finally green lines were the safest to travel on.

Marking out no-go areas for Irish traffic went against Captain Furey's basic instincts. He confesssed he would have liked to search every road in the Irishbatt area. His plan was accepted by UNIFIL and the driving discipline was adopted as a standard operating procedure. There are now areas where the Irish no longer drive although they do patrol on foot.

His scheme gave Irishbatt an edge over those militias and armies who chose from time to time to attack UNIFIL. If someone exploded a bomb on those routes taken by Irish soldiers the attack would be regarded as 'very personal'. The Irish in other words had to be the intended target.

In Lebanon all the warring parties played the politics of denial and counter-blame. The off-shoot faction which killed Hugh Doherty and Kevin Joyce emphatically denied any involvement in the crime. Amal never publically admitted Casfi had killed Lt Murphy. The DFF/IDF killings of Irish troops were always 'tragic mistakes' which never had any official sanction.

The restriction of Irish traffic to set routes sent out a signal to all factions in the area: 'If you set bombs on the only routes taken by our troops we will be sure you are responsible.' All armies learn by their mistakes. The Irish were no exception in Lebanon. Patrolling all the main routes in south Lebanon had left troops vulnerable to bombers and snipers.

Captain Furey's first twelve weeks in Lebanon proved to be busy as the newly formed SST unit began the painstaking task of search and clearance. Only a fortnight after taking over, his team discovered a huge bomb on the side of Hill 880 close to where Lt Murphy died. He believed this one was meant for a DFF patrol coming from Haddathah compound. It contained several hundred pounds of explosive packed into a number of anti-tank rounds. Captain Furey and his men blew the device up before it could do any damage. Perhaps the most startling thing about this bomb was the fact that Casfi's comrades offered information to the battalion about the device which he was believed to have placed on the hill.

In that period the new SST unit discovered and successfully isolated two landmines, one major roadside bomb and three unexploded artillery shells. The Irish battalion's area of operations is like an artillery range in that unexploded shells are found regularly by the SST. Some of the ordnance discovered by the unit are from the period prior to UNIFIL's establishment.

Captain Furey also noticed that the Moslem resistance was employing techniques he had seen before closer to home. On Hill 880 the SST found an initial device left at a path side containing up to 5 kg of explosive. It led to a firing position several yards away. Luckily the team was diligent enough to spot another device constructed out of a 105 mm artillery shell which had a separate firing position but was linked up to the first improvised bomb. The first device had been a 'come on' designed to lure troops into the area. The bomber would detonate that and soldiers would file into his killing zone. He would then trigger the second explosive which would catch his enemy unaware in a deadly trap. Captain Furey realised this was the type of trap set by the Provisional IRA in Northern Ireland. He also knew the man behind the latest Hill 880 bomb.

'It was definitely a Casfi job. He was big into secondary devices. This one had his prints all over it. The interesting thing is that this kind of operation turns up in places like south Armagh. The IRA probably use more sophisticated bombs than Amal but the techniques to lure their enemy into a trap are at times remarkably similar.'

The ingenuity of bomb makers in concealing devices impressed Furey. One search team was puzzled after discovering by chance an improvised explosive device buried into a wall in Brashit close to where Irish troops patrolled. They could not find any command wire leading to the bomb. They searched the area for hours before a private spotted something odd. A series of telegraph poles were placed beside the wall. The private noticed there were more lines on the pole than usual. After further investigation the searchers realised the command wire had been laid above their heads from pole to pole. In suspect areas the SST were told in future to count the power lines overhead.

Soldiers and civilians had an anonymous enemy in the south: the mole. The nocturnal animal unearths unexploded mines buried deep in the ground. Live artillery rounds from as far back as the first Israeli invasion in 1978 have been found at the peak of mole hills in fields tilled by local farmers. For that reason Captain Furey's team began to chart meticulously the location of 'war debris' scattered across their area.

As well as all their sophisticated detection equipment the SST also carried shotguns to protect themselves from another member of the animal kingdom, the snake. Captain Furey said each of the teams on his one-year stint in Lebanon used the shotgun.

'You would not believe the number of guys who were fearless when it came to approaching command wires which could have detonated massive bombs. Yet some of them were freaked out by snakes even though most weren't poisonous. It must be something to do with the fact that we don't see snakes in Ireland because when lads discovered them while searching for bombs it scared the hell out of them.'

As the SST was deployed throughout the area of operations the Irish contingent moved up the learning curve. They started to train units from other countries including the Swedes who were reported to be 'goggle-eyed' at the kind of equipment the Irish had at their disposal. The Swedes had been trained to clear minefields in conventional wars. They were not used to the type of terrain with which the Defence Forces had to cope at home or in Lebanon.

The battalion's SST searches six kilometres of road each day between the three company areas. Before returning home they will have cleared an impressive 600 miles of road, almost twice the length of Ireland. The daily searches are painstaking and meticulous.

When Captain Furey left UNIFIL he found a native 'shell' which was ideally suited for the mission. During one sweep of 'A' company area he thought he saw movement around rocks at a roadside. A soldier on patrol pointed his shotgun thinking it was a snake. On closer examination it was found to be a tortoise. Captain Furey suggested they should adopt it as their mascot. After all it was very like the SST in that it moved at a very slow speed, had a high protection factor and went about its business in a careful manner.

The SST's business is to save life by detection and prevention. The system seems to have worked well since 1989. The searches through roads, tracks, wadis and stony fields start at first light each day before a route is used by UN vehicles or foot patrols. For this reason the SST route clearance operation earned the codename 'Earlybird'.

The author went on an 'Earlybird' in June 1992 with soldiers from 'B' company who had to search and clear the route leading up to Hill 880. It began with an abrupt shake by Lt Neil McDonald shortly after 5.30 a.m. in the officers' quarters of 'B' company in Haddathah village. Each man was equipped with helmet, flak jacket and his particular piece of detection equipment. A soldier with the Vallon walked in front of his comrades and an APC drove behind. We walked on the side of the road slowly pacing along the route. The team leader carried a whistle. After halting every few yards to sweep an area en route, he blew the whistle to let us know it was safe and the patrol moved on. Luckily the team did not find any ordnance on the road that morning. The trek to Hill 880 took well over an hour.

By the time we reached the Irish position the morning mist had cleared and there was a breathtaking view of a snow-capped Mount Hermon to the east where the IDF have installed listening and observation posts which can spy deep into Syria. A soldier at the Irish post was playing with a hurley stick. He threw some stones in the air and volleyed them into the wadis below. DFF militia men observing our movements in the compound opposite looked on in bewilderment.

The troops' 'neighbours' opposite Hill 880 have their own crude way of clearing their routes out of the compound. Like other DFF positions, Irish soldiers noticed that the militia usually sent out one of their men in front of a half-track APC or tank. If there was a roadside bomb or landmine on the vehicle's route, the DFF man in front would get the full force of the blast. Such is the value attached to life by the warring parties in south Lebanon.

'We would never operate patrols the way the DFF do,' Captain O'Dea reflected. 'Everything we do out there is for the protection of life and to prevent incidents like the Brashit bombing ever happening again.'

The work of the EOD and SST teams has not just saved Irish lives in Lebanon. On 5 June 1992 local farmers working at the edge of Tibnin reported finding unexploded artillery shells in their fields. The war debris had been pushed to the surface by moles.

Irish engineers arrived at the scene. The farmers wanted to plough their fields. One bomb disposal officer put on a protective green suit which with its thick circular tyres made him look like a camouflaged Michelin man. He then donned a pointed blue helmet that looked like it had come from the set of a 1950s American science fiction film. The officer rigged himself with ropes and pulleys to a truck and made his way through the field to the unexploded shell. His coolness and courage was remarkable as he bent over the ordnance to see what it was. He then laid a tape around it and walked back to the Irish convoy. Having identified and isolated the shell, battalion engineers later blew it up. The farmers could get back to their land once more.

It had been a particularly busy month for the search and bomb disposal teams. An Israeli 155 mm shell had crashed into the wall of Tibnin hospital during the first week of June. Nobody was killed in the blast which the Israelis claimed was a mistake and the Irish had to clear up. Colonel Fawas, the head of the hospital and a senior official Lebanese army officer, praised the work of the Irish ordnance teams.

As he stood beside the gaping hole left by the Israeli shell in the wall of the hospital ward, Colonel Fawas said: 'One of the main reasons why the local population want Irishbatt to stay here is that they are so expert at finding and making bombs safe. I cannot even count how many of our own people's lives have been saved by your bomb search team.'

Blood Brothers

Even when not putting their lives directly on the line Irish soldiers gladly volunteer to shed their blood for the locals. Indeed Irish blood is literally flowing in Lebanese veins. It is donated to medical banks across the battalion area in order to save the lives of local people.

In centres like Tibnin local medics at the town's hospital find it difficult to get donors among fellow Lebanese citizens. Many Shia Moslems still refuse to give blood. Transfusion is taboo. Irish soldiers have stepped into the breach saving lives that would otherwise have been lost. It is for this reason that Colonel Fawas describes the Irish as the Lebanon's 'blood brothers'.

This visceral link between the Irish and the Lebanese is further enhanced by the work carried out by successive battalions in the south. Troops have rebuilt schools, hospitals, shelters and orphanages. The humanitarian side to every battalion's tour is as vital as the checkpoints, the searches, the Earlybird patrols, the reports, and the defence of UN positions.

There are also political dividends to be won in the 'hearts and minds' battle of the south. UNIFIL's ultimate aim is to create stability in the region and restore the authority of the Beirut government. In some parts of south Lebanon even since the first invasion in 1978 the Israelis had established a good image. In the Christian town of Marajayoun free medical services were provided for the population by IDF medics to Lebanese who wished to avail of them. The UN's concern was that the local population did not turn for help to Israel. UNIFIL was the *de facto* representative of the legitimate government in Beirut. Humanitarian aid and assistance in the south has helped strengthen the area's people's loyalty to the capital.

The mission was also determined to provide alternative sources of employment to locals who could easily earn a living carrying a gun for one of the militia groups. A volunteer with the DFF for instance earns up to $120 per month. On top of what is a reasonable salary in the poorest region of Lebanon his family can receive free medical care and support for their children's education from the Israelis. On the other side, young Moslems who join the Hizbollah can expect to be paid up to $200 per month from funds donated by the guerilla group's Iranian backers. If a Hizbollah fighter is killed in fire fights with the Israelis or the DFF his family will be compensated through Iranian-sponsored martyrs' foundations. In contrast, volunteers with the normally more moderate and pro-UNIFIL Amal movement only receive $25 every month.

By 1987 the 62nd Irish battalion and UNIFIL had drawn up a pro-gramme to provide aid to the civilian population. There was general concern among senior officers that the emerging militia groups on both sides were winning local support by lending assistance to civil-ians. In Kirbat Silm village, for instance, Irish intelligence officers noted that Hizbollah had acquired a doctor and nurse who were carrying out weekly visits to the surrounding area.

UN officers acknowledged that this form of aid had political implications, particularly in poorer villages at the edge of the Israeli security zone. The UN concluded that a co-ordinated 'peacekeeping humanitarian programme' was needed to counter-balance the growing influence of organisations such as Hizbollah.

In south Lebanon saving lives knows no boundaries for Irish troops. Even militia groups openly hostile to UNIFIL's presence have been helped for humanitarian purposes. Despite constant hassle throughout the mid-1980s, on several occasions Irish soldiers tended the very men who had made their lives a misery in the south. On 12 May 1984, for instance, the Islamic resistance mounted an attack on a checkpoint manned by a pro-Israeli gang set up near Yatar village. The 55th battalion had been constantly harassed by this gang during the IDF occupation. One member of the LAUI (Lebanese Armed and Uni-formed by Israel) was killed and another seriously wounded. The LAUI gang fleeing from the attack sought shelter in an Irish position down the road. A medical officer at the scene, Captain Rory Page, tended the wounded man, while soldiers removed the corpse of the other LAUI lying on the road. The wounded man was later released into DFF hands.

Ironically seven months later troops with 'A' company under the command of Lt Brendan McAndrew had one of their most serious confrontations with Israeli-sponsored Shia gunmen similar to the ones they saved in May. In Brashit the LAUI leader was known to Irishbatt as Hussein Abdul Nabi. On 4 November 1984 there was an attempted assassination against him after a funeral. As a result the LAUI closed their checkpoint in the village. The Irish did the same as a security precaution, no doubt expecting a confrontation to flare up as a result of the murder bid. The LAUI were thirsting for vengence. That same afternoon two unarmed UNTSO officers from Australia and Canada passed through the battalion's area. They had been coming from Beit Yahoun into the security zone. The officers ignored advice from their Irish colleagues to avoid the area after the Brashit incident. When the UNTSO officers tried to drive through the LAUI checkpoint they were pulled from their vehicle. Guns were put to their heads. The Irish at the scene spent the next few hours taking up positions and negotiating with the gunmen. Only after several hours of discussion were the UNTSO officers freed unharmed.

The bulk of Irishbatt's humanitarian work, however, concerned the local Lebanese Shia population. One of the most depressing sights Irish troops witnessed during Israel's gradual retreat into its self-declared security zone was the pathetic processions of helpless villagers fleeing from avenging IDF/DFF fire.

The evacuations became a ritual. The resistance would launch attacks on compounds or explode huge roadside bombs beside IDF/DFF convoys. The Israelis and their allies would then retaliate by directing heavy fire into Shia villages. Sometimes the IDF would even use their allies to expel people from villages. Once again, parts of south Lebanon had become virtual ghost towns as residents from small villages and hamlets fled in terror, seeking shelter with the United Nations.

The results of mass expulsions were and still are clear to see in south Lebanon today. Driving through villages inside and at the edge of the security zone there are entire population centres that are now completely empty.

On the road to an Irish post inside the security zone known to troops as 'The Black Hole' nothing moved except UN vehicles on one side and IDF/DFF traffic on the other. No one lives in the clusters of houses on the right-hand side of the road south any more. The fields were left untilled and sun scorched. There wasn't even a stray dog in sight. It was hard to believe people ever lived there. The clusters of solid three-storey houses peppered with huge holes from heavy machine-gun, artillery and mortar rounds resembled a deserted artificially built set for a Hollywood war movie. Only in this place the war was and still is real.

The Irish escort to 'The Black Hole' explained that the damage was caused by IDF/DFF reconnaissance fire. Armoured convoys during and after the 1982 invasion sprayed their bullets over the houses and in some cases into the very walls of homes as a warning to anyone not to dare attack their patrols. The strategy has given the Israelis and their allies a certain freedom of movement in the south. During a visit there on 5 June 1992—ten years after the second Israeli invasion—our UN convoy drove into the isolated Irish post past a patrol of IDF soldiers.

The Israelis filed past our Sisu armoured car walking on the road instead of the narrow footpath for fear of stumbling over booby traps laid by the resistance. It was an unusual sight as the IDF no longer tramp across ground in most of south Lebanon. But clearing the area of the locals who had lived there gives them the confidence to patrol at will. It is a policy that works brutally but effectively in a region that became a death trap for the IDF and their puppets during Israel's painful retreat from most of Lebanon since the mid-1980s.

An example of the policy of depopulation occurred on 30 December 1985 after two DFF men were killed by a roadside bomb on the road to Kunin village. In retaliation the DFF expelled every single person from the nearby area. As the terrified villagers ran from their homes DFF gunmen fired over their heads. The refugees fled northwards towards Irish posts.

Soldiers from the 58th battalion watched the refugees, mainly women and children, pouring into their area. They were given food, clothing and shelter for the evening. This time it was the victims of pro-Israeli gangs who were seeking help from the Irish. After the evacuation local muchktars wrote to the then Taoiseach, Garret FitzGerald, urging him to keep Irish troops in south Lebanon.

Throughout the winter of 1985 the Irish contingent was again on the receiving end from both sides in the conflict. On 11 November Comdt Rusty Keane and Lt-Col Wright stood in the way of IDF engineers attempting to blow up a house in Rashaf village which the Israelis claimed was used in resistance attacks against them. But for the presence of Irish officers at the scene the house would have undoubtedly have been demolished like thousands of others across south Lebanon.

In the same village three days later, three Irish soldiers had a miraculous escape when a Katushya rocket (commonly used by the

Lebanese Shia guerilla groups and the PLO) struck the UN's billet
there. This time UN intelligence discovered the rocket had been
fired by a resistance group from a position close to Shaqra.

On several occasions, the battalion had tried to prevent Israel and
its proxies depopulating the area. There was, however, little it could do
in the face of collective panic once the IDF or DFF started to pound
the villagers' homes. Formal protests were lodged with Israel at the
highest military and diplomatic levels including UN headquarters.
Ironically, on New Year's Day 1986, at the height of the attacks on
villages and the ongoing humanitarian relief programme, the United
States government announced that it was cutting $18 million from
UNIFIL's budget.

Although hamstrung by the overwhelming might of the IDF to the
south and the constant threat of resistance attacks coming from the
north, Irish battalions throughout the second half of the decade
continued to provide humanitarian assistance to the local population.

The battalion which has suffered the highest loss of life in Lebanon,
the 64th, was still able to get on with the job of improving life for the
locals throughout its six-month tour from November 1988 to April
1989. In the headquarters area around Tibnin the company at Camp
Shamrock donated $1,700 to buy diesel oil for the local hospital. The
battalion's medics set up new clinics in Ayta Az Zutt, Brashit and
Tulin with $1,000 out of humanitarian relief funds provided by the
UN and the Department of Foreign Affairs in Dublin.

As well as support for Tibnin hospital and the establishment of
new medical centres, the 64th carried out other 'hearts and minds'
operations ranging from buying glass for a damaged mosque in
Quabrika to giving $10 to a poor family in the 'C' company area so
that they could make an important phone call. Even at the end of the
tour, just one week before the Moslem resistance killed three Irish
soldiers in the Brashit bombing, the battalion was still risking its
men's lives to bring vital supplies to local Lebanese. Although it was a
city still under threat of IDF bombardment, on 14 March an Irish
convoy set out for Tyre to pick up flour to bring back to bakeries in
the battalion's area of operations. No one went without his bread.

During this year it was ironic that while the United States was
holding back on payments to UNIFIL and other UN missions,
blue beret peacekeepers were awarded the Nobel Peace Prize on 12
December 1988. The Irish Defence Forces were represented at the
award ceremony in Oslo that year by a soldier serving with the
64th battalion in Lebanon. Private Colin McGrath from 'A' com-

pany flew via Tel Aviv, Vienna and Frankfurt to attend the award. Four days later he returned to south Lebanon to continue his tour of duty.

Resistance attacks intensified throughout late 1988 into 1989 drawing the inevitable response from the IDF and their allies now settled behind the compounds built across ridgelines that fringed the security zone. Local lives were undoubtedly saved on April Fools' Day 1989 when a six-man DFF patrol seized two Lebanese at a waterhole used by Irishbatt at Ayta Az Zutt. The DFF tried to take them to Saff Al Hawa in the security zone for interrogation. The detainees were tied up at gunpoint and forced into an M113 armoured personnel carrier. Fortunately for the two men, Irish troops from 'A' company learned of the abduction and blocked the DFF patrol at At Tiri. As a stand-off developed that morning between DFF and Irish soldiers, an Israeli APC arrived at the scene. An Israeli officer got out of the vehicle and started to threaten the Irish at the checkpoint, warning them that they had ten minutes or they would be blown off the road. Although the Irish agreed to give way to the Israeli-led column, protests were immediately lodged with the IDF headquarters via Naquorra. Three days later the men were handed back to the UN.

Like all UNIFIL soldiers, the Irish were still in a no-win situation. Despite again saving the lives of local Lebanese Moslems, armed elements believed to be connected with the Hizbollah had attacked the Irish camp at Haddathah on 3 April firing up to 100 rounds from a light machine-gun and one RPG rocket. Angered no doubt about the battalion's inability, in their eyes, to stop the IDF abducting resistance suspects, the gang that fired on the Irish camp clearly forgot that the same UN troops had been threatened by Israelis only two days before while trying to save two Lebanese.

During the summer and autumn of 1989 the war between the resistance and the IDF/DFF was concentrated in the Ayta Az Zutt-Haddathah area under the control of 'A' company. The first contingent of troops with the 66th Irish battalion got their initial taste of action on the morning of their second day in Lebanon when resistance fighters launched an attack from the wadis near the DFF compound overlooking Beit Yahoun. The next morning a DFF foot patrol was caught in a blast from a roadside bomb. Retaliatory fire was unleashed against the villages below. The first victim in this latest outburst of attacks and counter-attacks occurred on 17 November when a young woman from Ayt Az Zutt was killed when her home was struck by a tank round fired from Beit Yahoun compound.

By 5 December the DFF were firing into the villages particularly in the Haddathah area where there were many resistance fighters. The fighting became so intense that Irish troops escorted the villagers out of their homes towards the north until the barrage ceased. Ten civilians were injured in the shelling and were evacuated by APC to Tibnin hospital. Ironically one of the families the Irish rescued from Haddathah that day was involved in a fire fight with troops in which two men died over two months later.

There were times however when the DFF fired into villages even though there had been no attacks mounted on their compounds. On the morning of 21 December 1989 a barrage of mortar and tank fire was directed at the 'B' company area and its surrounding villages. Two 120 mm mortars landed only 100 metres from the company's headquarters in Tulin. Nearby in Quabrika village two soldiers narrowly escaped death or injury after a tank round filled with high explosives struck their billet and flattened it. Miraculously two minutes earlier Sergeant John Wade, who was in charge of the post, roused the soldiers from their beds warning them about incoming fire. He ordered them to take shelter in the post's bunker. Had it not been for Sergeant Wade's prompt action in reacting to the incoming attack lives would have definitely been lost.

Soldiers from 'B' company survived the bombardment and four days later were able to celebrate Christmas Day in relative peace along with 100 local children at a party thrown for the kids by Irishbatt at Tulin, even though hardly any of the youngsters from Shia families knew much about the Christian feast!

After narrowly escaping with their lives from DFF fire, two months later Irish troops faced another life-threatening situation, this time on their flank from members of Amal.

The incident on 20 February illustrated how fickle the political and military situation in south Lebanon is. An Irish foot patrol searching houses in the narrow streets around Haddathah uncovered a machine-gun belonging to Amal. Local Amal fighters demanded the weapon back. Their organisation, however, had previously signed a co-operation agreement with UNIFIL over arms searches. Amal was after all officially pro-UNIFIL. Part of the troops' task was to confiscate weapons and try to prevent further attacks on the compound overlooking Shia villages.

There had been previous clashes at a local level between Irish troops and Amal militia men in the past but these were usually smoothed over by the UN and Amal's leadership. In Haddathah, however, Amal fighters took up firing positions close to the Irish at the north of the town. The militiamen opened fire on the Irish patrol wounding three privates including Riccardo Lucceshi from Dundalk who was seriously injured when he was shot in the chest. He was evacuated from the village and taken to Tibnin hospital where he recovered from his wounds.

In the gun battle, however, two Amal fighters were shot dead. Their parents had been among a number of people rescued from the village during heavy shelling by the DFF the previous December. Crisis talks were held between senior UN officers and Amal for several days after the shooting in a bid to defuse tension in the battalion's area. After the fallen Amal were buried their comrades hung two huge paintings of them at the south end of the village adjacent to an Irish observation post.

Oddly one of the dead men's portraits bears an uncanny resemblance to a republican terrorist involved with the Irish People's Liberation Organisation who was shot dead by a loyalist gang in Belfast later that same year. Perhaps the likeness is simply explained by the fact that propaganda murals to fallen insurgent fighters are the same the world over. The garish memorial to the brothers hangs in Haddathah today as a constant reminder to Irish troops of the dangers they face even in areas where the UN has a reputation for being friendly and fair.

Despite these infrequent skirmishes it is safe to conclude that like Amal at an official level the vast majority of people living in the Irish battalion area want UNIFIL to remain there. A good barometer of local opinion regarding the UN is local interpreter for the mission since 1983, Abbas Awala. A native of Tulin, Abbas has worked for the Nigerian and Ghanaian contingents as well as Irishbatt. He also works for the veteran reporter of Lebanese affairs, Robert Fisk.

Abbas explained that many local farmers are now able to tend fields lying underneath the DFF compounds which shield Israel's security zone. People he knew who fled the area have returned and have been encouraged to stay and rebuild their homes. The battalion's area has become in Abbas' eyes a 'haven of peace' because of the troubles in Beirut and elsewhere. While Israel remains in the south, the UN has failed to implement Resolution 425. Abbas does not blame the Irish. He said he feels UNIFIL has been hindered by outside interference, particularly Israel's strategic goals, militia groups opposed to the official Lebanese government and political ineptitude at UN headquarters in New York. He reflected the view of most local Lebanese leaders including one of Amal's rising commanders in the south, Abu Gawas, that Irish and other UN troops must remain until an overall political settlement is found not only for Lebanon but for the entire region.

Abbas pointed out that many young Lebanese have learned to speak the English language without having to study it in schools. Children have grown up living beside Irish camps and observation posts. They have heard English spoken in their home towns and villages since 1978. The English locals have picked up, however, is hardly the type read out over the BBC World Service.

In 'A' company, for instance, the children, particularly those born since 1978, speak in Dublin accents because troops in this unit mainly come from the capital and the surrounding county. At Majdal Selim for instance, Mohammed, one of the young boys who hangs around the Irish billet playing football with the troops speaks like a true Dub. He told the author that the Ireland soccer jersey he wears was given to him by a native of Ballymun. He related this story speaking in an accent as if he had just stepped out of Thomas McDonagh tower.

In Brashit local young people speak English with the same accent as troops from the west of Ireland. Beside the commanding officers' house 22-year-old Rosie Ali Haidar runs a mobile shop supplying troops with everything from Coca Cola to Persian carpets. She has run her shop beside 'C' company headquarters since 1985. As well as the shop, Rosie and her 15-year-old sister Khadige earn extra money washing and ironing Irish uniforms.

Her shop is a small cramped dimly lit hovel covered in post cards sent to her from all over Ireland. Physically she resembles her workplace, a tiny young woman who looks years older than she actually is, with a small fragile body that has been shielded from sunlight for a long time. Her English is spoken in a hybrid of accents from the west of Ireland. When the RTE broadcaster Treasa Davison visited Brashit several years ago she recorded Rosie speaking. After returning to Dublin Treasa played back the tape on air and asked listeners to ring in and suggest where Rosie was from. Galway, Mayo, Donegal and even Derry were among the suggestions callers sent in. Listeners on the radio were stunned when Treasa Davison informed them that the voice belonged to a young Lebanese Shia Moslem woman.

Rosie called her fellow Lebanese 'the civies'. When she explained something she amended her sentences by saying: 'Do ya get me, like?' She writes regularly to several soldiers back in Ireland. Her wish is to visit some of them one day but Rosie confessed that was probably unlikely because, as she put it, 'Me father wouldn't like it.'

She also reflected the views of most Lebanese in the area about the Irish force's presence: 'I don't want Irishbatt to leave the area because the other crowd [the DFF] would come into Brashit. When the Israelis were here it wasn't too bad. The other crowd were much worse. We're glad they're not in this area now, you know'.

Families like the Ali Haidars rely on UNIFIL's presence to make a reasonable living. The estimated monies spent in the entire peace-keeping zone is in the region of $50 million per annum. A whole economy now orbits around the UN presence since 1978.

Beside every Irish post there are 'Mingy' shops selling everything to troops from coffee to fake Cartier watches. The word 'Mingy' derives from the Congo where local tribesmen sold their wares to UN soldiers. The traders used the word 'Mingy' to describe the quantity of goods they had on sale. The expression was carried back by Congo veterans and has become a by-word for everything local in south Lebanon.

Electricity supplied from local generators rather than the UN or Lebanon's national grid supply is known as 'Mingy power' for instance. Fake designer clothes smuggled from Beirut and the Bekaa valley are known as 'Mingys'. Outside the UN headquarters in Naquorra there is a row of shops on one side of a dusty dirt track leading to the international camp known as 'Mingy Street'. This street sells everything from gold to CD players, always at a knock-down price. Soldiers normally go on a shopping spree in Mingy Street before returning home to Ireland via Israel.

The shops say a lot about Lebanon. It is a country where you can buy anything from the sacred to the profane. In one decorated with the flags of every UN contingent hanging on the outside window there was a vast collection of hard-core European pornographic videos, magazines and cards. But behind the counter hanging on the wooden wall was a morbid portrait of the Sacred Heart and wooden crucifixes nailed to the wall.

'Mingy Street Naquorra' is different in two important ways from the Mingy shops in the Irish battalion area. Some of the produce on sale at Naquorra is from Israel. The markings on the cans of juice and soft drinks are written in Hebrew rather than Arabic. The same is true for most of the non-European beer. Caught in the security zone, the Israelis are able to dump a lot of their surplus products onto local markets. The other more important difference is that the traders, even the Shia Moslems, in Naquorra pay 'taxes' to DFF commanders in the area. In real terms these 'taxes' (often up to 15 per cent of a trader's profits) are nothing more than an extortion racket in much the same way as nationalist and loyalist terror groups raise finance in Northern Ireland. Ironically in south Lebanon the profits made from the pockets of Irish and other UNIFIL soldiers partly help fund the very militias that harass and at times kill them.

In the hills, however, Irishbatt's spending power and humanitarian efforts have more benign results. The Lebanese are masters at mimicking the customs and background of their Irish guests. In Total village the two local Mingy shops are called Dunnes Stores and the Ilac Centre. Several of the shops in other parts of the battalion area have shamrocks and tricolours with the words 'Welcome Irish' painted in green. The locals even refer to their own businesses as Mingy shops. The Lebanese businessmen can also outcompete the UN. Calling home to Ireland in Camp Shamrock costs three dollars per minute on the UN-supplied phone system. I wanted to call Belfast from Tibnin one Saturday morning in June 1992. Instead a local teenager arrived at the entrance of Recce company's headquarters in Caltex House carrying a huge black portable phone with an elongated aerial. He said his name was Ali and that he could tap into the Israeli portable telephone network to make cheap calls abroad. He was charging the troops $1.50 per minute to call Ireland. I decided to take up his offer and phoned home speaking to my parents on a clear uninterrupted line for five minutes at half the price the UN was charging. Suffice to say Ali's service became extremely popular with Recce company.

As the 1990s began, normal life was slowly returning to the area under Irishbatt's control. One indication of this was the reopening of Tibnin orphanage in 1990. It was originally established by the Dutch but then closed after the invasion and the war in the south. Hassan Fawas, a native of Tibnin, who also works as a translator for UNIFIL, pointed out that it can only survive by the supplies of food, fuel and equipment donated by the Irish and the Norwegian maintenance company beside Camp Shamrock. In 1990 it housed twenty children; three years later it has over forty-three kids orphaned by the war or simply abandoned by their parents. While Irishbatt provides medical support and special projects such as the provision of extra beds for new children entering the orphanage, the Norwegians see that clothing and books are catered for.

Mohammed Fawas, the principal of the orphanage, said that without the UN's help the project would close down tomorrow. He gave some of the history of the orphanage building which was opened by a local Melkite Christian priest with the help of Dutch-batt in 1978. The priest fled the area after the Israeli invasion and died in 1987. After the Israeli withdrawal in 1985 the building was occupied by Amal fighters. Backed by UNIFIL Mohammed then negotiated with Amal for several years to get it handed back to the orphans. He recalled that the 70th Irish battalion raised money for children's clothing and also repaired the damage caused to the building's structure during the occupation. Along with UN troops and the International Red Cross in the region the orphanage is now run by three volunteers including 16-year-old Mariam Sabra whose mother was killed during IDF shelling on the Tibnin area during the early days of the 1982 invasion. In a classroom inside the orphanage the children, ranging from one to fifteen years old, repeated phrases from a French grammar textbook used by schools the world over.

Like Mohammed's orphanage, the local Red Cross volunteers work in tandem with the Irish and provide assistance to anyone regardless of their religion or political allegiances. The Lebanese Red Cross team based on the edge of Tibnin is regarded by Irish officers serving in the south as an exceptionally brave band of men and women. Eleven local Red Cross volunteers have been killed in just over a decade, with sixty-eight badly injured and two who were kidnapped and, like Private Kevin Joyce, are regarded as 'missing presumed dead'.

One of the aid workers who co-operates closely with Irishbatt is 25-year-old Mahmoud. Inside his headquarters overlooking fields to the south of Tibnin, Mahmoud has access to a 'hot line' to Camp Shamrock in case he needs Irish troops to help escort ambulances into trouble zones.

Mahmoud's team also co-ordinates with their Christian counterparts in Marajayoun where the DFF has its main headquarters. Apart from the UN his volunteers with their two ambulances are the only local Lebanese in the area who have access to the security zone.

Although the ambulances at the Tibnin headquarters bear the Islamic Red Crescent rather than the Christian cross on each side, Mahmoud insisted his volunteers have to be seen as very neutral in the conflict.

'We don't decide who to help on the basis of whether they are Moslem, Christian or Druze. We have contacts with all the militias and armies.' One of his team's more grisly tasks is to go into the security zone to pick up the dead bodies of resistance fighters killed in attacks on IDF or DFF compounds.

Mahmoud was particularly grateful to Irishbatt and other UNIFIL contingents for the blood they donated to save the lives of his patients. 'When we need blood we call the Irish regimental aid post at Camp Shamrock to help us. This happens quite a lot and we are never let down by the Irish. We can rely on the Irish to clear roads and tracks we have to travel in case there are mines or bombs around. The lives of our volunteers have undoubtedly been saved by Irishbatt. This is no exaggeration.'

As well as providing armed escorts for the Red Cross, UNIFIL evacuates some of their more seriously injured patients by helicopter to the American University hospital in Beirut.

Framed above Mahmoud's desk inside his HQ is a prize cherished by every one of his volunteers. In 1988 the Lebanese Red Cross won the organisation's World Cup for being the best first aiders on earth.

Irish medics working from Camp Shamrock scored a victory of their own in early 1992. It was the Irish contingent's second triumph in At Tiri, this time without any bloodshed. At Tiri has been so devastated and deprived that it was populated by less than one hundred old people with little or no contact with the outside world beyond the Irish troops based in the village. The battalion's MIO, Comdt Jim Goulding, made At Tiri target number one for Irish medical teams operating in the area. Escorted by troops from 'B' company, a fortnightly clinic was established in the village. Conducted by Comdt Nora Curran, from Mount Vernon in Dublin, the clinic attracted the whole population and became a kind of social occasion.

One of Comdt Curran's team, Captain Tony Margiotta who worked as a GP in Finglas before leaving for Lebanon, admitted that the medical benefits of the clinic to the locals are limited but the social contact is vital in helping to keep the shattered community together. The key achievement for UNIFIL is that this latest development keeps the UN and Irish flags flying in such a politically and strategically important area.

The medics of the 71st battalion had further success when they opened a second clinic in Bint Jubyal, another desolate village lying at the edge of the security zone. The Regimental Aid Post at Camp Shamrock also attracts people from villages close to and even inside the Israeli-occupied area. Nobody is turned away.

Over the last three years Irishbatt has had several other successes in the battle to restore normal life to the area. Families reliant on olives as one of their staple products can now harvest them during the season even though many of the groves lie beneath the shadow of

DFF compounds. A few years ago this would have been impossible as the DFF suspected that the resistance were using olive pickers to attack their positions.

Irishbatt has now set up a communications system with local DFF commanders to inform them when the UN will escort the farmers into their fields. Troops in each company area ensure that only those known to the UN and local village leaders are allowed into the fields during harvest time. The agreement has boosted the local economy, with olives now replacing tobacco as the number one export crop in the south. The region has become stable enough even for Shia Moslems in Beirut travelling south to work alongside their relatives in the olive groves.

UNIFIL also donated $1,000 in 1992 to the local farmers' co-operative in Tibnin to purchase an olive press in order to export olive oil abroad. Farmers even from inside the Israeli-controlled security zone now travel to Tibnin to use the press.

Land in south Lebanon, particularly in built-up areas, is normally cleared when a house is shelled. But one open space in bombed-out Brashit has been created by Irishbatt for a more positive purpose. Soldiers with 'A' company in the 72nd battalion started to build a children's playground with a see-saw, swings and slide in the local school. The project was given $800 out of a special fund which is administered by the second-in-command of each battalion. 'A' company designed the equipment and got the material from local suppliers. The extent to which the return to normality is going to be a long, slow process for the people in south Lebanon is illustrated by the fact that play itself had to be taught anew.

Captain Pat Aylward explained that before the children were allowed into the playground the equipment had to be shown to the teachers. Some of those teaching at Brashit school had never seen a playground in the war years. The teachers had to be taught how to use the swings and roundabouts! The sight of grown men, all soldiers, playing on see-saws and climbing frames was an extreme but moving demonstration of the lengths to which Irishbatt has gone to try and bring peace and stability to Lebanon.

 GASBATT

Irish soldiers witnessed at first hand the lethal results of Saddam Hussein's chemical arsenal well before the invasion of Kuwait and the second Gulf War.

When Sergeant Martin Malone picked his way through the deserted streets of Halabjiyah in northern Iraq, Saddam's regime was still an ally of the western world. It had just fought a bitter eight-year war with the fundamentalist Islamic state in Iran boosted by western military hardware. An estimated one million died in a struggle reminiscent of the trench warfare of World War I. And one side, the Iraqis, were willing to use First World War tactics in horrific mass gas attacks on Iranian forces at the front.

Sergeant Malone arrived in Halabjiyah three months after the Iraqi armed forces dropped chemical bombs from the sky on its rebellious Kurdish citizens on 6 March 1988. The Irish military policeman was sent there by the United Nations Iran-Iraq Monitoring Group (UNIMOG) to investigate reports that almost the entire population of several thousand people had been wiped out in a chemical attack. A number of other Irish MPs were stationed in Iraq to oversee the exchange of prisoners and the collection of war dead along the de-militarised zone with Iran. At its peak fifty-four Irish observers were stationed along the former front from Kurdistan to the Persian Gulf.

Martin drew the short straw. Along with other UNIMOG observers he was escorted everywhere by Iraqi soldiers in the northern Kurdish area still at war with the Baghdad government. Every time he tried to take pictures in Halabjiyah his Iraqi shadow would prevent him. It was obvious that hardly anyone had been spared in the gas attack. The remaining survivors were pushed off the streets just in case they spoke to the UN soldiers about the slaughter.

'There were no people left that I could see or talk to,' Martin reflected, 'but all the buildings still stood intact. It was eerie to think what happened in the streets where we were walking. No collateral damage at all, just a population which seemed to have disappeared off the face of the earth. It was as if someone had dropped a neutron bomb.'

Two years later fellow Irish soldiers were living under the constant fear that they and the Lebanese civilians around them might suffer the same fate as the Kurds at Halabjiyah. Sergeant Malone's comrades in the 68th Irish battalion serving in Lebanon were preparing to cope with an Iraqi chemical attack if caught in the crossfire of another all-out Middle East war.

Their protection against this impending horror had to be taken everywhere during their tour. While sitting on the toilet, eating in the cookhouse, driving out on mobile patrols and sleeping in bed, their Nuclear, Biological and Chemical suits (NBCs) became constant companions for soldiers serving with the 68th battalion.

As the new Gulf crisis of 1990–91 moved inexorably from Operation Desert Shield to Desert Storm there was a growing threat that the Iraqis might use chemical weapons against the allied forces massing in the Saudi desert and against Israel to the west.

The 68th took no chances. The indirect threat to them was all too obvious. In some outposts they were, after all, within sight of the border with Israel which Saddam Hussein had threatened to attack with his vast arsenal of chemical warheads. Every one of the 700-odd troops travelling to Lebanon in October 1990 was issued with the suit. Prior to their departure they were taken on a one-day training exercise at Kilbride camp to learn the basics of putting the protective clothing on in the event of a gas or chemical attack.

The suit became the symbol of the 68th tour of duty. It was for that reason that it gained the nickname 'Gasbatt'.

The NBC was the most sought after commodity in south Lebanon. When the Gulf War was at its height many worried locals, fearful that incoming Scud missiles might miscue and fall on Lebanon instead of their southern neighbour, were willing to pay upwards of $1,000 for the protective kit.

Nicknamed the 'Noddy Suit' it consisted of a rubber suit, gas mask, a set of inner and outer gloves, galoshes, special rubber boots, protective hood and a respirator.

Private Phillip Thorpe from Athboy remembered being approached early on the tour by locals anxious to purchase the suit. Others didn't bother paying. Several NBCs were stolen from a warehouse in 'A' company shortly before the war started. The company did manage to retrieve the suits after local interpreters and militia leaders intervened with the thieves. It was as well because, as Phillip Thorpe remembered, each soldier was only issued with one full kit and there were inspections every week to ensure that each still had it in his possession. Private Thorpe, one of the few black soldiers serving with the Defence Forces, had one major problem with his lifesaving kit. His feet were too big. There were no size 12s in the NBC stock.

'I might have survived a gas attack with the boots on, but my feet would have been in bits after,' he joked.

As well as the NBC, troops were given a booklet of white papers which were to be stuck around the living and working areas in their bases. The papers changed to blue if there was a gas or chemical emission in the atmosphere. The tiny square booklet became the soldier's best early warning system against an incoming gas attack on the region. Special antidote tablets and injections were also handed to every member of the battalion.

Fears that Scud attacks on Israel might indirectly pose a threat to them drove thousands of Lebanese out of the south towards the relative safety of Beirut and the Bekaa valley. The impending war in the Gulf may have been a long way away but Saddam's bellicose threats to Israel were enough to cause collective panic in the UNIFIL zone.

Israeli cities such as Haifa were, after all, only eighty miles from the battalion's area of operations. UN soldiers and civilians alike waited for a doomsday scenario as the year turned around. The impending war also had an economic effect on Lebanon. Many Shia Moslems in the south work in the Gulf states and send money home to their families. Thousands fled Kuwait and Saudi Arabia as a result of the invasion and later Desert Storm. A large proportion of these migrant workers never returned when the conflict was over.

On the same evening that Saddam Hussein's forces pushed into Kuwait, the father of a young Irish army private was piloting a Kuwaiti Airways jet along the Gulf. His destination was Kuwait city. On hearing on his radio about the Iraqi invasion Maurice O'Sullivan turned back the jet just in time and headed back towards the safety of Saudi Arabia. Mr O'Sullivan had lived in the Middle East, working for Kuwaiti airways. His son Eamon grew up in Beirut and learned Arabic as a child in the Lebanese capital. Less than a month after Iraq's defeat on 28 February Gunner Eamon O'Sullivan arrived in Lebanon with the 69th battalion to relieve his comrades in 'Gasbatt'. Nicknamed 'The Arab', Gunner O'Sullivan was able to translate for officers and read the Arabic graffiti daubed on the walls by Shia guerilla groups in the battalion area.

Private O'Sullivan's father had been lucky enough to escape being trapped in Kuwait and thus ending up as another western 'human shield' held hostage by the Iraqis for several months. Up to the outbreak of war there were, however, other potential Irish hostages caught in the danger zone when Iraq invaded Kuwait.

The thirty-six-strong unarmed Irish contingent with UNIMOG remained in the Gulf when the Kuwaiti crisis flared up. Indeed eight of the team, led by Lt-Col Joe Young of Athlone, were on leave when the invasion occurred and returned to Iraq via Jordan. Like their comrades in Lebanon the observers were issued with NBC suits, primarily to protect them against contaminated war debris such as unexploded artillery and rocket shells containing toxic substances on the battlefields between Iraq and Iran. At the time of Saddam's occupation of Kuwait all thirty-six men had service passports and were therefore not strictly entitled to diplomatic immunity.

By Christmas 1990 the United Nations had initiated plans to evacuate the families of twenty-one soldiers serving across the Middle East with UNTSO. The officers and NCOs who serve for two years in the region are normally accompanied by their wives and children. They were deployed throughout Syria, Lebanon, Israel and Cyprus. As with their colleagues in UNIFIL, the UNTSO personnel were issued with NBC suits, respirators and water bottles.

In the Irishbatt zone, despite the tension, troops had time to relax over the festive season. On Christmas Day Corporal Paul O'Reilly from Belfast remembers one of his comrades dressing up in a Santa Claus outfit for local Moslems at their post near 'A' company headquarters in Tulin.

Corporal O'Reilly's main memory of the weeks leading up to the war was that mail from home became more scarce as the number of flights into Israel were reduced. Letters were arriving up to three weeks late whereas before it was only taking around a week to get through to the troops.

Telephoning Ireland also became more difficult during this period as the system had to go through the Israeli network. With more people phoning friends and relatives in Israel, inevitably lines to the outside world were harder to book in south Lebanon.

Seven days before war finally broke out the remaining eleven Irish UNIMOG officers were evacuated. UN headquarters in New York decided to scale down their presence in Iraq and close the UNIMOG office in Baghdad. Ten of the military policemen were flown by a chartered plane to Cyprus. The UN, however, wanted to retain a presence in the area so that its forces would be in place to monitor any possible settlement when the war ended. Comdt Brian O'Sullivan was transferred from the Iraqi capital to Tehran for that reason.

In Lebanon the build-up to war in the Gulf concentrated the minds of troops who had served in the region before. Sergeant Martin Walsh had been out previously with the 46th and 51st battalions. On his third tour he was appointed to the Force Mobile Reserve at Quana. He had seen action at the Battle of At Tiri and had been under fire on his second tour.

This time he confessed he was much more apprehensive: 'When we were given the NBC suit I thought that's it. This time I might not get out of here again. It does hit you when you see that suit. I knew I would be close to the Israeli border during my tour because the FMR goes almost everywhere in south Lebanon. We would have been in particular danger.'

Sergeant Walsh and his comrades learned that in the event of the Gulf War spreading west to Israel and Lebanon UNIFIL had drawn up plans for an emergency evacuation of the entire force. Rumours were widespread that the blue berets were to move north to Beirut to be taken by helicopter to American aircraft carriers with the US 6th Fleet in the Mediterranean. Phillip Thorpe said at one stage he was even told the entire battalion would be sent home.

In the early hours of 17 January the allied forces launched a huge air and missile attack on Iraqi cities and military installations. Irish troops in Lebanon sat glued to their television sets as CNN relayed the first reports of the blitz on Baghdad in which one reporter with the news network tastelessly described it as 'being lit up like a Christmas tree' with the anti-aircraft fire shooting hopelessly at the allied planes overhead.

The opening day of the conflict prompted a new exodus of local Lebanese heading as far as they could from the Israeli border. Phillip Thorpe remembered seeing car roof racks packed with every conceivable household commodity including the kitchen sink as families fled the UNIFIL zone. A few stalwarts remained such as Ali Saad and the infamous Monsewer, a trader who made a living selling food, clothes, beer and gifts to soldiers stationed at Total.

'A lot of people were on the move in the first week of the war. They took everything with them. There was little we could do to stop them. But others like Monsewer wouldn't have left the area if they dropped the atomic bomb. He liked making money too much,' said Phillip.

The local Lebanese fears about a missile strike on northern Israel were justified only 24 hours into the war. Iraq's answer to allied superiority in the air was to launch Scuds against Israel. The Soviet-designed missile with a maximum range of 550 miles was primarily used by Saddam for its political potential. An attack on Israel would, he believed, draw the Jewish state into the war. Arab nations in the coalition mounted against him could not fight on the same side as the Israelis and the fragile unity of the allied forces would fracture. The Scud attacks, with the ever pervasive threat that the missiles contained chemical warheads, also played on deep psychological fears in Israel. An Arab leader unleashing gas attacks on a state founded from the ashes of the Nazi gas chambers chilled Israel.

The first wave of Scud attacks could he heard during the night across the Irish battalion area. Troops on isolated listening posts reported that the missiles sounded 'just like thunder' when they impacted on their targets. On Hill 880 and on the roof of Recce company's Caltex House, soldiers could see the arced light of the Scuds travelling through the sky towards their final destinations, Tel Aviv and Haifa. After the first few days scrambling into the protective suits the troops started to treat the Scud attacks like a spectator sport. They stood on Caltex roof and Hill 880 in their ordinary uniforms watching the firetrail of the missiles over the southern sky.

Martin Walsh recalled that the entire area of operations was completely illuminated by IDF flares in the first week as the Israelis feared pro-Iraqi guerilla groups might attempt to open up a second front against their state from Lebanon. Irishbatt reported an increasing number of overflights by Israeli jets and remote-controlled Drone spy-planes.

Aside from the gas threat, Irishbatt and other UNIFIL contingents were on a state of increased vigilance in case local militias increased their activities during the Gulf conflict. UN commanders feared that Palestinian factions would try to infiltrate the south and launch direct attacks on Israel.

This scenario would have been more likely had Saddam's attacks on Haifa and Tel Aviv drawn Israel into the war and split the allied coalition. An Israeli strike against an Arab state would have increased the danger of a second front opening up in south Lebanon. Instead, after the initial few days of the war, fears of the conflict spreading to the UNIFIL zone dissipated. Officers reported instead that their tour had been one of the quietest in recent years. One reason for this was that Syria actually joined the coalition against Iraq, sending an entire brigade to Saudi Arabia. The Syrians had some measure of control over militias in the region, particularly Amal. It may also have been due to the fact that Shia Moslems were not ready to die for Saddam Hussein whose regime had butchered their co-religionists in southern Iraq and Iran during and after the first Gulf War. Iran remaining neutral in the conflict meant the militia they sponsored in Lebanon, Hizbollah, was unlikely to widen the war to Israel's northern border.

There was, however, considerable confusion among the local population about the allied-led war against Iraq. Many were aware that Operation Desert Storm had been sanctioned by the United Nations Security Council. In the minds of some locals, Irish soldiers serving under the UN flag in Lebanon were no different from their western counterparts in the Gulf.

Corporal Paddy Keeley from Raheny, Dublin, said he was asked on several occasions about why 'UN soldiers' were serving in the anti-Iraq coalition. He described the mood and ambivalent attitude the Shia had towards Desert Storm.

'Many of the locals would walk up to you and say "Hey, why are you attacking Iraq?" They didn't see the difference between peace-keeping and what the allies were doing in the Gulf. Many of them didn't understand. The funny thing was while during the war some locals accused us of attacking fellow Arabs; after the Allies won the same people came up and shook our hands congratulating us on "our victory". Others in the villages just wanted to know what was going on. They were very frightened that missiles might land on the area. Every day during the war they would come up to the camp and ask for news about it.'

While the number of reported overflights by Israeli aircraft increased the only serious ground incursion by the IDF took place shortly after Christmas Day. An Israeli armoured column of half-track troop personnel carriers drove through Tibnin into the heart of Irishbatt's area. Irish soldiers from 'A' company along with an armoured escort from Recce company blocked off opposite ends of the village and trapped the IDF column in the town. After quick negotiations the Israeli commander agreed to leave the UNIFIL area and turn back towards the security zone. The battalion's quick response prevented the Israelis from flexing their military muscles deep inside their area.

On 27 February Kuwait was finally in allied hands. After the air strikes came the 100 hour ground war which routed the Iraqi army in the desert. The Iraqis had been driven out and their retreating forces from Kuwait city annihilated by British, French and American fire power at the Mutla ridge along the road to Basra.

Two months later, with the oil fires ignited by Iraqi engineers during the occupation still turning day into night, Irish officers returned to Kuwait. On 11 April the UN Security Council formally established the United Nations Iraq-Kuwait Observer Mission. Its task was to monitor the demilitarised zone established by the allies between Iraq and Kuwait. In recognition of the Irish army's experience in the region the UN appointed Lt-Col Peter Feely, the c/o of the Second Infantry Battalion at Cathal Brugha barracks, to take charge of one of the three sections of UNIKOM. In total ten Irish officers were selected for the mission area. Prior to leaving for the region they were carefully schooled about the dangers of mines which littered Kuwait's roads and desert tracks.

A further twenty-one members of the 68th battalion volunteered to join UNIKOM. The contrast between UN peacekeeping in Lebanon and the active armed operation sanctioned by the UN against Iraq was glaring.

The most suprising thing perhaps about the period was that Irishmen were serving in both areas. In British regiments such as the Queen's Royal Irish Hussars, I met entire Challenger tank crews from the Republic of Ireland. Some of them had previously served in the Irish Defence Forces before switching their allegiance to the British army in the pursuit of better pay and prospects.

Perhaps the most noticeable difference between Irish soldiers (along with their English, Scottish and Welsh comrades) in Lebanon and their fellow countrymen in the British brigades in the Gulf was their attitudes to the local Arabs. In Lebanon diplomacy at street level is everything. Dealing with people, treating them fairly and respecting their religious and social customs is as important, if not more, than knowing how to fire a rifle or drive a tank. There were, of course, customs to be respected in Saudi Arabia. While there I was told by British officers not to wear a crucifix or Star of David around my neck. Never mention Israel, Salman Rushdie or ask questions about the monarchist dictatorship that rules the kingdom. These restrictions were imposed on all foreign journalists as well as western armies during the crisis.

Many of the British soldiers I met simply ignored them. They brought hard-core pornography purchased in German sex shops with them to the Gulf even though Page Three of *The Sun* had been cut out on the strict orders of the Saudi military. They treated their Saudi guests with amusement and contempt referring to the women completely veiled in their black chadors as 'stealth bombers'. Worst of all, they had a nickname for the unfortunate guest workers who flocked to the region in search of jobs the Saudis would not do. They called the migrant labourers 'chokies'.

It was a patronising description for men who toiled for hours on end both for the allied armies and their Saudi masters. To be fair to the British contingent, the 'chokies' I met preferred to work for them rather than their Arab and Moslem brothers, the Saudis.

One Egyptian student working in Saudi Arabia to earn enough money to pay for studies at home got a job at the British camp in Al Hala outside the Gulf port of Al Jubayal. He opposed the allied operation and supported Saddam Hussein. He wanted to see the overthrow of pro-western Arab regimes in the region. And yet here he was in Al Hala working for the same 'imperialists' propping these regimes up. He sarcastically explained why: 'I need the money and although the British are imperialists they treat us better and much fairer than our Arab brothers. The Saudis mistreat us all the time. We are their slaves.'

When I visited the 69th Irish battalion in Lebanon several months later the first thing I noticed was the change in attitude towards local people. The word 'Mingy' was only used in an affectionate way to describe everything local. Soldiers bent over backwards to avoid insulting their Lebanese hosts. Most Irishmen expressed sympathy for the plight of the Lebanese. There was little or no macho parading by the Irish contingent, unlike those allied troops who strutted around Kuwait city like a conquering army. Perhaps the greatest contrast between the two forces was that the average British squaddie was about five to ten years younger than his Irish counterpart serving in Lebanon. Most of the soldiers driving Challengers I met outside Kuwait city were still in their teens or early 20s. There were very few fresh-faced teenagers in the 69th Irish battalion at all.

Seven months after the Gulf War ceasefire the 'New World Order' had failed to touch south Lebanon. Hundreds of thousands had gone to war supposedly in defence of a UN resolution aimed at stopping Iraqi aggression in Kuwait. There had been high talk about the rule of international law. Acts of 'naked aggression' as US President, George

Bush, described the Iraqi invasion would be met by the force of united global armed force under the UN's auspices. But there was no such action to enforce UN Resolution 425. The continued violation of 425 didn't provoke even the same kind of verbal outcry on the international political stage even though soldiers wearing UN flashes and flying the organisation's flag were in the firing line. But of course there was one critical difference—Lebanon did not have oil.

Irish troops on the ground were left to pay the price of the New World Order's inaction when it came to Lebanon. Soldiers with 'C' company endured renewed and sustained attacks by the Israeli-backed DFF throughout September. In the first week the Irish post at Brashit was fired on ninety times by DFF gunners from their compound above the village. The post was actually hit on twenty-four occasions but remarkably no soldiers were injured as they constantly scrambled in and out of their protective bunkers on the codeword 'Groundhog' for hours on end. It had been the heaviest attack on the post in five years with mortars, anti-tank rockets and heavy machine-gun fire directed at the Irish position.

The local population was not so lucky. Two thousand of them in the company area fled their homes after the DFF renewed the bombardment following an Islamic resistance attack on the compound which left two pro-Israeli militia men injured. After the lull during the Gulf War south Lebanon was returning to its old brutal ways.

By 3 September the Irish had to provide food and water from their own stores to the remaining 1,000 people trapped in Brashit. UNIFIL commanders guessed that the barrage was a fresh attempt to depopulate the village which the IDF/DFF suspected was a launching pad for resistance fighters.

As well as helping the beleaguered population, 'C' company ignored a DFF-imposed curfew on Brashit. The Irish put themselves in the direct line of fire from the compound every time they patrolled through the village in defiance of a curfew the UN could not accept. As a result of the bombardment and the threats to UNIFIL personnel, the Defence Forces in Dublin issued an official complaint to the Israeli military attaché in London, Brigadier-General Tamir. Shortly after the the diplomatic parleying between Dublin and the Israeli embassy, Irish troops on the ground reported a reduction in the number of DFF attacks. The lesson was clear. The puppet masters could control their surrogate force whenever they liked.

The bombardment of Brashit came at a crucial time for the Lebanese government which had proposed a general amnesty for political crime in a desperate bid to end the sixteen-year-old civil war and move towards the final release of all western hostages. The fresh violence launched from the resistance, namely Hizbollah, also had to be viewed against the backcloth of the Middle East peace process which was kickstarted by the Americans after the Gulf War. Hizbollah, along with radical Palestinian factions, formed part of a rejectionist front opposed to negotiations with the Israelis. Increased attacks on the Israelis and their allies in south Lebanon were encouraged by the rejectionists' Syrian and Iranian backers.

In October the DFF switched their attacks to the 'B' company area firing at Haddathah village in retaliation for renewed Hizbollah sorties on their compounds. Mortar and anti-tank rockets were used again in indiscriminate shellings. Given the renewed ferocity of these attacks it was tragically inevitable that Irish lives would be lost. Within less than a month the fears of Irish commanders about renewed DFF activity were realised. And once again At Tiri was the venue.

At 9.00 p.m. on 16 November Corporal Michael McCarthy led a five-man foot patrol out of their post in the 'Irish house' in At Tiri after reports of a DFF incursion on the northern side of the village. As the patrol got to the western edge of At Tiri, having walked down the main street, they were fired on from very close range. Corporal McCarthy and Private Richard McGrath were in front of their three colleagues. In the fire fight that followed Private McGrath was shot in both legs and sustained a superficial flesh wound to his lower back. Corporal McCarthy was hit in the head and died instantly. A DFF militia man was also killed in the shooting incident.

Despite the Irish patrol shouting out that they were UN soldiers, the DFF continued to fire. An APC rushing to relieve the men under fire was attacked despite its distinctive flashing yellow beacon and illuminated UN flag and painted sign.

Private McGrath was taken from At Tiri to Tibnin and then flown by helicopter to the UN field hospital in Naquorra. The loss of Corporal McCarthy brought the Irish death toll in Lebanon to thirty-three. Twelve of these men were killed in action. The 33-year-old corporal was a native of Buttevant, Co. Cork and had two young children.

The killing caused another public outcry back in Ireland. The then Minister for Foreign Affairs, Gerry Collins, told the Israeli ambassador to Ireland and Britain, Mr Yoav Biran, that the Irish government held the Israeli authorities responsible for the murderous activities of its puppet militia.

The Israeli ambassador offered what appeared to be a feeble excuse for the DFF's attack, that it was a case of mistaken identity. Mr Biran insisted that the Israeli army had no control over the actions of its DFF allies who, he said, had mistaken the Irish for Hizbollah guerillas infiltrating the area. Although he conceded that 'everybody appreciates the role of UNIFIL' he lectured the minister that the only way to prevent similar incidents to the one in which Corporal McCarthy died would be to prevent 'terrorists' from acting in the area.

This was rejected by Mr Collins during their 30-minute meeting. He pointed out that Irish troops were well known to the Israeli-backed group in At Tiri. It was simply untrue to claim the IDF exercised no influence over their allies on the ground in south Lebanon.

Michael McCarthy made the ultimate sacrifice for the cause of peace in Lebanon. Six months later his wife and children's grief was compounded by a wrangle about an insurance policy taken out in his name. The insurance company told Mrs Margaret McCarthy that it refused to pay £25,000 under a mortgage protection policy on a Cork County Council mortgage to the family. The company claimed that a clause in their contract stated that it did not have to pay out the money if the holder was killed in a war zone.

The decision caused a furore. The former Defence Minister, John Wilson, intervened on the family's behalf pointing out that Corporal McCarthy had not joined the 69th battalion to fight in a war zone. He was in a peacekeeping area of operations.

After a wave of protests from the family, the Defence Forces union PDFORRA, politicians and community leaders, the Department of Defence eventually agreed to pick up the tab for the mortgage. The debate, however, as to when a peacekeeping zone becomes a theatre of war is still raging. PDFORRA has since urged its members to check their insurance policies to ensure there are no such similar exclusion clauses.

Margaret McCarthy's compounded grief turned to anger in December 1992 when it was revealed that the very bullets used by Irish troops in Lebanon were bought from the country which armed and supplied the De Facto forces that killed her husband. She was outraged at the fact that the very army backing the militia was profiting from an arms sale to Ireland. Mrs McCarthy urged her government to pull out of the trade. A deal to buy ammunition from Israel was, however, agreed after lengthy discussions with the Irish government on 1 December. The deal was worth £600,000 to the Israelis.

The Department of Defence in Dublin defended its procurement claiming it had no diplomatic significance. The 5.6 mm bullets were for use in the army's Austrian-made Steyr assault rifles, the space-gun shaped weapon introduced into the ranks of the permanent Defence Forces in 1989. Moreover, the new helmets worn by Irish troops are made in Israel. Even Hebrew words can be found inscribed inside the helmet. The irony was not lost on soldiers who sometimes had to scramble into their bunkers when incoming artillery, mortar or tank fire rained down on their positions from Israeli or DFF compounds. Their last line of physical protection during such barrages directed from Israeli-made artillery pieces, tanks, mortars, machine-guns, helicopter gunships and planes was after all an Israeli-made helmet.

The Gulf War proved to be the apocalypse that never happened in southern Lebanon. It was true that the resistance had been relatively inactive during the war. After the hostilities were over, however, a new war started to break out in the region as Hizbollah vied with Amal for dominance in the Shia Moslem heartlands.

Irishbatt and other UNIFIL contingents tried to encourage the official Lebanese army to return to the south. A battalion of Lebanese troops began to deploy around Tyre while Amal handed over its heavy weapons to the government in Beirut. There were indications that the government was beginning to reassert its authority in the area after years of chaos and foreign invasion. But the relative peace in south Lebanon during the Gulf War had been a phoney one. Hizbollah was preparing for a new offensive against the Israelis and the DFF. And the unfortunate Irish were still stuck in the middle.

THE SUN NEVER SETS

Pauline Ward has suffered at the hands of two opposing factions in Lebanon. Her husband was killed by an Islamic fundamentalist guerilla group determined to drive Israel out of their country. Her brother was shot dead by a militia armed, trained and supported by Israel.

The two men's deaths sum up the dangerous dilemma of peacekeeping in Lebanon where troops are caught in the middle of a renewed civil war living under the constant threat of being shot by both sides.

Corporal Peter Ward was within two weeks of completing his third tour of duty in Lebanon when he was shot dead. He had joined the army in May 1980. He had previously served with the 51st Irish battalion in 1982, with the 63rd in 1988, and in 1992 with the 71st. His wife Pauline, along with neighbours in Athlone's McCormack Park, had been planning a homecoming reception as he neared the end of his latest tour. Pauline had bought a new outfit for the celebration. His four children, 8-year-old twins Emma and Louise, Martin (5) and Kim (3), were also anxiously awaiting their dad's return.

Corporal Ward had been scheduled to arrive home around the same time as his mother's birthday. His sister-in-law Mrs Connie Cooley said he had called his mother from Lebanon pretending that he would not be home for another month. He intended to spring a surprise for his mother turning up for her birthday celebrations unexpectedly. Tragedy in the Lebanon had touched Pauline Ward's family before. Her brother Willie O'Brien was killed by the DFF on 6 December 1986. He had been shot dead during a DFF gun attack on Brashit camp.

Corporal Ward died on 29 September 1992 at Al Journ checkpoint in a shoot-out with Hizbollah guerillas. Al Journ is one of the most strategically important crossroads in south Lebanon. It is a

stronghold for the Iranian-backed Islamic fundamentalist movement which frequently launches attacks on the Israelis and their
DFF allies. In the run-up to Ward's death there had been a number
of Hizbollah attacks mainly on nearby Tulusa compound.

One such attack shortly before the Al Journ shooting was actually
prevented by troops from 'A' company. The soldiers set up a checkpoint blocking the route to the compound after reports that Hizbollah
fighters were seen in the area. An Irish patrol also discovered a roadside bomb close to Tulusa. The device was later defused by army
engineers. As a result of the checkpoint and the discovery of the bomb
Hizbollah called off the attack.

When the guerillas returned from their abortive attack they
passed the Irish position at Al Journ. As they reached the village the
fighters opened fire on Post 645.

Troops at the post radioed for help. Among the reinforcements sent
to the village was an armoured personnel carrier from Brashit where
Corporal Ward was based. He was the gunner in a Sisu armoured personnel carrier which raced to Al Journ after reports to 'A' company
headquarters that the Hizbollah had taken up firing positions facing
the Irish checkpoint. The column was sent to back the 21-man
checkpoint.

When the APC reached its destination the guerillas opened up
without warning with Kalashnikov rifles and RPG rockets which
were fired over the vehicle. During the exchange Peter Ward manned
the heavy machine-gun set on one of the hatches of the Sisu. Thousands of rounds were discharged and one of them hit Corporal Ward
in the chest.

Medical aid was given to the seriously wounded corporal in the
APC as he was taken back to Brashit. He died, however, as he was
being prepared for helicopter evacuation to hospital.

Another member of the 71st battalion, Private Neil Coleman of
Keeper Road Park, Drimnagh, was wounded in the stomach during
the attack. He was in one of the dug-out positions around the checkpoint when the Hizbollah opened fire. Some of the Irish troops at the
scene returned fire on a much smaller scale. After the shooting
stopped both sides arranged for negotiations and shortly afterwards
the Hizbollah fighters backed off, escaping from the area.

The loss of another Irish life occurred once more during rotation
time between the 71st and 72nd battalions. Seven soldiers have been
killed during these 'hand-over' periods when numbers on the ground
are at their thinnest.

An upshot of the investigation into Corporal Ward's death was that the Hizbollah fighters involved were found not to be from the battalion's area. They had penetrated the area from the Bekaa valley where the organisation is armed and trained.

Comdt Noel Loughnane, 'A' company's commander during the 71st battalion's tour, later said that none of the men who carried out the shooting was known to UNIFIL personnel.

He recalled that, following the killing, a delegation of local muchktars came to Tulin along with Moslem holy men to express their sympathy and offer their condolences to the Ward family.

'The delegation told me they were horrified that this should have happened to someone who was there in Lebanon to ensure the safety of them and their families. The gesture did help. It convinced my men that the majority of people were not against them.'

Irish troops' main task at the checkpoint is to search cars for weapons and deny entry to armed elements infiltrating the area to attack the DFF/IDF compounds ringing the Israelis' self-declared security zone. The posters on the wall beside the Al Journ checkpoint are deceptive. Pasted there are the portraits of Amal leader, Nabbi Berri, and the movement's founder, the Imam Moussa Sadr. The posters might lead you to believe that the normally pro-UNIFIL Amal dominates Al Journ.

Al Journ, however, is close to the village of Majdal Selim whose telephone poles are decorated with the truculent portraits of the Ayatollah Khomeini and the murdered Lebanese leader Sheikh Moussawi. It is a nervous, suspicious place where young bearded men follow you around the streets while on patrol. While on a brief visit to the area in June 1992 these young Hizbollah supporters were happy to show the burnt-out remains of an Israeli rocket fired into a house adjacent to the Irish checkpoint in the village. They denounced the Israelis who in their helicopter gunship attempted to assassinate a local Hizbollah leader in the village. They pointed out wall posters showing the corpses of children killed in Israeli air raids on Beirut. All of them refused to give their names.

They did not have the same rapport with Irish soldiers as the youngsters in the village of Tulin. They do not play football with the Irish troops in Majdal Selim any more. None of them wears an Ireland soccer shirt or speaks English with a distinctive Dublin accent.

These quiet, serious young men represent the up-and-coming force in Lebanon. Militant fundamentalism is on the march. The

Hizbollah is gaining at the expense of Amal which in 1991 handed over its heavy weapons to the official Lebanese army. The problem for Irishbatt is that Hizbollah is opposed to the UN's presence. It wants all foreign armies off Lebanese soil (with the exception of their Shia brothers in the Iranian revolutionary guards in Baalbek), including UNIFIL. While Hizbollah continue to oppose the renewed Middle East peace process the attacks on the security zone and subsequent Israeli/DFF retaliation will go on for the foreseeable future.

Meanwhile the entire future of peacekeeping across the world is undergoing a quiet revolution. The current UN secretary-general, Boutros Boutros Ghali, has drawn up a blueprint in his document 'Agenda For Peace' which will radically alter the whole nature of peacekeeping. His proposals include establishing reserve UN battalions to be ready at short notice to join new missions across the globe. The upshot is that regular UN contributors like Ireland will have soldiers on file whom it can call up for overseas peacekeeping tours in a very short period of time. The secretary-general's plan effectively means the formation of an American-style rapid deployment force for peacekeeping zones. The very ethos of peacekeeping is thus changing towards a more offensive mode as the UN's role in policing conflicts expands.

The big plans for the UN army in the organisation's glass-fronted skyscraper in New York contrast absurdly with the reality of its outdated Byzantine bureaucracy. The former UN under secretary-general Marrack Goulding has admitted that the organisation does not even have a reserve stockpile of weapons, transport, protective clothing or uniforms. So unprepared is New York for any new mission emerging that headquarters has not even bothered to build up a reserve stock of blue berets and UN flags.

Goulding is sceptical about building the UN's blue berets into a global army styled on conventional military forces. He fought against moves to adopt such a 'Pentagon-style' approach. Some officers want a war room with electronic maps and gadgets. While the nature of UN military action is changing, Goulding points out that the primary aim of the blue beret forces is to prevent wars rather than make them.

But how do you differentiate between UN peace missions and outright war? The new buzz word 'peace-enforcement' stretches the meaning of peace to a new, absurd level. Enforcement means going on the offensive, taking the initiative, imposing a settlement. Peace becomes war.

More than 60,000 peacekeepers are scattered around the world in fourteen separate operations. Ireland sends soldiers to Cyprus, Lebanon, Syria, Israel, Egypt, Iran, Iraq, Pakistan, Afghanistan, Russia, Cambodia, El Salvador, Angola, the Western Sahara and the former Yugoslavia. A new batch of eighty troops has arrived in Somalia in the latest UN mission—UNOSOM 2.

Apart from the 700-odd soldiers in Lebanon there are twenty Irish officers working with UNTSO across the Middle East. The Defence Forces have two officers and seven NCOs in Cyprus under the command of Major-General Pat Minehane. Two Irish officers are serving with OSGAP (Office of the Secretary-General, Afghanistan/Pakistan) monitoring developments in Afghanistan following the Soviet withdrawal in 1988.

Two other officers are working with ONUSAL (United Nations Mission El Salvador) checking on the peace process between the government and left wing rebels. A further six officers are serving with UNIKOM (United Nations Iraq/Kuwait Monitoring Mission) which inspects the Gulf War ceasefire line imposed in April 1991. Two officers are attached to UNAVEM II (United Nations Angola Verification Mission) which was originally set up to monitor and plan free elections which were held in 1992. This mission has been tormented by violence following the election. The South African-backed UNITA party led by Dr Jonas Savimbi has refused to accept the outcome of the election which gave the left-wing MPLA governing party a larger share of the popular vote than Bill Clinton received in the American presidential election. Once again the 'force of international opinion' has failed to force another warlord to accept a UN resolution. Savimbi simply ignored the UN-monitored election's outcome. His forces continue to defy the UN and the elected government. Calls for the UN to impose a settlement against Savimbi have been few and far between compared to the clamour for intervention in Bosnia. Hundreds of thousands have died in Angola but the international community seems for the moment to be less concerned about the plight of that African nation than with the slaughter in the Balkans.

Irish soldiers are also currently involved in an even more controversial UN mission in Cambodia which has brought the greatest mass murderers since Hitler and Stalin back to political respectability. UNTAC (the United Nations Transition Authority in Cambodia) has taken charge of running the war-ravaged country until elections are held. Twelve Irish officers, along with 40 gardai, are in Cambodia working under the blue flag. The mission is one of the most dangerous Irish personnel have ever served on because of the continuing guerilla war waged by one of the factions in the struggle, the genocidal Khmer Rouge.

In the mid-1970s the Khmer Rouge led by Pol Pot killed an estimated two million people before they were toppled by the Vietnamese who invaded at Christmas 1979. Despite their record, Pol Pot's government were allowed by the UN security council to occupy Cambodia's seat in the UN general assembly. The UN-sponsored peace accord between the Khmer Rouge, their allies and the Vietnamese-installed government allowed Pol Pot's henchmen to return to the country and participate in the transition to a new government.

Ireland has a long, noble record in UN peacekeeping missions across the world. Cambodia is the blot on the landscape. The UN's role in Cambodia has been morally dubious to say the least. In official-speak, UN officers no longer even refer to the word 'genocide' when talking about the Khmer Rouge's policies while in power from 1975. The Khmer Rouge is accorded the status of a respectable political party who have a rightful place in the country's government. It seems the UN suffers from collective amnesia about Pol Pot's crimes. Whether Irish troops and police should remain in Cambodia while the Khmer Rouge continues to be protected under the UN's umbrella is very much open to question.

Irish officers have held commanding positions in various UN missions including the former Yugoslavia where an Irish commandant held the line for the international community in besieged Sarajevo long before larger contingents of blue beret troops arrived.

Comdt Colm Doyle was the European Community's chief observer in the city during the first half of 1992, reporting on the plight of Sarajevo's beleaguered citizens for the EC's special envoy Lord Carrington. It is a measure of the esteem officers of Doyle's calibre are held in that Carrington, Britain's former Foreign Secretary, insisted that the Irishman remain in the position when his official tenure of office was over.

The tasks Irish officers have to undertake for the UN now go beyond simply monitoring ceasefire lines and conventional peacekeeping. Their brief has been extended to include checking on human rights violations, supervising elections and overseeing the destruction of weapons of war.

Many of the officers involved in these new tasks have learned the ropes of UN service in Lebanon. In 1990 Comdt Noel Loughnane spent a year as a UN observer in Nicaragua. A former platoon commander in Lebanon, Loughnane arrived in the Central American country in December 1989 shortly after the Contra war against the former left-wing Sandinista government ended.

His job went beyond the normal limits of military operations. For one, he had to investigate incidents of initimidation against political opponents of the Sandinista government in the capital, Managua. Along with Lt-Col Jimmy Farrell and Lt-Col Sean McCarrick, Loughnane was part of an international team of observers who were there to ensure that the elections due in early 1990 would be fought on a free and fair basis.

All three Irishmen were billeted in a house in Managua. They were uniformed but unarmed. The spartan conditons they had to endure did not worry Loughnane. 'It didn't bother me at all. Irish officers are well accustomed to UN missions throughout the world now. We can be ready for almost anything.'

The most exhausting part of their year-long stint was a three-month tour of eight special centres where the right wing Contra rebels were handing over their weapons to the international observers. The first thing Loughnane and his colleagues did was to meet the Contra fighters in demilitarised zones close to the Honduran and Costa Rican borders. They were then ordered to hand over their weapons to his team. Loughnane remembers that a special battalion of Venezuelan soldiers under their command was used to physically destroy the Contras' weapons, which ranged from rifles to heavy mortars.

'We had a machine which looked like a huge pair of garden shears,' he said. 'It actually cut rifles and RPG launchers in two. This part of the mission was the busiest. We were working around the clock overseeing the destruction of these weapons. By the time we were finished I was sick of the sight of guns.'

Loughnane contrasts the relative success of the mission in Nicaragua with the ongoing situation in Lebanon. 'There was a willingness on both sides in Nicaragua for peace, unlike the Lebanon.'

Irish troops have continued to stand between these warring parties in the most dangerous terrain in south Lebanon. While they physically stop the DFF entering Shia villages or carry out dangerous night-time patrols in deep wadis to ward off guerilla fighters infiltrating the area the risk is great. The Irish do not expect (or want) any favours from either side in the renewed conflict. Nor should journalists. The undercurrent of hostility I encountered in Majdal Selim from the young Hizbollah supporters was matched that same week by the howls of protest ranged against me from the Israeli military.

Shortly after that visit to Al Journ and Majdal Selim I was warned by the battalion's head press liaison officer that the Israelis had complained about my presence in the area. Prior to arriving in Lebanon I had written a report for *The Sunday Press* on a helicopter gunship attack which nearly cost the lives of several Irish soldiers at the Majdal Selim checkpoint. While in Irish headquarters in Camp Shamrock I was handed a faxed copy of the article which the Israelis presented to UNIFIL in Naquorra. They complained about the 'tone' of the report which they suggested made it look like their helicopter crew had deliberately targetted the soldiers at the UN post. Obviously someone back in Dublin had been doing his homework. *The Sunday Press* would not, after all, be widely available in Israel or Lebanon.

During a previous visit to the south the year before, I encountered a very different kind of disapproval from the Israelis' proxies. As I drove with an armed escort from Tibnin to Naquorra our jeep approached a series of gates on the road parallel to the coast inside the security zone. The gates are manned by armed DFF men who sit smoking in cramped sentry boxes looking either bored or menacing.

At one gate we encountered a young DFF guman who was no more than sixteen or seventeen. UN troops rather than the militia have to open the swing gates on the road outside Naquorra. As one Irish soldier got back into the jeep the young DFF man muttered an obscenity and then spat into the vehicle narrowly missing me with his jet of saliva.

Several hours later, after lunch in Naquorra, I left for Israel with an Irish military police sergeant who had a leave pass. Along with his overnight bag he carried a pair of pale brown desert boots. At the final DFF swing gate before the Israeli checkpoints we were stopped in our car by an overweight middle-aged militia man called Mahmoud. The Irish sergeant dangled the boots out of the window until Mahmoud snatched them out of his hand.

'God bless you Irish! You are a very good man,' he cried as he ran towards his comrades standing around the sentry box and paraded his new footwear. 'That'll keep him happy and stop hassling us at the checkpoint for a while', the sergeant remarked as we drove off towards the heavily fortified Ros Haniqra border post. The incident was a minor illustration of the trials Irish and other UN troops have to put up with while travelling into the security zone from their battalion areas.

Because they are at the sharp end in Lebanon, Irish troops in particular are under severe stress while on their six-month tour.

They are constrained by their standard operating procedures which severely limit what they can do as soldiers. Unlike other armies, UN peacekeepers only fire back as a last resort in self-defence. Peacekeeping in Lebanon requires every Irish soldier to suppress a lot of their basic instincts as fighting men.

The vast majority are able to cope with the savage pressure weighing down on them. Some, however, find it difficult to re-adjust to life after Lebanon. Sergeant Harry Higgins, based at the Air Corps headquarters in Baldonnel, confessed that he encountered feelings of alienation and isolation after he returned from the Middle East. He found it difficult to readjust to normal life, to get used to basic commodities like clean running water and electricity which were rationed while on his tour. His sleep patterns were disturbed for several months.

'One of the first things that struck me when I came home after the last tour was that people in Dublin were drinking water from bottles in pubs and paying for it! I just couldn't believe that in Ireland, with our water system, people were willing to fork out money to drink it from a bottle. We had to pay a lot for water in the Leb. I never thought anyone at home would want to do the same.'

From his work as a PDFORRA representative Harry encountered other Lebanon veterans with more serious problems some of which led to marital breakdowns, domestic violence, alcoholism and illness. The military authorities are beginning to take the problem of soldiers suffering combat stress more seriously. The Defence Forces now has a Personal Services Section which helps soldiers and their families cope with the problems faced by overseas veterans. One of the section's latest innovations was to issue leaflets to the entire 73rd battalion and their families advising them on how to cope with the period during and after the six-month tour. Returning troops can also avail of new counselling services from the specially trained section.

Several soldiers have found it difficult to cope while out in the Lebanon. One of the most tragic cases involved Private Sean Courtney, who was convicted of the murder of Mrs Patricia O'Toole in Dublin in early 1993. He claimed he was a victim of Post-Traumatic Stress Disorder following an incident in the Lebanon in which Private Patrick Wright of the 63rd battalion was found dead in a toilet, having shot himself accidentally.

Courtney was in bed in Ayta Azutt camp on that evening when he heard shouting outside the barracks. He went outside, heard a bang, and thought it was someone throwing rocks at the toilet cubicles. When the door of one of the cubicles was opened, Private Wright's body was found. He had died of a shotgun wound to the stomach and because of the velocity, the body was badly mutilated.

After being put on duty the next day Courtney complained to his officers he could not stay in Lebanon any longer. It was his third tour with UNIFIL and he was determined it would be his last. 'I just had to get out of there. That place isn't worth the life of one Irish soldier,' he said.

Courtney related his story about finding Private Wright's body while on trial for the murder of Dublin insurance agent, Patricia O'Toole, on 31 August 1991.

He claimed at the time of the killing he was suffering from a severe case of Post-Traumatic Stress Disorder after his experiences in Lebanon. Prior to the horrific discovery in the toilets at Ayta Azutt Courtney had come under fire from both sides of the conflict in the space of a few hours on 13 June that same year.

After surviving an Israeli tank barrage which was directed close to the Irish post, local Lebanese villagers later surrounded their barracks and threatened him and other troops with Kalashnikovs and RPGs.

During the latter incident Courtney was posted on the roof of the camp. He recalled seeing one of the Lebanese taking out a grenade. Courtney believed the Arab was going to throw the grenade into an Irish armoured car. He fired in the direction of the man with the device and hit him in the leg. As a result of the incident Courtney was moved to another post because the villagers threatened to wreak their revenge on him.

In his defence during his murder trial, Courtney admitted killing Patricia O'Toole in the Dublin mountains but claimed he did not intend to do so. He said he was mentally ill at the time of the murder. The jury rejected his plea that he was suffering from PTSD. They reached a majority verdict of 10–2 on 21 January 1993 and found him guilty of murder. He was sentenced to life with penal servitude and is currently being held in Dublin's Arbour Hill prison.

The trial caused acute embarrassment to the Defence Forces and the military authorities. Throughout his trial Courtney wore his army uniform and was actually held for a considerable period of time on closed bail at Dublin's Cathal Brugha Barracks. As a result of the Courtney case the Department of Defence later changed the law so that soldiers could not wear the uniform while in court unless authorised by an official order. Like Michael McAleavey before him, Sean Courtney was also discharged with ignominy.

As for Courtney's plea of insanity it is worth noting that the Defence Forces' union, which has strongly argued that UNIFIL veterans have suffered from combat stress, is cynical about his claim. As one representative with several overseas tours under his belt commented: 'Lots of lads got out to the Lebanon and come home suffering from post-traumatic stress disorder. They might take to drink, lose their jobs or end up ruining their marriage. But PTSD is not an excuse for murder. Hundreds, perhaps thousands, have suffered from stress but that doesn't mean they take a woman against her will up the Dublin mountains and beat her face in with a brick.'

The presence of foreign armies seems increasingly to be a permanent feature of life in south Lebanon. The Israelis have invested heavily in their self-declared security zone, building up a complex network of listening stations, helicopter pads, tank parks and defensive compounds. Even the way the UN used to describe these Israeli positions in Lebanon is steeped in the language of permanency.

One such position, a listening post with a huge red and white pylon sticking up from a sand-banked compound which faces onto the Irish battalion area, is called PV41. This stands for 'Permanent Violation'. The language is almost a reluctant acceptance of the continued presence of the Israeli army in defiance of Resolution 425. The entire region resembles a militarised south Armagh only magnified a thousand times. It is unlikely that the Israelis will simply tear down their highly sophisticated line of defence in the south for the foreseeable future.

The Irish battalion's own presence in the region has a permanent feeling about it. A new headquarters is now nearing completion which will replace Camp Shamrock. North of Caltex village, the new HQ is modelled on the design of the DFF compounds. Officers who brought me to the huge site just a few kilometres from Recce company's base stress that the earth mound structure will be more secure from attack than the old headquarters outside Tibnin. This suggests UNIFIL command and the military authorities at home expect the mission to continue for a considerable time to come.

Despite ongoing attacks on the security zone and the inevitable retaliation by the Israelis and their allies, UNIFIL has been successful in rebuilding south Lebanon's political and economic structure. It has focused the international spotlight on the region and provided a buffer between the Israelis and their enemies. But for how long should the multinational force remain simply as a protective shield between the warring parties?

Its military role could be enhanced to the extent that it replaces the IDF and is capable of securing Israel's northern border. That would mean beefing up the UN army and taking in new units from western and eastern Europe actively backed by the Americans in order to secure a full Israeli withdrawal.

This proposal, however, flies in the face of the original aims of UNFIIL which were to restore the legitimate Lebanese government's authority in the south and allow its forces to deploy right up to the actual border with Israel. The goal should be to reduce the number of foreign forces in Lebanon, not dramatically to increase them.

The danger, however, in reducing UNIFIL's strength at present to around 2,000 men, the bulk of whom would be constituted by unarmed observers, would be to send a signal to Jerusalem that the international community accepts Israel's presence in the south.

A middle course might be for the force to continue to help the Lebanese government's forces deploy deeper into the south as they are currently doing in the area of Tyre. On top of this, UNIFIL's ultimate role in south Lebanon could be as the logistical base for further free elections to the Beirut parliament. UN officers, including those like Comdt Loughnane, already have the experience in supervising elections in other parts of the world. The force would not be found wanting in this regard. It should be noted, however, that in the 1992 elections the party most opposed to peace talks with Israel, the Hizbollah, did exceptionally well along with the pro-Syrian Amal, whose policies are indirectly linked to the interests of Damascus.

The optimistic scenario is dependent on wider Middle Eastern issues. Since 1991 Syrian involvement in Lebanese affairs has deepened. The Treaty of Brotherhood between Beirut and Damascus allows the Syrian army to remain in Lebanon. While the Syrians stay put, it is highly unlikely the Israelis will be persuaded unilaterally to give up the security zone. In Israeli eyes an extension of Lebanese authority right up to the border means that Syrian influence moves southward as well.

The security zone, in the words of Lebanese scholar Fida Nasrallah, has become like the Golan Heights: it is a 'bargaining chip' between Israel and Syria in the wider Middle East game. Nasrallah is pessimistic about the prospects for ending the Israeli occupation. Unless Syrian military and political influence on Lebanon is drastically reduced, he believes it would be easier from the Israelis' point of view to give up the Golan rather than the security zone. Outright final withdrawal from Lebanon by the IDF depends ultimately on the future of the current fragile Middle East peace talks. Given the likelihood that these negotiations will be long, slow and tortuous, the situation in south Lebanon will remain the same. UNIFIL's presence will still be required for several years yet, perhaps even into the next century.

The Irish Defence Forces have been involved in overseas UN missions now for thirty-five years. Consistently, Irish officers have held key posts in missions around the world. For a relatively small army, the Defence Forces have played a crucial role in promoting the UN despite major difficulties. As well as its role on the ground, the army has had a high profile at UN headquarters in New York. In 1992 Comdt Dermot Farley returned from headquarters staff after serving as a military adviser to the secretary-general for four years.

The army has faced unfair jibes that it is a relatively inconsequential force that would be overwhelmed by an invading army reaching Ireland's shores. In its defence the record of the country's armed forces working for the United Nations is second to none, given the size of Ireland and its limited resources. They continue to hold the thin blue line in dangerous missions overseas sometimes putting their own lives in danger to save local people and prevent conflicts escalating. Ireland is constantly called upon to provide personnel due to its unique position as an English-speaking post-colonial neutral nation. Even in the era of the so-called 'New World Order' the country's troops are set to continue to serve in the cause of peace abroad. The unbroken link from the Battle of the Tunnel in the Congo to the sacrifices at At Tiri is set to stretch into the twenty-first century. To adopt a catchphrase of Victorian imperialism: 'The sun never sets on the Irish UN commitment.'

Across the area under Irish control in south Lebanon there are memorials to soldiers who have died serving in the peacekeeping mission. Outside 'C' company headquarters in Brashit village, under the control of soldiers from the west of Ireland, there is a small grotto protected by white-washed concrete T-squares.

It faces onto the men's mess under the shadow of a large three-storey Lebanese house rented from a local family and now occupied by an Irish company commander and his junior officers. Inside the house itself is a morbid memento to the dangers facing Irish troops in southern Lebanon. Embedded in the wall of the officers' mess is a machine-gun bullet just over the dining table. It is framed in glass and below it there is an inscription: 'To the officers of 'C' company courtesy of big Antoine Lahad.' The 'gift' from the DFF's new commanding officer Major-General Lahad arrived in Brashit camp during a DFF gun attack on the Irish base in 1990. Sometimes a weird sense of humour is required to cope with the strains of peacekeeping.

The grotto outside is tended by every new troop contingent stationed in the village. It is fenced off with white stones and looks like a small graveyard. Around the edge of the grotto is a cluster of wreaths with red, white and yellow roses. The centrepiece of the memorial is a cross with three stones, each bearing the names of soldiers who died in Lebanon.

In front is a statue of St Joseph holding the baby Jesus in his arms. Flanking the statue on either side are vases containing flowers. The white marble stone on the left bears the names of the men who died in the Brashit bombing of 1989. In the middle the stone reminds soldiers and visitors of 'Those who fell and gave their life in foreign lands. They stood for peace. Please stand for them.' It remembers Corporal Dermot McLoughlin and Private William O'Brien, both victims of the DFF.

The final memorial stone recalls all the other names of those who died both of natural causes and in action while serving with UNIFIL. It includes Hugh Doherty. But as with the graveyard overlooking the Atlantic on Inisheer two thousand miles away, there is still one name missing from the Brashit memorial—Kevin Joyce. Like the Defence Forces' own UN commitment, the sun has never finally set on his tragic story.

EPILOGUE

7 May 1993, Israel-Lebanon border

Four hundred kilometres north of the electrified border fence sep-arating Israeli and Lebanese territory a football game kicked off in Beirut. It was the first time since the Lebanese civil war broke out in 1975 that an international soccer game was played in the capital. For the record Hong Kong beat Bahrain two-nil in a World Cup qual-ifying game. Another sign of some normal life returning to Lebanon.

Outside Kibbutz Za'it just yards from the border young Israeli soldiers patrolling the strip of sand beside the security fence were unaware of the big soccer clash in the city they had occupied eleven years before. Nothing was new or normal here. Peace for the Israelis still meant a low intensity war. For them the remnants of the Palestinian fighters and the pro-Iranian Hizbollah in Lebanon con-tinue to pose an 'existential threat' to the state of Israel.

Overhead an IDF helicopter arched away just above a UN post in Lebanese territory. The helicopter carried an Israeli brigadier-general who was on a morale boosting visit to his troops stuck in the strip of Lebanese land occupied by the IDF.

A 28-year-old major from Tel Aviv who said he was a veteran of Israel's Lebanon war explained what would happen to anyone trying to breach the fence. 'If they get into Israel itself we kill them,' he said smiling. 'Once they escape into our country it's difficult to find them. The terrain in northern Galilee makes it easy for them to get lost.'

He called himself Major Z, a boyish looking diminutive character who kept smiling while he rattled off the names of suspected Lebanese Shia fighters some of whom (including Jeywad Casfi) were known to Irish battalions in UNIFIL. Major Z's job was to direct military intelligence for an entire division deployed along Israel's frontier with Lebanon. The fence, he pointed out, was electrified and when touched would alert nearby Israeli troops who, Major Z claimed, could be at the scene within four minutes.

We were standing right up beside the fence which is about ten feet high and crowned with barbed wire and menacing spikes. Beyond it to the north IDF engineers have placed mines and an elaborate early warning system which alerts Israeli troops if someone is trying to infiltrate southwards.

On the Israeli side there is a thin strip of sand running alongside the fence. Every morning troops sweep the strip for footprints and other signs of infiltration. From positions in the Irishbatt area it is possible to see this continuous sand strip snaking its way across the scrubbed hills and wadis that separate the two countries.

'Our aim is to try to make life for Israelis living one kilometre from the border as normal as it is for those in Tel Aviv. That is why we need this security zone.'

The young major revealed that on average there are about twenty-four attacks on the IDF and their DFF allies per month inside the self-declared security belt, the majority coming now from the Hizbollah. 'If the security zone was not there some of these attacks would be on Israel proper. I am not blaming the Irish or other UN forces. They have a job to do which I would not like. But quite honestly they are not able to stop the terrorists. It's up to us to protect Israel first of all.'

But what about the spate of incidents directed by the IDF in the zone which have sometimes claimed the lives of Irish and other UN soldiers? 'From time to time there will be accidents. South Lebanon is a pressure cooker and sometimes tempers boil over. We want no trouble with the Irish, I can assure you.'

Major Z had an extensive knowledge of the main resistance fighters based in the Irish battalion area. He was well acquainted with Jeywad Casfi, the bomber who targeted Lt Aengus Murphy in the Hill 880 explosion. 'He was an important player, a very dangerous man who, we suspected, killed our soldiers in roadside bombs. I know of two soldiers from an Israeli infantry brigade in this division whom he definitely killed. I also know he killed one of your soldiers too.'

As the helicopter above veered westwards towards the Mediterranean Major Z asked me to come with him to a nearby Israeli village overlooking the border.

It started to pour rain when we got to Gragnot Hagilah ten minutes later. The grey clouds over Mount Hermon and the Sea of Galilee had been threatening to burst all afternoon. Just off the main street the rain started to fill up a three-foot wide crater on the road between a cluster of bungalows.

This was all that remained of the spot where the Katushya rocket fell on the village the year before, killing an eight-year-old girl. The family has left Gragnot Hagilah. Their home is up for sale. So far there have been no takers. The rocket had been fired from south Lebanon. The culprits, the Israelis suspect, were members of the Hizbollah.

The crater on the road was exactly similar to hundreds of similar ones which peppered the roads and village streets of south Lebanon. Like the one in Gragnot Hagilah the craters in the Irish battalion zone were reminders to the local population of the deaths of their civilians killed in IDF/DFF shelling, mortar fire and air raids.

Irit Kalechman, a local artist and chairwoman of the local council in the Israeli village, pointed at the crater where the child died. I asked her about the security zone. Was it not time for the Israeli Defence Forces to pull out of Lebanese territory? Weren't the rockets still falling on Galilee despite the IDF presence across the border? And weren't Israeli soldiers till dying in Lebanon eight years after the withdrawal from most of the country's territory?

In her bohemian dress and flowing blonde and grey hair Irit looked more at home at a peace camp or serving up lentil soup in a radical chic resource centre. But instead she was a woman on a constant war footing, adamant that her troops remain in Lebanon for the time being.

'I know that before Operation Peace for Galilee in 1982 life here was intolerable. Women could not let their kids out to play on their own. They were afraid they would be attacked by terrorists infiltrating down from Lebanon. There were whole days which we spent in air raid shelters. That must never happen again. It is bad enough when the terrorists fire the Katushyas but it would be worse if they were to come across.'

Irit waved her hand to dismiss suggestions that UNIFIL would be able to protect her community if the force was able to fulfil its mandate and deploy to the Lebanese border. 'I only trust my own army,' she said. 'UNIFIL were in Lebanon since 1978 and never prevented the PLO from attacking our settlements.'

Her comments were almost identical to the complaints made by some local Lebanese across the border who believe UNIFIL have not done enough to protect them and fulfil their mandate.

Even the most ardent peaceniks in Israel, such as those living in a Kibbutz founded by the Israeli Communist Party not far from Ros Haniqra, are sceptical about giving up the security zone. Red flags still hung from the telegraph poles on the Kibbutz alongside the blue-and-white Israeli flag. The red flags were up to celebrate Mayday. Igal is a supporter of the left-wing Meretz Party. He said he believes in giving up land for peace and recognising a Palestinian homeland on the West Bank and Gaza Strip.

But even Igal is unwilling to support unilateral Israeli withdrawal from south Lebanon. While the security zone was one of the bargaining chips on the table of the Middle East peace talks held in Washington that same month, Igal wanted Israel to hold onto the strip in the short term. As we stood outside one of the air raid shelters he helped to build, he pointed out that the Lebanese border was only two kilometres away.

'We can give the security zone up if it means peace but only a peace with which we Israelis can feel safe. I think most of the people in Lebanon want peace too. But there are terrorists who want to destroy us, like the Hizbollah. We can only pull out once there is a real peace treaty between Lebanon and Israel with guarantees for our security.'

East of Gragnot Hagilah is Israel's most northern city, Kiryat Shemona. Here they are less generous towards the Lebanese, particularly the Shia living across the border. Many residents, such as American-educated Susan Peretz, regard the Shia as fanatical enemies and UNIFIL as a completely ineffective force.

Mrs Peretz, a chain smoking slender woman in her mid-40s, revealed a long-standing connection with south Lebanon. As a former major in the IDF she was part of a technical team which armed and supplied Saad Haddad's De Facto forces. She even showed me the apartment Haddad used to rent in Kiryat Shemona where he would spend weekends recuperating with his wife after the daily slaughter and sectarian warfare north of the border. A Jewish immigrant family now lives there.

'The Shi'ites are fanatics', Susan stressed after we left the city's museum which included a film on the history of the settlement. 'There is no reasoning with the Shi'ites.'

In contrast Susan believed, like many other Israelis, that the Christians in Lebanon were the 'most reasonable type of people'. Pointing out the atrocities their Christian allies have committed against the Lebanese Moslems, Palestinians and even UN soldiers including the Irish, does not wash with her or with most Israelis you meet on the northern border.

Haddad's successors in the DFF are a welcome buffer force, a 'shield of Galilee' in the words of the IDF press office in Jerusalem. Senior Israeli officers were at pains to defend the militia Haddad founded. They rejected charges that the DFF were involved with the Christian Phalange in the massacre of Palestinians of Sabra and Shatila in 1982. When pressed on the murders carried out by the DFF in south Lebanon, including the revenge killings of Irish soldiers such as Tom Barrett and Derek Smallhorne, the IDF brass turned to a well-worn excuse.

They suggested that the DFF operate 'Lebanese morals'. The militia did not adhere to the standards of the Israeli army, said one Lt-Colonel who was in Beirut in 1982. It exacted its own form of revenge and there was little the IDF could do about it. While they defended the DFF, the Israelis did not provide any interviews with militia commanders. The DFF remained hidden from view and scrutiny.

One Israeli officer well known to Irishbatt, Major David, admitted that he could never make a DFF man into an IDF soldier. 'These people are Lebanese with their own code of conduct,' the burly liaison officer to UNIFIL protested. 'We have common interests with them but not all our interests coincide.'

But what about the murder of Irish and other UN soldiers at the hands of your allies, I asked? Do you know that Mohammed Bazi is still at large despite being the prime suspect in the Barrett-Smallhorne murders?

'I know of these people,' Major David said, swinging his baton around with which he pointed to a map of south Lebanon. 'They are more of a clan than a family. One of their fathers is currently in Israel receiving hospital treatment at the minute.'

He claimed he did not know Mohammed Bazi personally. Most of the IDF officers I met also denied any knowledge of the man from Blida village.

The only visible sight of the DFF were the compounds on the ridgelines looking into the UNIFIL zone. Thousands of Lebanese Christians, many of them supporters of the DFF, pass through a gate north of Kiryat Shemona every day to work in Israel.

If Irishbatt and UNIFIL's current humanitarian aid programme is really going to succeed then it will have to persuade Lebanese like those passing through the 'good fence' at Metullah Gate to stay and earn a living in their own country.

The Israeli authorities, whether at the foreign ministry in Jerusalem, in the country's parliament, the Knesset, or on the army's general staff, are clearly worried about the impact of UNIFIL's presence in south Lebanon and the strain it has put on bilateral relations with contributing countries, particularly Ireland.

In April 1993 the IDF's education corps drew up a new leaflet to be issued to troops on the northern front aimed at clarifying UNIFIL's role in Lebanon. It warns IDF soldiers not to point their weapons at UN soldiers who are described as a 'foreign but not alien force'. They are advised that 'a relatively small incident could potentially arouse widespread reactions that may cause a large amount of damage to the state of Israel. Therefore, we must try and prevent any kind of damage to UNIFIL positions and/or personnel.'

The new charm offensive by the Israelis aimed at healing the wounds between them and UNIFIL is a far cry from the country's former attitude to the international force. The old attitude of suspicion and hostility towards the UN was summed up by one of the founding fathers of the Israeli state, David Ben Gurion, who used the expression 'UN blah, blah ...' in reaction to certain unfavourable UN security council resolutions.

Senior figures connected to the political establishment in Israel are keen to stress their understanding of the predicament UNIFIL battalions, particularly the Irish, are in. The chairman of the Knesset's defence and foreign affairs committee, Ori Orr, acknowledged that Irishbatt was in a 'mission impossible in Lebanon'. Mr Orr, a Labour member of the Knesset and former c/o of Northern Command, claimed the IDF had intelligence that Lebanese resistance groups deliberately used Irish and other UN positions as shelter when they attacked the Israelis and their allies in south Lebanon.

'The mandate of each UNIFIL battalion is a mission impossible because there is still no effective Lebanese government. When an incident occurs involving Irish and Israeli troops your government complains to ours. That is because there is an address to write to. But when Hizbollah fires on your positions or kills one of your people there is no address to write to. Perhaps you should direct your attention more to Tehran because the Lebanese government is not effective,' Mr Orr said.

Orr, an influential member of the largest party in government and a former acquaintance of UNIFIL c/o, Lt-General Bill Callaghan, accepted, however, that Irish troops had to watch their back constantly from attack by resistance fighters who from time to time turned their guns on the international force.

He expressed confidence that Israel's own pet militia group in Lebanon was slowly changing its attitude towards UNIFIL. One wonders, however, if the specially produced IDF leaflets dealing with the blue beret force will be translated into Arabic for the benefit of the DFF?

Wherever you go in Israel, whether on the settlements along the border or in the suburbs of Tel Aviv where I met Ori Orr, there is a widely held feeling that the IDF will hold onto the security zone for the foreseeable future.

Israelis of every political persuasion protest that they want out of the Lebanese mire, that the 1982 adventure was a massive mistake, and that the IDF could never have imposed their own hand-picked government on Lebanon. They point, however, not to Beirut as the solution but to Damascus. As long as the Syrian garrison remains and its proxies attack the IDF in the south, Israel stays put in its security zone.

Back in Jerusalem yellow-and-black flags were flying from taxi cabs, telegraph poles and house windows. As in Beirut the Jerusalemites (the Israelis at least) were celebrating their own soccer triumph. Their local side, Maccabi Jerusalem, had won the Israeli National League the week before.

Many of the football fans waving scarves and flags from cars and buses were Israeli soldiers returning from duty in the last occupied strip of Lebanon. After the weekend celebrations they would return to their positions in the north.

Despite such brief chinks of normality, the war in south Lebanon continues.

The returning Maccabi fans did not have long to wait for hostilities to resume. Throughout the early summer Hizbollah launched a flurry of Katushya rockets at northern Galilee. Predictably the IDF responded to these attacks with renewed ferocity. The old pattern of attack and counter-attack was reappearing again.

In the last week of July Irishbatt headquarters recorded one of the heaviest ever Israeli bombardments on the UNIFIL zone. In that period 5,300 155 mm shells fell on the battalion's area. The Israelis fired a further 420 tank rounds, 60 mortar rounds, 130 bombs from fixed wing aircraft and 130 helicopter missiles.

In one incident two unexploded 155 mm shells fell on an Irish post at Brashit. The Irish base there took five direct hits during the Israeli operation which one senior UNIFIL officer said showed that 'selectivity by the Israelis is not a prime consideration'. Three soldiers from Western Command were treated for shock after the shells landed on their base.

The UNIFIL officer added that there were suspicions that targetting Brashit was part of a new strategy to force the UN out of the village and eventually incorporate it in the Israeli declared security zone. The Israelis for their part vigorously deny this.

Irish troops spent hours on end sweating it out in their bunkers in 'Groundhog' while the IDF pounded the surrounding villages which it claimed were the launching pads for Hizbollah attacks against Israel.

The barrage, codenamed 'Operation Accountability', cost more than a hundred Lebanese lives. The aim of the bombardment was to force Shia villagers north to Beirut and put pressure on the Lebanese government to halt Hizbollah's holy war.

But less than a month later, on 17 August, it was reported that Hizbollah launched fresh attacks on DFF compounds and an Israeli patrol. On the surface at least, the Israeli exercise seemed to have been futile.

Nevertheless, the Israelis pointed to the deployment of the Lebanese army within days of the end of Operation Accountability. The regular Lebanese army sent 300 troops to the south, many of them taking up positions in Irishbatt's area.

The Israelis hoped, a little in vain perhaps, that the Lebanese army would be sent to control the activities of Hizbollah. Even news reports in Irish papers noted super-optimistically that the deployment of the regular Lebanese army marked a new turning point towards peace in the south.

Irishbatt veterans knew otherwise. Many remembered that the Lebanese government forces had been more or less ineffective in stopping Palestinian forces operating independently against Israel from Jebel Amil more than a decade before. Now this same regular army was up against an indigenous Lebanese force driven by theological conviction and fighting on its home turf.

The most telling reason for Israel's brief but bloody bombardment of south Lebanon came during an interview the present author had with an Israeli official almost one month to the day after Operation Accountability began. He explained the 'political goals' behind the massive retaliation. It was, he said, a message not ultimately to Beirut but to Damascus, to the seat of power held by Hafed Assad.

The message was clear and brutally simple: if Syria allows its own proxies to pin-prick Israel during peace negotiations then there will be a price to pay. It was missile rather than megaphone diplomacy at work. South Lebanon was once again a battleground in the wider unsolved Middle East war between Israel and Syria.

In the battalion area the villagers have returned after their brief exodus north. Irish troops have started the slow painful work of helping to rebuild the shattered zone again. Hizbollah, meanwhile, re-organises hoping to capitalise on deepening Shia resentment against Israel and their allies.

Several months before, with the peace process under way and the south's economy starting to regenerate, it looked as if Irishbatt and UNIFIL were watching the emergence of some form of stability. Instead, Operation Accountability has returned the unfortunate villagers to the late 70s and early 80s when the region was turned into a charnel house by warring factions and invading armies.

But Irish troops with UNIFIL are now used to the shifting patterns of calm punctuated by violent sectarian eruptions and foreign invasions. Irishbatt continues to operate in a land trapped in political and military gridlock. Once again Irish soldiers are between a rock and a hard place, peace-keeping in a war without end.

INDEX

UNIFCYP, 21
UNIFIL, 3, 4, 7, 42, 50, 93, 120, 158
  age of troops, 16
  and Amal, 112–13, 117
  bomb disposal, 115
  budget cut, 128
  Callaghan in command, 98–9,
    101–9
  death toll, 3, 4, 13
  defends At Tiri, 46–56
  established, 28–41
  future role, 154–5, 161–3
  and Gulf War, 141–5
  'hearts and minds' campaign,
    124–5, 133, 134–7
  and PLO, 9
  relations with IDF, 44–5, 165–73
  and 'Rubicon', 70–73, 76–7
  and SLA, 34–5, 51, 58
UNIKOM, 145, 155
UNIMOG, 138–9, 141–2
UNITA, 155
United Nations, 163, 170
  extent of operations, 20, 155–7
  Gulf War, 144
  'peace-enforcement', 154–5
  Security Council, 21
  Security Council Resolution 425,
    28, 66, 101, 131, 147, 161
  use of force by, 20–21
United Nations Emergency Force
  II, 22
United Nations Veterans
  Association, 16
United States, 7, 19, 25, 38–9, 59,
  71, 101, 162
  attitude to UNIFIL, 77, 128
  multi–national force, 54, 77, 106
UNOGIL, 25

UNOSOM, 155
UNTAC, 155–6
UNTSO, 21, 22–3, 24, 126, 141, 155
  and Joyce kidnap, 8, 10
  officers killed, 78–9
  and UNIFIL, 28, 29
Urquhart, David, 37

Vartam, Zavan, 59, 65
Venezuela, 157
Vincent, Captain Patrick, 59, 64
'Voice of Hope', 68

Wade, Sergeant John, 130
Walsh, Sergeant Martin, 142, 143
Walsh, Pauline, 117
Walsh, Private Thomas, 116–17, 118
Walsh, Tony, 117
Ward, Rev. Alan, 8
Ward, Pauline, 151
Ward, Corporal Peter, 33, 151–2
Warren, Harley, 78
Weizmann, Ezer, 45
West Bank, 71, 168
Wickham, Comdt Thomas, 23
Wilson, John, 149
Wright, Lt-Col, 127
Wright, Private Patrick, 159–60

Xeros, 21

Yatar, 125
Yeats, Sergeant Edward, 67
Yom Kippur War, 22–4, 80, 101
Young, Lt-Col Joe, 141
Yugoslavia, 155, 156

Zaire, 20